African Journal of Science, Technology, Innovation and Development (AJSTID)

Vol. 4, No. 2, 2012

Contents

RESEARCH NOTES

BOOK REVIEWS

African Journal of Science, Technology,
Innovation & Development
AJSTID

African Journal of Science, Technology, Innovation and Development (AJSTID)

Volume 4, Number 2, 2012

Editorial Board

ISSN: 2042-1338 (print)
ISSN: 2042-1346 (online)

Cover Design: Asia Iftikhar
Layout Artist: Jan B. Mwesigwa

http://www.adonis-abbey.com

Also visit the journal website: http://www.ajstid.com

Adonis & Abbey Publishers Ltd
P. O. Box 43418
London, UK,
SE11 4XZ

Adonis & Abbey Publishing Co
P. O. Box 10546
Abuja, Nigeria
Tel: +234 (0)8165970458

AJSTID is a multi-disciplinary and refereed international journal on science, technology, innovation and development in Africa and other low-income countries. It was established in appreciation of the role and importance of innovation in the development processes and the recognition of the relative absence of research in this area in Africa. AJSTID encourages research along the following broad areas:

- Role of science, technology and innovation in the processes of industrial growth and development.
- Emergence and the making of innovation systems in the context of broader socio-economic development.
- Exploring the inclusion of innovation and knowledge in sub-national, regional, global and local innovation networks and cross border integration processes in Africa.
- Research on the interaction among governments, industries, businesses, universities and communities in the use and application of science, technology and innovation policies; particularly comparative works that have implications for all developing economies.
- Critiques of science, technology and innovation policies and their applications in Africa.
- Exploring co-evolutions, broad-based innovations and indigenous knowledge systems in the context of African development.

Submitting Papers

Authors are required to submit original papers, that is, papers submitted should not have been previously published or be currently under consideration for publication elsewhere. All papers are refereed through a double blind process. You may send an electronic copy of your paper (MS Word file attached to an e-mail) to:

editor@ajstid.com

For detailed guidelines: visit **http://www.adonisandabbey.com/**
Also visit: **http://www.ajstid.com**

African Journal of Science, Technology, Innovation and Development
Vol. 4, No. 2, 2012
pp. 7-10

Notes from the Editors

Mammo Muchie, Angathevar Baskaran
& Oghenerobor B. Akpor

The term human capital was invented by the economist Theodore Schultz in the 1960s to express the contribution of differentiated human capacities and skills. The concept was defined, like any other capital, as a correlation between labour and skills that humans have in relation to how they are able to build capacities through education, training and skills upgrading to bring about improvement in the quality and level of production. Human capital development is critical to reduce unemployment, particularly among youth. In many African countries training for human capital building is critical. It appears that coordination and linkages amongst the production of the skilled and educated trainee remains a big challenge to many African countries. Human capital is one of the critical factors for building the national system of innovation in Africa and Africa needs an education revolution to create a human capital foundation that can sustain a robust system of innovation. It also needs to launch an engineering and design revolution. The science, technology and engineering revolution can serve as a spring board for re-designing an African development agenda where agriculture, manufacture and services are interlinked in the African national economic space. The goal is to expand the industrial foundation of a strong and integrated African economy.

In addition to building the capital of the mind and skills, Africa needs to build social capital which together with human and financial capital can provide the necessary conditions that serve the development engine of Africa. In addition to the technical innovation of converting R&D and knowledge into innovation, Africa needs a social innovation where the collaborative and partnering values of African society grow by combining traditional values that support development with values from the globalizing world that are worth incorporating without defying the logic of building the African system of innovation (ASI).

The concept of national systems of innovation (NSI) has come under close scrutiny from researchers who have witnessed the overwhelming sweep of the globalisation and internationalisation of research and innovation. Questions are being raised on whether the NSI concept is nearing its sale-by date as international and regional networks of innovation overtake them in the production of knowledge. The 'hollowing out of NSI', though not adequately researched, is an ongoing trend that any proposed review of NSI in Africa and beyond would have to address. Research has barely begun on how to harness the positive outcomes of the internationalisation of innovation systems for national development and on the policy implications for maintaining NSI in the face of sweeping internationalisation of innovation networks. Therefore, it may be useful and interesting to pay more attention to networked innovation systems with boundaries of various nature giving way to the facilitation and incentivisation of networks that are often self-organising and self-maintaining. However, national systems of innovation remain important as laws and policies are still framed with a national context and by national governments notwithstanding the high visibility of regional and supranational networks and systems of innovation. The national state despite the corrosion of sovereignty by globalisation, is still important and the governance and stewardship of networks of innovation rests largely on the national state or on the supra/international organisations where the role of the national state is decisive.

This issue carries five research papers, four research notes, and two book reviews. The research papers and research notes in this issue are an eclectic set that deal with a number of areas from human capital; international collaboration in R&D; financial lending and investment in small-scale agribusiness in Sub-Saharan Africa; assessment of technological innovation in the oil sector; quality in engineering design; broadband connectivity model for rural areas; rural development under different policy regimes, industrial appraisal, and environmental impact of underground natural gas.

The first research paper is by Victor E. Dike on human capital development, technological capabilities and the Nigerian national development where he argues failure to build human capital poses threats to national development.

The second paper by Gonzalo Ordóñez-Matamoros, Susan E. Cozzens, Margarita García-Luque deals with identifying the actors that undertake R & D collaboration in Colombia. The research work identifies that "the number of members holding doctoral degrees and the characteristics of the team leader have the strongest explanatory power of the collaborative behaviour of teams in Colombia"

The third paper by Oluseye O. Jegede, Abiodun A. Egbetokun, and Willie O. Siyanbola deals with assessment of technological innovations in selected indigenous oilfield servicing firms in Nigeria. The research's findings demonstrate that "the overall innovation of the firms for innovations was mainly expressed in organisational changes; product and process innovations in the sub-sector were mainly incremental."

The fourth paper by Zeundjua Tjiparuro is on a guide for enhancing quality in engineering drawings. The paper establishes that the literature fails to appreciate that different checking methods apply to different drawing scenario and identifies two distinct drawings scenarios one based on drawings-for-prototyping and another drawings-for-documentations.

The fifth research paper is on by Benjamin Olatunbosun which examines the impact of climate change to reverse existing disconnect between smallholders and small-scale agribusinesses and financial institutions. His finding demonstrates that the collaboration between financial institutions and smallholders is an appropriate foundation for relationship building which will ease credit constraints, improve information asymmetry and increase agricultural investment.

The first research note is by Nseabasi S. Akpan which explores the rural development in Nigeria under alternative civilian and military regimes. Paradoxically the move from military to post-military regimes have not significantly changed the rural development landscape in Nigeria. The author recommends that a much broader conceptualization of rural development is necessary to include in agricultural development and enhancement of living standard, a broad range of social opportunities to improve the general capabilities of the rural areas.

The second research note is by Fatuma Simba, Lena Trojer, and Zaipuna O. Yonah on sustainable broadband connectivity model for rural areas of Tanzania. The objective is to expand rural broad band connectivity. The paper suggests that the way to do it is to construct robust private, public and peoples partnership.

The third research note is by Oluwatoyin O. Akinola and Olusola A. Olaolorun on lithogeochemistry and industrial appraisal of Igbetti Marble in south western Nigeria. The authors show that the dolomitic Igbetti marble is a very viable refractory raw materials for the steel plant, flux stone in iron smelting, manufacture of sheet glass, furnace lining and production of magnesia lime.

The last research note by Charley I. Anyadiegwu and Emmanuel E. Anyanwu on the environmental impact of natural gas storage discusses the various control measures and recommend that both advanced technology and skilled human capital are critical for improving the environmental safety during the operation of natural gas transportation and storage systems.

In addition to these research papers and research notes the issue carries two book reviews. The first is by Anthony O. Agwuele which reviews the book *Postethnophilosophy* by Sanya Osha, Amsterdam Value Inquiry Book Series, Rodopi Publishers, Amsterdam, New York (2011: 265 pages).

The second book review is by Oghenerobor B. Akpor which reviews the book by Akpor Strydom HA and King ND (editors), *Fuggle & Rabie's Environmental Management in South Africa,* (2nd edition), JUTA Law: Cape Town (2009: pages 1142).

What emerges as a common and shared problem that the authors are grappling with is the importance of human capital, the national system of innovation and the capacity to manage and improve the function level, quality and productivity of the various specific activities the researchers chose to select and investigate with a view to make and add new contributions and recommendations for policy learning. We invite readers to use and engage with the work of the various authors who are mostly from the developing world.

African Journal of Science, Technology, Innovation and Development
Vol. 4, No. 2, 2012
pp. 11-28

Human Capital Development, Technological Capabilities and National Development: The Nigerian Experience

Victor E. Dike*

Abstract

The neglect of education, especially technical and vocational education and science-based technology education in Nigeria has made a review of the poor investment in human capital development and national development rather compelling. The political leaders have always raised the people's hope by painting glowing pictures of their development plans and how they would stimulate the economy and improve the people's living conditions. Thus, they swore that they would give priority attention to human capital development and national development and empower the citizens particularly the poorly educated, unskilled, and unemployed youths with relevant human skills capital (HSK) and entrepreneurial skills to enable them to contribute profoundly to national development. Yet the political leaders have over the years failed to adequately fund education and strengthen the infrastructure and institutions that would drive the economy and create employment for the teeming population. Both the new breed politicians like the old politicians before them are promising to transform the nation into an industrialized society and the people cannot hold their expectations. The reality though is that Nigeria cannot become an industrialized society without investing handsomely on human capital development (education and health) and technological capabilities.

* School of Engineering & Technology, National University (Sacramento Campus), California, USA. Email: vdike@cwnet.com

Keywords: Human capital development, Human skill capital, Entrepreneurial skills, Technological capabilities, National development, Nigeria.

JEL Classification: O21; O30; O55.

1. Introduction

This paper examines the forces that have prevented the leaders from utilizing effectively the abundant human and natural resources at their disposal to build up the technological base of the society and transform the nation into an industrialized country. The population of Nigeria is estimated to be about154 million and rapidly growing without commensurate economic growth rate and development to sustain the teeming population (NBS, 2009). Unemployment rate is over 14 percent and public schools lack adequate funding to provide quality education to students; and the few private schools in the society are beyond the reach of the common people (NBS, 2009; Kakwagh and Ikwuba, 2010).

And teachers at all levels of the educational system (primary, secondary, and tertiary) are not properly motivated to effectively perform their duties. As a result, they are always on strike to force the government to pay their basic salaries and benefits; the government has over the years been promising to improve their conditions of services, but has each time failed to honour its promises. And the teachers' frequent industrial actions have more often than not disrupted regular academic calendars (NBS, 2009). Consequently, experienced and high quality teachers who are disgusted and cannot any longer tolerate the poor conditions of services they found themselves in and are leaving in droves to other neighbouring countries with better working conditions. These are among the major causes of the dwindling standard of education in Nigeria. Poor investment in human capital development (education and health) and particularly the neglect of technical and vocational education and training (TVET) and science-based technology education has contributed in no small measures a lack of highly-skilled technical manpower and "technological capabilities" (Mahon, 2003) to drive the economy and transform Nigeria into an industrialized society and improve the living conditions of the teeming population.

Experts in human capital development ranging from classical scholars such as Schumpeter (1942) and others, to the contemporary scholars such as Schultz (1993) and Hanushek and Kym, (2005) have identified some dimensions of human capital: entrepreneurship skills (or human skills or human skills capital); technological progress that results from Joseph Schumpeter's 'creative destructive'; and accumulated human knowledge and skills that are as important as physical capital in the production process; and of course social capital (relationship between individual-social or institutional capital. These are some of the positive results of long-term investment in human capital development (education and health) (Piazza-Georgi, 2002).

But poor leadership and governance are the integral part of the causes of the problems facing the nation, as they have made investment in human capital development difficult. Economic growth and development are difficult if not impossible in any society that does not seriously invest in human capital development. And that is the crux of the matter with oil-rich Nigeria where the majority of the political leaders are not working for the well-being of the citizenry but for their selfish purposes. They are known to have diverted public funds allocated to education and other national development programs to their private bank accounts. In addition to the poor investment in human capital development is the neglect of the infrastructure and institutions that drive the economy. Today, these structures are in shambles, leading to unfriendly business environment. Many of the business organizations, particularly manufacturing industries are closing down, leading to rising unemployment and crime. The industries that can afford it are relocating to neighbouring countries with alluring business environment.

It is unquestionably a Herculean task to govern a society, but it becomes much more daunting in a society such as Nigeria with an uncertain sociopolitical and economic environment. The state and fate of Nigeria is today defined by the ineffectiveness of the political leaders, non-functional institutions and dilapidated infrastructure that have crippled the economy and pauperized the people. Thus, the myriad sociopolitical and economic problems facing the society today are exerting untold pressure on the people who are utilizing every available opportunity to pour out their anger and frustration. The question is can the greedy and 'me first' new breed politicians lead Nigeria to true democracy, true capitalistic system, and economic prosperity?

2. Purpose

The purpose of this paper is to examine the obstacles to Nigeria's quest for national development, from the point of view of investment in human capital development, technological capability, and good governance and leadership. Thus, the paper seeks to discuss the issues in an attempt to suggest some solutions to the policymakers.

3. Research Methods

The data for this case study were derived from the research and analysis of scholars, analysts and practitioners, government documents and recent newspaper and journal articles. This is to say that the primary method of study was an extensive review of available literature for an in-depth analysis of the problems facing the Nigerian educational system and the economy. The sources of information were carefully evaluated and analyzed to determine their veracity. The educational system of any society is designed to transmit the beliefs, values, attitudes, and norms from one generation to another as well as to train skilled technical manpower to drive and sustain the economy.

4. Problem Statement

Over the years Nigeria has been investing less on education, infrastructure, and institutions that are critical to building to a viable economy. Yet the political leaders think that Nigeria can be transformed into an industrialized society without these necessary preconditions. The political leaders of Nigeria do not appear to be working for the people's welfare, but for their own. Thus, the people should check their enthusiasm whenever they make their usual paper promises. The developed countries around the globe could not have become what they are today without investing in human capital development, good governance and leadership, and technological capability.

5. Research Questions

This paper focuses on the following research questions: Can Nigeria become an industrialized society without functional fundamental institutions and infrastructure (such as effective judicial system, stable electricity supply, functional educational system, good network of roads, security, good leadership and good governance)? Are Nigerians (leaders and followers) making good efforts to resolve the challenges facing the nation and her quest for national development? Can Nigeria meet her challenges for national development without copious investments in human capital development and technological capabilities? Can the people (the leaders and followers) build the technological base that will transform Nigeria into an industrialized society?

6. Challenges Facing Education and the Nigerian Economy

This paper will discuss the myriad forces that have prevented Nigeria from investing in education and the emerging instructional technologies so as to empower the citizens with employability skills through quality education directed by highly trained and motivated teachers. From the foreground it has convincingly been argued by human capital development gurus that without investment in human capital, physical capital, and social capital, economic growth and development will be difficult if not impossible.

7. Human Capital Development

Both ancient and contemporary human and social capital thinkers have been confronted by the issue of human capital development for decades because they recognize their critical role human capital and physical capital development play in individual worker's productive capability, the prosperity of a nation, and the overall living condition of the people (Schumpeter, 1942; Schultz, 1993; Becker, 1993; Hanushek and Kym, 2005; Bell and Pavitt, 1995).

However, Becker (1993) who is widely known for his work on human capital development observed that human capital theory tends to draw a distinction between general education and specific training. He observed that the key focus of human capital theory is how education increases human productivity by improving human knowledge and skills and increases an individual worker's the productive capacity, future income, and lifetime earnings. Thus, the neglect of this important element has a far-reaching consequence on the welfare of a nation. According to Becker (1993) general education creates general human capital, and technical and vocational education provides specific human capital. In human capital framework the economic prosperity and progress of a nation depends precariously on the stock of its physical and human capital.

This author anchors his work on this perspective because no nation can talk about the manpower planning, growth and development, and the creation of employment to improve the lives of the citizens without bringing education (formal, non-formal and informal) or learning into the equation. This is because the shortage of manpower (this author emphasizes technical education) has the tendency to impede individual worker productivity, national productivity, and economic growth. In other words, human resource development has an essential role to play in the economic health of a nation (Perkins *et al.*, 2001).

Recognizing the importance of education in national development, the UNESCO international experts in their meeting in Bonn, declared that "since education is considered the key to effective development strategies, technical and vocational education and training must be the master key that can…, improve the quality of life for all and help achieve sustainable development" (UNESCO, 2004: 107). One of the major problems facing the Nigerian democracy and economy is that the nation, which is aspiring to transform into an advanced economy, is not investing in the necessary institutional and infrastructural conditions.

Social thinkers in the field of human capital and social capital theory have observed that worker's productivity capability is determined by the many variables, including its human skills and ability, health, motivation, and job satisfaction (Judge, May 2001). Experts in this field as well as social analysts have also observed that the majority of the sociopolitical and economic issues facing Nigeria can be attributed to its poor investment in human capital and physical capital development, poor governance, and visionless leadership (Dike, April-September, 2010; Ferriss, 2006; Lewis, 2004).

Nigeria's underdevelopment status can also be traced to inept leadership, which breeds corruption that has become pandemic in the society (see *San Francisco Chronicle*, 2007; Dike, April-September, 2010). And this appears the undisputable reason for the lack of investment in institutional and infrastructural structures, human capital development (particularly health, technical and vocational education and training, and science-based technology education) that will enable that nation to develop a good stock of highly-skilled technical manpower that drive economic growth and national development and improve the health of the nation (Krueger and Mikael, 2001).

Thus, a lack of long-term investments in human capital and the accumulation of knowledge and human skills and "physical capital development" or the "stock of equipment and structures that are used to produce goods and services" (Mankiw, 2008) constitute a bottleneck to economic growth and development and creation of employment for the citizens (Hanushek and Kym 2005; Becker, 1993). Specifically, poor investment in human capital development and physical capital development (poor electricity distribution, poor potable water supply, poor network of roads, railways, airways, congested sea ports, poor postal system, etc.), has contributed in no small measures to the poor performance of the economy, and by extension, the dwindling standard of education in Nigeria.

Over the years employers of labour in Nigeria have been complaining that most of the recent university graduates lack employability skills and problem-solving abilities and other competencies that are the main variables that determine an individual worker's productivity capabilities (Mankiw, 2008; Dike, 2002). Yet Nigeria's educational administrators and policymakers have done very little, if anything, to improve the quality of human capital, which has direct bearing on workers' productivity (Perkins *et al.*, 2001).

However, because of the role of 'human skills capital' (HSK) on individual productivity and by extension their profit margins, organizations around the globe are said to be spending billions of dollars annually to educate and upgrade their employees' 'human skills capital'(Piazza-Georgi, 2002). More often than not workers are rewarded for their higher productivity and the high quality of their goods and services, which influences their firms profits margins (Clayton, 1995). A journey back to the memory lane shows that before independence in 1960 the schools in Nigeria were properly funded and managed and the students were well behaved and the quality of graduates was equal to those from advanced nations (Dike, 2002). But today, the schools lack adequate funding to hire quality teachers' and purchase the necessary instructional technologies to produce high quality graduates and enhance technological development. Studies show that no nation can make any meaningful socioeconomic and political stride without a good pool of skilled technical manpower (Hanushek and Kym, 2005) and technological capabilities (Mohan, 2003; Bell and Pavitt, 1995).

Instead of Nigeria's schools to be properly funded and developed into a place for high quality-research, technological innovation, and for good character formation, they have become a breeding ground for cultism and other destructive social behaviours. Today, 'values education', good 'moral values' and civic responsibility, which shape the character of nations, have become a thing of the past (Dike, 2002). As Lickona (1992) has aptly observed 'respect and responsibility are the two foundational moral values' that a society should teach its citizens. Others admirable qualities include honesty, fairness, tolerance, prudence, self-discipline, helpfulness, compassion, cooperation, courage (the virtues of Aristotle) among other democratic values. Thus, 'taking responsibility for the things we do wrong as well as the things we do right' (Lickona, 1992) is important for national development.

As noted earlier, as the nation's quality of education is rapidly deteriorating so is also the economic environment. In its 2010 report on 'Doing Business in Nigeria 2010-Through Difficult Times', the World Bank ranked Nigeria 125 out of 182 economies surveyed in its Global Doing Business Report. The report showed that about 90 per cent of Nigerian businesses that operate in the informal sector lack access to credit. One would add that similar problems are being faced by those in the formal sector of the economy. And in its 2008 Review of World Development, the United Nations Development Programme (UNDP) ranked Nigeria 157 out of 177 in Human Development Index; Nigeria was also among the 'Least Liveable' nations (UNDP, 2008).

Some of the problems facing Nigeria today require common sense solutions, but others would involve sophisticated framework of ideas and application of advanced technologies. As Albert Einstein observed decades ago, "the specific problems we face today cannot be solved at the same level of thinking we were at when we created them" (see quote from Albert Einstein, n/d). Thus, for the economy to grow and for businesses to thrive and create employment, Nigeria should employ or elect political leaders with proper skills, knowledge and vision as well as political courage to adopt and implement policies to meet the challenges facing the nation.

8. Leadership and Governance

The issue of the role leadership in the direction of organizations and development of nations has continued to prompt debates as leadership appears to have many meanings (Marquis and Huston, 2012). Although there is no single definition of leadership it is imperative for this paper to consider some perspectives. Ward (2009) has defined leadership as "the art of motivating a group of people to act towards achieving a common goal" and not a selfish objective. And as Northouse (2007: 3) has aptly noted, leadership "is a process of getting things done through people"; it "means responsibility" - having "passion for the purpose and the mission of the organization" or society one leads.

However, because of poor leadership or 'leadership without a purpose' the state of the polity appears to be rapidly deteriorating because very few of the leaders of Nigeria, if any, work to improve the living conditions of the citizenry. Over the years a wave reform programs have been undertaken, but the society still lacks the leadership with political will and commitment to implement effective policies to transform the economy and tackle the sociopolitical problems facing the nation. The political leaders do not seem to understand that leadership is assuming responsibility for something. They appear good at prescribing solutions to economic problems (Dike, 2003) without providing the institutional and infrastructural framework to help the economy grow (Acemoglu, 2003; Edison, 2003).

And more often than not, their policies are hastily put together and poorly executed. The political landscape is littered with wreckage of unreasoned policies and those involved in such activities appear to enjoy the nation's underdeveloped status (Dike, 2003). Given the foreground, the activities of the leaders shape the reality of the nations they lead (UNDP, 2008). To resolve the leadership challenge facing Nigeria today and transform its organizations into productive entities (Kouzes and Posner, 1995) Nigerians must elect or appoint men and women of proven integrity, drive and know-how to transform (Burns, 2003) and manage the affairs of the nation. This is because without meeting the ethical and leadership challenges (Johnson, 2005) and improving organizational effectiveness (Bass and Avolio, 1994) Nigeria may not achieve her objectives. The nation's economic growth and development rests with good leadership and governance. Thus, for Nigeria to move forward the leaders as well as the followers must clean up their act and invest in the fundamental infrastructure and institution that will promote technological innovation, transform the economy, and develop the society.

Related to the leadership problem is governance, which has among others, been defined as a system of values, policies, and institutions by which a society manages its economic, social, and political affairs through interactions within the state, civil society and private sector. Put differently, governance comprises the mechanisms and processes for citizens and groups to articulate their interests, to work together and mediate their differences, and exercise their legal rights and obligations with rules, institutions and practices that set limits and provide incentives for individuals, organizations and firms (UNDP, 2008). Thus, good governance (political, economic and social governance) - the three dimensions of governance (Shabbir-Cheema, May 2005) refers to the question of how a society can organize itself to ensure equality of opportunity and equity (social and economic justice) for all citizens. Good governance promotes people-centered development; but 'bad governance', which is the opposite of good governance (Shabbir-Cheema, May 2005) is among the major cause of the problems facing Nigeria. For instance, the people are not allowed equal economic opportunity and freedom to participate in the political process. And this is threatening to destabilize the polity and undermine Nigeria's democratization process.

According to Sen (1999), 'unfreedoms' leave the people with little choice to exercise 'their reasoned agency, and "Freedoms are not only the primary ends of development, they are also among its primary means". Thus, development whether social, political and economic, "requires the removal of major sources of unfreedoms" (Sen, 1999: 36-37). Because of bad governance (and thus corruption) Nigeria's system lacks checks and balances (or mechanisms) to control the autocratic tendencies in government and to hold political actors accountable for their actions. The politicians do not practice ethical politics and their actions do not add values to the system. Lack of 'ethical politics and values' and politics of hate and destruction have contributed significantly to the economic and political hiccups in the society. Corruption (Smith, 2008) is, however, a greater part of the problems facing Nigeria as it leads to bad governance that has hampered socio-political and economic development.

9. Bribery and Corruption

Although corruption is a global scourge, Nigeria appears to suffer the most from it because the leaders are pathologically corrupt. Is Nigeria born to be corrupt? Everyone appears to believe that Nigeria has a 'culture of corruption' (Smith, 2008). Over the years, Nigeria has earned a lot of revenue from crude oil, which has gone down the sinkhole created by corruption. An article in the *San Francisco Chronicle*, 11 March 2007, described Nigeria as a rich nation floating on oil wealth ,but almost none of it flows to the people' "Oil giant that runs on grease of politics." This is evidence in the fact that top public servants are very rich because they harbour the mentality that public money belongs to no one (Dike, April-September, 2010; October-March, 2011).

Nigeria appears a hotbed of corruption and the so-called 'war against corruption' seems like trying to contain the wind. The country has become synonymous with corruption. Majority of the elected officials, appointees, and top government are corrupt. They often extract bribes from the citizens (business owners, those seeking to do business with the state, etc.) while performing their official duties. The magnitude of high-profile political corruption in Nigeria tends to dwarf any genuine efforts to enhance economic growth and nation development and diminishes the peoples' trust in government. National dailies are awash with news of how public officials are acquiring million-dollar homes (within and outside Nigeria) and stockpiling stolen public money in financial institutions abroad. Thus, corruption scandals are strewn all over the society like a straw hut in a hurricane (*BusinessDay,* 14 May 2010; 15 May 2010; and 17 April 2012).

There are two sides to every problem; private individuals are also involved in corrupt activities. A spate of studies shows that corruption leads to "poor governance and low growth" and hampers social development (Rose-Ackerman, 2004). And the leaders of Nigeria have demonstrated their unwillingness to reform the society despite the number of top government officials involved in corruption (*BusinessDay,* 14 May 2010; 15 May 2010; and 17 April 2012). For instance, the former governor of Delta State, James Ibori, who eluded the Economic and Financial Crimes Commission (EFCC), was arrested in Dubai recently (*BusinessDay,* 14 May 2010) on money laundering charges.

Since corruption is an anathema to political stability and economic prosperity this author can hazard to conclude that Nigeria's problems are not from the "harshness and the niggardliness of nature" (Keynes, May 1932), but corruption that prevented the society from investing in human capital development, particularly technological capabilities that would drive the economy, create employment, and put the nation's abundant human and resources into productive use.

If the political leaders want to fight corruption they should start by fixing the economy because some of the petty corrupt activities are caused by poverty. For instance, the roads and highways in the society are roadblocks manned by police officers who are virtually thieves in uniform; they are ill-trained and poorly paid (Dike, April-September, 2010; October-March, 2011). In addition, to breathe a new life into the nation's ossified economy

Nigeria must strengthen her critical institutions and infrastructure that drive the economy.

10. Infrastructural and Institutional Challenges

Any person familiar with Nigeria would agree that among the challenges facing the economy is ineffective institutions and dilapidated infrastructure (bad roads, erratic power supply, limited access to potable water and basic healthcare, and ineffective regulatory agencies, et cetera).The plethora of reforms and development policies are ineffective due to shoddy infrastructure and institutional failure (Hoff and Fall, 2003). In particular, electricity supply is poor and expensive; and investors are not impressed. In a country where electricity takes about 40 percent cost of production improving electricity supply would lure foreign investors into the society and spur the sluggish economy (*Daily Sun,* 07 June 2010). Without functional infrastructure and effective institutions and with good education system Nigeria can be turned into the Singapore of West Africa. Singapore is said to have 'one of the world's best-educated populations and busiest port' (*The Economist,* 25 February 2012: 80).

As economists have observed, building a vibrant economy or restoring growth to an ailing economy takes resources. To ensure long-term growth and prosperity, Nigeria must use its resources wisely, invest in science-based technology education to train a good stock of highly-skilled technical manpower to build and maintain the critical institutions and infrastructure without which the economy will not gain from the "power of productivity" (Lewis, 2004). A nation enjoys higher standards of living if the workers can produce large quantities of quality goods and services for local consumption and extra for export (Mankiw, 2008). Without technological capabilities, however, the economic will remain in shambles, productivity will remain low, the quality of goods and services will remain poor, and Nigeria will be unable to produce enough food to feed its teeming population and will not effectively compete in the global marketplace.

11. Technological Capabilities

This paper posits that the problems facing the Nigerian economy (including the low capability utilization of domestic industries and firms) hinge precariously on the nation's poor investment in human capital development (education and health) and a lack of long-term investment in education, particularly science-based technology education and technical and vocational education and training (TVET) that will enable the country to develop a good stock of highly-skilled technical manpower training to provoke system innovation, technological development and economic growth that will sustain its industrialization process.

Put differently, the 'growth tragedy' (Easterly and Levin, April 1997), of the Nigerian economy has its roots in ineffective and inefficient domestic development policy design and implementations and the failure of the policymakers to learn from the impressive history of economic growth and development of the East Asian countries, that are today branded Asian Tigers. Thus, to move forward technologically Nigeria has to copiously invest in technical education and develop "an effective national system of innovation" (Mohan, 2003), which is a precondition for rapid technological development. The pace of technological change in any society is a reflection of the health of its infrastructure and institutions, and of courses its social capital, which will encourage innovative system activities and enhance industrial capital accumulation and technological transformation and national development (Mohan, 2003).

As in human capital development, physical capital development in the form of technological capabilities and innovation will drive a sagging economy and create employment. Some studies show that there is a correlation between the underdeveloped status and soaring unemployment in developing nations, including Nigeria, to their lack of technological capabilities and a good stock of highly-skilled technical manpower to drive the economy and create employment (Rose, 2009; Mohan, 2003; Sen, 1975; Dike, October-March, 2011).

Thus, because of a lack of investment in science-based technology education and technical and vocational education and training (TVET)Nigeria is suffering from a shortage of highly-skilled technical manpower to build and maintain its critical infrastructure and produce quality goods and services at a least cost and compete effectively in the global marketplace. And the ongoing global financial and economic crisis that started in 2008 has worsened the already bad economic situation in Nigeria, including rising youth unemployment (Kakwagh and Ikwuba, 2010), social crisis and lawlessness (e.g. kidnapping for ransom and the *Boko Haram*, a militant Islamic group) onslaught (*Daily Trust*, 18 August 2010; *ThisDay*, 09 January 2012).

Social scientists, especially economists have aptly noted that modern economy demands technological skills to enhance innovation and to function effectively and efficiently (Rose, 2009; Offor, 2007; Freeman, 1987). In particular, development economists have noted that socio-economic changes or transformations are impossible in any society without the preconditions, one of which is technological capabilities (Webb and Grant, 2003; Soubbotina, 2004). In addition, studies show that no nation has developed without 'technological capabilities' (Kim, 1980, 1997; Bell and Pavitt, 1995; Mohan, 2003).

For Kim (1980) "technological capability" is "the ability to make effective use of technological knowledge in efforts to assimilate, use, adapt and change existing technologies" (Kim, 1980: 254-277). In fact, experts have noted that 'technological capability' is an essential component for "sustainable development", which is a 'development' that 'meets the needs of the present generation without compromising the ability of future generations to meet their own needs' (United Nations, 11 December 1987; Smith and Rees, 1998). In spite of some flickers of development efforts (some people would argue that the efforts are not meaningful-that they are mere political rhetoric), the economic environment remains very unfriendly with industries and organizations still facing a huge hurdle. However, because of the poor employment opportunities most of the youth are frustrated and desperate to leave the country. Stories abound of how desperate Nigerians, mostly youth, take extraordinary risks to travel to Europe, the United States and even to some African nations in search of an elusive better life. Some of them have been arrested, tortured, and maimed or imprisoned in foreign countries; and some of them have died in the deserts of North Africa in the process of trying to escape economic hardship (Hamoon, 13 May 2006; Fletcher, *BBC News*, 05 December 2007).

12. Concluding Remarks

System Innovation and Technological Capabilities

Does Nigeria possess the needed skilled technical manpower for system innovation and technological transformation? The world economy is rapidly changing and the only countries that are capable to compete effectively in the global marketplace are those that are investing in human capital development and technological innovation. Nigerians are tired of being hungry in the midst of plenty. Investors (both domestic and foreign) are not motivated to invest in the domestic economy because of the unlimited hurdles posed by the shoddy infrastructure and institutions.

It is impossible for Nigeria to meet her technological and system challenges and move along with the changing global economy without investing copiously in technological education and research and development. To transform her economy and effectively compete in the global marketplace tomorrow Nigeria should begin today to nurture and strengthen the infrastructure and institutions that makes technological development possible. Technological innovation will give rise to new entrepreneurs and knowledge-driven industries that will push down the barriers to economic growth and development.

Thus, no nation can grow and thrive in the present knowledge-intensive global economy without a long-term investment in human capital development (education and health), system and technological innovation. No society can grow and thrive in the present twenty century knowledge-driven global economy without copious investment in human capital development (education and health), research and development (R&D) and technological innovation either by developing serious indigenous technological innovation (fresh thinking) or copying and adapting other nation's technological ideas in the cheapest possible means.

China and other serious nations have gone through this route to become technological giants. And today, China possesses the technological clout to gain from the power of productivity (*The Economist,* May 26th – June 1st, 2012). To move forward, Nigeria should adopt and adapt the economic policies and technological innovation of successful nations. Nigeria can become an industrialized nation either by developing her indigenous technology or copy and adapt other nation's technological ideas by the cheapest possible means.

Thus, without creating a hospitable environment to lure investors into the economy; and without ensuring that the Constitution and rule of law is respected and business contracts honoured; and without investing in human capital development, particularly technology education Nigeria will continue to dream of being an industrialized nation.

References

Acemoglu, D. (2003), 'Root Causes: A historical approach to assessing the role of institutions in economic development', in *Finance and Development,* June, 40 (2): 27-30.

Bass, B.M. and Avolio, B.J. (1994), *Improving Organizational Effectiveness through Transformational Leadership*, Thousand Oaks, CA: Sage.

Becker, G.S. (1993 [1964]), *Human Capital: A Theoretical and Empirical Analysis, with Special Reference to Education,* 3rd edition, Chicago: University of Chicago Press.

Bell, M. and Pavitt, K. (1995), 'The Development of Technological Capabilities', In Hague, I. U. (ed.), *Trade, Technology and International Competitiveness,* Washington, DC: The World Bank.

Burns, J.M. (2003), *Transforming leadership,* New York: NY: Grove/Atlantic, Inc.

Business Day (2010), 'EFCC seeks Ibori's extradition from Dubai', May 14.

Business Day (2010), 'I resigned to face corruption charges-Ogbulafor', May 15.

Business Day (2012), 'Ibori jailed for 13 years', April 17.

Clayton G.E. (1995), *Economics: Principles and Practices*, New York: Glenco, McGraw-Hill.

Daily Trust (2010), 'Experts Proffer Solution to Collapse of Buildings', August 18.

Daily Sun (2010), 'In Nigeria, power is about 40% cost of production – John Aluya, MD, TechnoGlass', June 7.

Dike, V. E. (2002), 'The State of Education in Nigeria and the Health of the Nation', in *NESG Economic Indicators*, Jan-March, 8(1): 45-50

Dike, V. E. (2003), 'Nigeria: Economic Growth and Institutional Factors', in *NESG Economic Indicators*, October–December, 9 (4): 46-50.

Dike, V.E. (2010), 'Review of the Challenges facing the Nigerian Economy: What is the Way Forward?' in *NESG Economic & Policy Review*, 17(2&3): 45-53.

Dike, V.E. (2011), 'Can Nigeria build its economic future?', A Critical Review of Issues Facing the Nation', in *Economic and Policy Review*, 17&18(4&1): 24-32.

Edison, H. (2003), 'Test the Links: How strong is the links between institutional quality and economic performance?' in *Finance and Development*, June, 40(2): 35-37.

Easterly, W. and Levin, R. (April 1997), 'Africa's Growth Tragedy: Policies and Ethic Divisions', Available at: http://williameasterly.files.wordpress.com/2010/08/17_easterly_levine_africasgrowthtragedy_prp.pdfon (Accessed: 17 February 2012).

Einstein, A. (n/d), Available at: http://www.quotedb.com/quotes/11 (Accessed: 28 March 2011).

Ferriss, A.L. (2006), 'A Theory of Social Structure and the Quality of Life', in *Applied Research in Quality of Life*, May, 1(1): 117-123.

Fletcher, P. (2007), 'Mirage of rich Europe Lures Job-Hungry Africa', *BBC News-online*, December 5.

Freeman, C. (1987), *Technology and Economic Performance: Lessons from Japan*, London: Pinter.

Hamoon, S. (2006), *Africa Transit Migration through Libya to Europe: the Human Cost,* May 13, Cairo: FMRS/AUC.

Hanushek, E. and Kym, D. (2005), 'Schooling Labour Forces Quality and Economic Growth', *NBER Working Paper 5399,* Cambridge, MA.

Hoff, K. (2003), 'Paths of Institutional Development: A view from Economic History', in *The World Bank Research Observer,* Fall, 18(2): 205-226.

Judge T.A., Thoresen, C.J., Bono, J.E. and Patton, G.K. (May 2001), 'The job satisfaction–job Performance relationship: A qualitative and quantitative review', in *Psychological Bulletin,* 127(3): 376-407.

Johnson, C.E. (2005), *Meeting Ethical Challenges of Leadership,* 2nd edition, Thousand Oaks, VA: Sage

Kakwagh, V.V. and Ikwuba, A. (2010), 'Unemployment in Nigeria: Causes and Related Issues', in *Canadian Social Science,* 6(4): 61-67.

Keynes, J.M. (1932), 'The World's Economic Outlook.', *The Atlantic,* Available at: http://www.theatlantic.com/unbound/flashbks/budget/keynesf.htm (Accessed: 04 December 2006).

Kim, L. (1980), 'Stages of Development in Industrial technology in a Developing Country', in *Research Policy,* 9(3): 254-277.

Kim, L. (1997), *From Imitation to Innovation: The dynamics of Korea's Technological Learning,* Boston, MA: Harvard Business School Press.

Kouzes, J.M. and Posner, B.Z. (1995), *The Leadership Challenge: How to keep getting extraordinary things done in Organizations,* San Francisco: Jose-Bass.

Krueger, A.B. and Mikael, L. (2001), 'Education for Growth, Why and for Whom?' in *Journal of Economic Literature,* 39(4): 1101–136.

Lewis, W.W. (2004), *The Power of Productivity: Wealth, Poverty, and the Threat to Global Stability,* Chicago: University of Chicago Press.

Lickona, T. (1992, October), *Educating for Character: How Our Schools can Teach Respect and Responsibility,* New York: Bantman Books.

Mankiw, N. G. (2008), *Essentials of Economics,* 5th edition, South-Western: CENGAGE Learning: Australia.

Marquis, B.L. and Huston, C.J. (2012), *Leadership Roles and Management Functions in Nursing*. New Delhi: Wolters Kluwer, Lippincott Williams and Wilkins.

Mohan R. (2003), *Facets of the Indian Economy: The NCAER Golden Jubilee Lectures*, New Delhi, India: Oxford University Press.

National Bureau of Statistics (NBS) (2009), 'Federal Government of Nigeria-Statistical Fact Sheet on Economic and Social Development', Nigeria: Abuja.

Northouse, G. (2007), *Leadership theory and practice*, 3rd edition, Thousand Oak, London, New Delhi: Sage Publications.

Offor, E.N. (2007), 'Refocusing Science and Technology Education toward National Development', in *Knowledge Review: A Multidisciplinary Journal of NAFAK*, 15 (6): 53-55

Perkins, D.H., Radelet, S., Snowgrass, D.R., Gillis, M., and Roemer, M. (2001), *Economic Development*, 5th edition, W.W. Norton Company. See in particular Chapters 8 and 9.

Piazza-Georgi, B. (2002), 'The role of human and social capital in growth: extending our Understanding', in *Cambridge Journal of Economics*, 26: 461-479.

Rose-Ackerman, S. (2004), 'Governance and Corruption', In Lomborg, B. (ed.), *Global Crises, Global Solutions*. Cambridge: Cambridge University Press.

Rose, K. (2009), 'Enhancing Innovation in Developing Country Systems: A Synthesis of Case Studies and Lesson from Uganda', in *African Journal of Science and Technology, Innovation and Development*, 1(2&3): 89-114.

San Francisco Chronicle (2007), 'Oil giant that runs on grease of politics', March 11.

Schumpeter, J.A. (1942), *Capitalism, Socialism and Democracy*: Harper (reprinted by Harper Colophon, 1975).

Schultz, T.W. (1993), *Origins of Increasing Returns*, Oxford, Blackwell.

Sen, A. (1975), *Employment, Technology and Development*, Oxford: Clarendon.

Sen, A. (1999), *Development as Freedom*, New York: Anchor Books (see Chapters 1-3), pp.36-37.

Shabbir Cheema, G. (2004), 'From public administration to governance: the paradigm shift in the link between government and citizens', *Paper presented at the 6th Global Forum on Reinventing Government: Towards Participatory and Transparent Governance*, 24-27 May 2005.

Smith, C. and Rees, G. (1998), *Economic Development*, 2nd edition, Basingstoke: Macmillan.

Smith, D.J. (2008), *A Culture of Corruption*, Princeton and Oxford: Princeton University Press.

Soubbotina, T.P. (2004), *Beyond Economic Growth: An Introduction to Sustainable Development*, 2nd edition, Washington DC.: World Bank Publications.

The Economist (2012), 'Business in Rwanda-"Africa's Singapore?"' p. 80.

The Economist (May 26 - June 1, 2012), 'How strong is China's economy?' p. 11.

This Day (2012), 'Jonathan-Boko Haram Has Sympathizers in Govt', January 9.

United Nations (1987), 'Report of the World Commission on Environment and Development', General Assembly Resolution 42/187, December 11. Available at: http://www.un-documents.net/a42r187.htm (Accessed: 06 September 2010).

UNESCO (2004), *Learning for Work, Citizenship and Sustainability*, Final report, UNESCO International Experts Meeting, Bonn, Germany, 25-28 October 2004:107.

UNDP (2008), 2008 Review of World Population, New York: The United Nations.

Ward, S. (2009), 'Leadership', About.com. Canada: Small Business; Available at: http://sbinfocanada.about.com/od/leadership/g/leadership.htmon (Accessed: 18 March 2012.

Webb, C. J. and Grant, C. (2003), 'Economic Transformation: An Implementation Framework', *Tertiary Education Commission Research Paper*, Wellington: Tertiary Education Commission.

African Journal of Science, Technology, Innovation and Development
Vol. 4, No. 2, 2012
pp. 29-68

Who Collaborates Internationally on R&D in Colombia?

Gonzalo Ordóñez-Matamoros*, Susan E. Cozzens**
& Margarita García-Luque***

Abstract

This paper delves on the determinants of international research collaboration involving developing countries, and provides evidence on the effects of both structural and functional factors on the design of collaborative strategies at the research team level. In particular, it studies the characteristics and collaborative patterns of 1889 Colombian research teams working in all scientific areas. It explores the effects of team size, team age, the number of team members with doctoral degrees, the characteristics of the team leader, the performance of the team, the sector of operation, the characteristics of the institution of affiliation, and the characteristics of the region they are

* University of Twente, Institute for Innovation and Governance Studies (IGS), Dept: Science, Technology, and Policy Studies (STePS), NL-7500 AE Enschede, Netherlands; Univ Externado de Colombia, Centro de Investigaciones y Proyectos Especiales (CIPE), Bogotá, D.C. Colombia.
Email: gonzalo.ordonez@uexternado.edu.co; h.g.ordonezmatamoros@utwente.nl

** University of Georgia Institute of Technology, School of Public Policy, Dept: Technology Policy and Assessment Center (TPAC), Atlanta, GA, USA.
Email: susan.cozzens@iac.gatech.edu

*** Universidad Externado de Colombia, Bogotá, Colombia.
Email: mgarciluque@hotmail.com

located. A logistic regression model is used to account for the factors affecting the collaboration modality (hosting foreign researchers, working in projects with foreign funding, and co-authoring with colleagues working overseas) as well as the type of partner involved (partners from Northern and Southern countries). It finds that the number of members holding doctoral degrees and the characteristics of the team leader have the strongest explanatory power of the collaborative behaviour of teams in Colombia. It concludes outlining policy implications and recommendations.

Keywords: International research collaboration, Research collaboration patterns, R&D collaboration, North-South research collaboration, Colombia.

JEL Classification: O31; O34; O55.

1. Introduction

International research collaboration is a growing social phenomenon (Wagner and Leydesdorff 2006; NSF-NSB 2008). It results in part as a strategy to deal with increasingly complex problems and the rising costs of research (Luukkonen *et al.*, 1992; Gibbons, Limoges *et al.*, 1994; Adams *et al.*, 2005), as well as a result from government policies oriented to favour globalization (Georghiou, 1998; Wagner *et al.*, 2001). The continuous fall of communication costs and the increased mobility of scientists and students across borders are some of the factors facilitating this phenomenon.

According to the US National Science Foundation (NSF), the number of international articles with authors from at least two countries more than doubled in share between 1988 and 2003 from 8% to 20%. The number of countries collaborating on an article also expanded. In 2003, more than 60 countries had co-authored with other countries, compared with 32 in 1996 (NSF-NSB 2006). Over the period, 1995-2005, intercontinental co-authorship increased as a percentage of total article output for the US (from 17% to 27%), for the EU (from 18% to 26%), and for Asia (from 16% to 19%)(NSF-NSB 2008), resulting in an increasing level of international interdependence of the research enterprise (Narin *et al.*, 1991; Glänzel and Schubert, 2004; Glanzel and Schubert, 2005; NSF-NSB, 2008).

This trend is not only taking place in developed countries but is arguably happening at a particularly rapid pace in developing countries. In fact, Wagner and Leydesdorff (2005) show that the global network has become denser and that more countries can be counted as part of the core component of the global S&T network (Wagner and Leydesdorff, 2005; Wagner and Leydesdorff, 2006).

More importantly, policy discourse and literature increasingly claim positive effects of international collaboration on local scientific and technological capabilities in these countries. It is assumed to give local scientists and engineers in developing countries access to new knowledge and research resources they would not have otherwise within their national boundaries. It is said to raise the quality of the research performed in those countries, increasing the possibility for local scientists and engineers to benefit from the expertise brought about by international partners.

The purpose of this paper is to contribute to a better understanding of the determinants of international research collaboration in developing countries, using Colombia as a case study. In fact, knowing the factors that affect the choice of collaborating internationally by teams located in developing countries will help to better design policies aimed at creating the necessary conditions for local research teams to benefit from the internationalization process currently underway within the R&D community.

2. Why Research Collaboration?

In the literature, research collaboration is mostly portrayed as an important enabler of science and technology development. It is considered to be 'better' than individualistic research in several respects. Many argue that research collaboration has greater epistemic authority (Wray, 2002; Beaver, 2004); facilitates diffusion of information and ideas; increases access to new knowledge and research tools; and offers visibility and feedback (Crane, 1972; Beaver and Rosen, 1979; Rigby and Edler, 2005). These are crucial elements for the use and production of new knowledge and technology.

More importantly, most of the literature on the topic claims that research collaboration is an important source of creativity (Farrell, 2001; Burt, 2004; Levine and Moreland, 2004; Uzzi and Spiro, 2005), which in the right set of conditions may increase: a) scientific productivity (Beaver and Rosen, 1979; Landry *et al.*, 1996; Adams *et al.*, 2005; Lee and Bozeman, 2005; Turner and Mairesse, 2005), b) research quality (Diamond, 1985; Katz and Hicks, 1997; Basu and Aggarwal, 2001; Frenken *et al.*, 2005; Rigby and Edler, 2005), c) innovative capacity (Allen, 1977; Georghiou 1998; Le Bas *et al.*, 1998; Tsai and Ghoshal 1998; George *et al.*, 2002; Landry *et al.*, 2002; Belderbos *et al.*, 2004; Granovetter, 2005), d) science and technology human capital (Coleman, 1988; Rogers and Bozeman, 2001; Seibert *et al.*, 2001; Bozeman and Rogers, 2002; Bozeman and Corley, 2004), and e) help the consolidation of research agendas and the expansion of research areas.

Others, however, warn about the negative impacts of research collaboration on productivity (Fox and Faver, 1984; Landry and Amara, 1998; Carayol and Matt, 2004; Cummings and Kiesler, 2005); output quality (Herbertz, 1995; Kleinman, 1998); innovative capacity (Gelijns and Their, 2002); human capital (Behrens and Gray, 2001; Stephan, 2001; Slaughter *et al.*, 2002); and relevance of the research (Kleinman, 1998; Florida, 1999; Sagasti, 2004; Shrum, 2005). Risks and costs identified include the privatization and capture of traditional 'public' knowledge, the 'mercantilization' of knowledge and human capital as resulting from public-private research partnerships, opportunity costs, and crowding out effects.

The literature defining research collaboration and giving accounts on the characteristics and on the determinants of such enterprise is rather abundant. Katz and Martin (1997) define research collaboration as the working together of researchers to achieve the common goal of producing new scientific knowledge. A variety of 'collaborative activities' has been identified as falling under this broad concept. As Bordons and Gomez (2000) claim, these include the expression of opinions, the exchange of ideas and data, working together during the course of a project, working separately on different parts of a project with the purpose of integrating the results at the end, sharing equipment, and exchanging personnel.

However, as Katz and Martin (1997) acknowledge, both the concept of 'working together' and the assumption of a 'common goal' as a distinctive characteristic of a collaborative activity are rather conceptually and empirically problematic since, a) it is not clear how closely researchers have to work together in order to constitute a collaboration, and b) either no two researchers ever have precisely the same goals, or, conversely, every single researcher in the world is in fact a member of a big collaboration called 'scientific community' for they all work to advance scientific knowledge and are all somewhat interrelated: they all exchange ideas on what experiments to do next, what hypothesis to test, what new instrumentation to build, how to relate their latest experimental results to theoretical models, and so on.

As Bordons and Gomez (2000) acknowledge, if we take a narrow definition and agree that collaboration is defined as two or more scientists working together on a joint research project, sharing intellectual, economic and/or physical resources, a wide range of situations still can be included, and a wider array of contributions will in fact be excluded under such definition.

It seems therefore that, as the authors acknowledge, a research collaboration has a very "fuzzy" or ill-defined border, and exactly where that border is drawn is a matter of social convention and is open to negotiation. Furthermore, perceptions regarding the precise location of the 'boundary' of the collaboration may vary considerably across institutions, fields, sectors, countries, actors, and purposes over time. The fact is that, as any other social process, research collaboration is mainly governed by the complexity of human interactions, which we still don't understand completely.

Nevertheless, several types of collaboration are identified in the literature. As Bordons and Gomez (2000) point out, they can be theoretical or technical, the former being based on the exchange of ideas, the provision of advice, or criticism, and the latter being based on the share of resources, methods, etc. Another typology of collaboration is offered by Hagedoorn *et al.* (2000), who claim that research partnerships can be either formal or informal and can involve any type of partners (i.e. scientists, technicians, students, employees, etc.), belonging to universities, enterprises or government agencies committed to research projects. While formal research partnerships include research corporations (equity joint ventures focusing on research, and research joint ventures) and contractual arrangements such as strategic technical alliances, etc., informal agreements includes short-term research project-specific endeavours, and less visible but not less important social contacts.

3. What is International Research Collaboration?

Contrasting with the abundant literature on research collaboration that related with its international dimension is less prolific. Arguably, the similarities between local and international research collaboration are greater than the differences between the two. However, distinctive aspects of the latter, besides the 'obvious' condition that partners are located in different nations, include a different set of drivers, enablers, modalities, and consequences.

According to Wagner and Leydesdorf (2004), the drivers of International Research Collaboration include: a) location of specific resources. Marine research for example would probably require accessing different ocean resources from different countries; b) unique expertise. The treatment of some disease may well require local expertise in those areas where it has developed and being investigated from the past; c) location of large-scale equipment. A space research initiated in Russia would probably need to work at NASA to do some of their experiments; d) global problems requiring global solutions. Global warming would probably require research performed in different places of the planet to monitor and understand the cause.

As for the enablers of international research collaboration, one can identify in the literature the following: a) the return to home country of former 'brain drained'. It is well known (thought barely tested empirically) that one of the factors driving international research collaboration are the social networks created by foreign students and professors who return to their home countries and (either because of personal reasons or because they have been attracted in the framework of explicit institutional or policy strategies) maintain their contacts with their mentors, colleagues or students in the countries where they spend part of their academic lives (Melin, 2004); b) the Diaspora. Many of those who do not return to their countries of origin keep the contacts made in the past or develop new ones with their co-nationals they meet in international workshops or other academic and social events (Basu and Kumar, 2000; Chaparro *et al.*, 2004); and c) the Cultural-, geographic-, historical-, linguistic-, proximity, as one is more likely to collaborate with whom one shares more basic characteristics than with those radically different (Frame and Carpenter, 1979; Narin *et al.*, 1991; Katz, 1994; Farrell, 2001; Lee, 2004; Levine and Moreland, 2004; Wagner, 2005); In addition, relatively low costs of transportation and communication have contributed importantly to the collaborative enterprise across borders.

Finally, some of the barriers to international research collaboration identified in the literature include: a) low absorptive capacity. According to Cohen and Levinthal (1990), it is the lack of absorptive capacity of the knowledge and technology produced in developed countries what keeps developing countries from benefiting from the advances of the modern world. In fact, very often, researchers from developing countries are not able to take advantage of the knowledge and techniques offered by partners working in developed countries mostly because they lack the basic resources and knowledge necessary to exploit such opportunities (Bayona *et al.*, 2001; Penner-Hahn and Shaver, 2005); b) strong intellectual property regimes, which adds high transaction costs to the collaboration enterprise (Forero-Pineda and Jaramillo-Salazar, 2002); and c) political reasons oriented at controlling migration, ensuring national security, encouraging patriotism, etc.

4. International Research Collaboration and S&T Capabilities in Colombia

International Research Collaboration is said to boost local scientific and technological capabilities in developing countries (Wagner *et al.*, 2001). Based on the analysis of more than 5,400 journal articles published by Colombian scientists and engineers between 1980 and 2005, Ordonez (2005) found that the country's recent good performance was explained by its increased international collaboration. As Figure 1 shows, while the number of articles published by Colombians alone was rather small, that published in collaboration with foreign partners was large and rising rapidly.

Furthermore, in a more recent research, Ordonez (2008) studied 1889 Colombian research teams and found that international research collaboration was positively and strongly associated with both team output (as measured by the number of bibliographic items produced) and teams' ability to contribute to local knowledge (the extent to which a team involved the country either as unit of analysis, laboratory or the object of the research performed). The study shows that such effects depend on the type of collaboration chosen and the type of partner involved, however.

Figure 1: Publications and Research Collaboration: 1980-2005

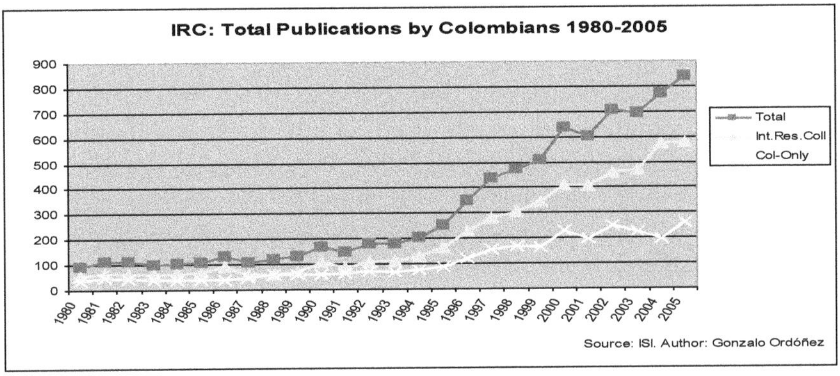

Particularly, it shows that while co-authoring with colleagues located overseas or receiving foreign funding increases team output, hosting foreign researchers does not seem to affect a team's productivity once all other variables are held constant. It also found that collaborating with partners from the South yields greater productivity counts than collaborating with partners from the North, and that funding from southern countries is associated with greater productivity rates than any other combination of collaboration activity and origin of partners. The study also found that hosting foreign researchers did not appear to be associated with the probability of teams to involve Colombia in their research process either, and that receiving foreign funding or co-authoring with colleagues located overseas increased a team's probability to contribute to local knowledge. Similarly, the study found that collaboration with partners from northern countries was strongly associated with a team's ability to contribute to local knowledge, while collaboration with partners from southern countries was not (Ordonez, 2008; Ordonez *et al.*, 2010).

5. Research Question

If International Research Collaboration (IRC) positively affects local S&T capacity in developing countries, the issue is a clear policy challenge, as knowing what factors affect teams collaborative choice is determinant to design successful public policies aiming at the internationalization of the domestic R&D community as a way to improve local S&T development.

The questions that remain to be answered are: *What factors explain the collaborative behaviour of Colombian research teams? What makes teams more collaborative with international partners than others?* These are the main focus of this paper.

Ordonez (2005) shows that the Colombian S&E community has been experiencing a rapid process of internationalization. That is, the Colombian scientists and engineers worked between 1998 and 2005 in collaboration with colleagues and institutions from 118 countries. While in 1998 local scientists collaborated with peers from 54 countries, in 2005 they co-authored with scientists and engineers from 70 countries, that is, an increase of 30% (see Table 1). While in 1998 there were 559 foreign institutions collaborating with Colombian researchers; in 2005 there were almost twice that number. In 2005 almost 68% of the articles published by Colombians were written with foreign partners.

Table 1: IRC: Co-Authorships

Year	Articles	Authors	Total Addresses	IRC-Articles	% IRC-articles	Partner Countries	Internat. Addresses
1998	498	2069	589	314	63.1%	54	559
2005	886	3909	1134	600	67.7%	70	1098

Source: ISI. Author: Gonzalo Ordonez

Moreover, Ordonez (2008) found that between 2003 and 2005 more than 800 foreign researchers and technicians were associated with more than 540 Colombian research teams coming from 59 countries. Among the 1889 teams studied, 736 collaborated either by co-authoring with partners located overseas, by working on foreign funded projects, or by hosting foreign researchers. 1153 teams did not collaborate internationally at all, therefore running with high opportunity costs.

What factors then explain the collaborative behaviour of those teams? What makes teams collaborate? What are the drivers and enablers that "push" them to collaborate internationally? Alternatively, what explains the "domesticity" of those teams that do not collaborate internationally? These are relevant and complex questions that we acknowledge cannot be fully answered with the information at hand. However, we attempt to make here a valuable contribution to the debate on the issue. The following are the hypothesis investigated.

6. Research Hypotheses

We identified five hypotheses about the factors affecting the choice of teams to collaborate with foreign partners. These include team's intrinsic characteristics, their field of specialization, the characteristics of their home institution, the sectors the teams operate in, and the characteristics of the overall environment where they are physically located. The following is the description of the hypotheses investigated.

Hypothesis 1: *The choice of collaborating internationally may be a function of team's intrinsic characteristics.* Larger teams are perhaps more likely to collaborate internationally than smaller ones as each team member may act as a collaborating agent: more agents equal more opportunities for collaboration. Older teams may be more likely to collaborate than younger teams because of their longer exposure to the international scrutiny and the maturity and recognition attained in their field. The more PhD holders a team has, the more likely it is to collaborate internationally as team members with PhDs tend to be good counterparts of foreign scientists and engineers, and because they may have had international experience during their personal and professional career. Teams led by someone who writes well in a second language tend to be more likely to collaborate internationally than the other teams, as language is one of the main enablers (or barriers) for collaborating with foreign partners. Similarly, teams led by a researcher who in the past studied overseas tend to collaborate internationally more than comparable teams as their leader may help the team to establish international linkages that may result in collaboration with their mentors, classmates and/or research associates located in the host country. Finally, highly dynamic teams both in terms of the number of R&D projects active and of the number of bibliographic products done tend to engage more in international collaboration than teams that are less dynamic.

Hypothesis 2: *International collaboration may also be a function of the field the team specializes in.* It is well known, for instance, that while R&D projects in physics tend to be highly collaborative, one can hardly find collaboration around projects on philosophy. One can argue that teams working in the natural sciences may be more collaboration-prone than comparable teams working in the social sciences or the humanities given the idiosyncratic nature of the latter types of teams, which may keep them from working with scientists of different origins and epistemic grounds. Similarly, one expects that the teams working in the agricultural sciences as well as those working in the medical sciences appear more likely to collaborate internationally than teams working in other fields due to their acclaimed international reputation in tropical agriculture and in tropical medicine research respectively.

Hypothesis 3: *International collaboration may also depend on the characteristics of the sector they operate in.* Teams working in the academic sector may be more likely to collaborate internationally than comparable teams working in the business sector. Allegedly, while the former type of teams tend to work on issues of public interest and therefore are expected to be more 'open' to interact with their peers from overseas, teams working in the business sector tend to work on issues with strategic value that may keep them from sharing information and interacting with foreign partners.

Hypothesis 4: *International collaboration may also depend on the characteristics of their home institutions.* As collaborating with foreign partners requires both financial and institutional support, teams affiliated with big institutions are expected to be more internationally oriented than teams affiliated with mid-size or small institutions. Competition among teams of the same institution may also help to explain collaborative behaviour, and such competition is typical to big institutions.

Finally, Hypothesis 5: *International collaboration may also be affected by the characteristics of the cities teams are located.* Teams located in/or near big cities may be more likely to collaborate internationally than teams located in mid-size or small cities. The assumption is that the teams of the first group tend to have more opportunities to access valuable information from foreign peers, may be more visible given their greater participation in international workshops, and may engage more human resources of higher productivity than teams located in small cities.

The following section describes the data and the methodology used to test the aforementioned hypotheses.

7. Data and Methodology

We relied on Ordonez' (2008) data composed by the information on 1889 teams registered at Colciencias (the Colombian National Science Foundation) by the end of 2005. Appendix A describes the sampling strategy used.

For the purpose of this research, a "team" is defined as a) two or more people who claim they work together on common research problems or interests; b) are recognized by their home institution and Colciencias as such; c) work on at least one R&D project active during the period of observation (2003-2005); and d) produce research outputs jointly or independently that are attributed to the team's work[1].

To answer to the main research questions, the following models were tested using logistic regressions.

Pr(International Research Collaboration in 2005=1) = F(Team Size, Team Age, Total PhDs in 2003, Total Projects in 2003, Total Bibliographic Products in 2003,

Leader Writes Well in a Second Language, Leader Studied Overseas, Scientific Field, Sector, Size of Home Institution, Size of City of Location)

Where International Research Collaboration is captured in different ways: collaborations that involve different modalities: foreign researchers working in local research teams, "ircpeople05," foreign funding, "ircproj05," or co-authorship[2]. Collaborations with different types of partners: partners from Northern countries, "ircN05," or from Southern countries[3], "ircS05." Collaborations that involve different combinations of modality and type of partner: collaboration with teammates from Northern countries, "peopN05," or from Southern countries, "peopS05;" funding from Northern countries, "projN05," or from Southern countries "projS05. In all cases, if the team collaborated internationally between 2003 and 2005 it is coded, 1 and zero otherwise. "IRC05" is used to distinguish between collaborating and non-collaborating team.

Team size, "Core03," is an interval-level variable for the number of researchers and technicians the team had active in 2003.

Team age, "age03," is an interval-level variable for how long the team had been in existence in 2003.

The total number of PhDs, "totphds03," is represented by an interval-level variable for the number of members with PhD degree the team had in 2003.

The characteristics of the team leader are captured in two forms: "leadwrit05," is coded 1 if the leader writes well in a second language, zero otherwise; and "leadstudo05" is coded 1 if the leader studied overseas, zero otherwise.

Team dynamism is measured by an interval-level variable, "totprojects03," for the number of R&D projects the team had active in 2003.

Team productive capacity is measured by the total number of bibliographic products done by 2003, "totbibprod03."

Scientific field is represented by seven dummy variables (agricultural sciences, "agroscs," medical sciences, "medscs," social sciences, "social," humanities, "human," engineering, "engi," and other sciences, "othscs"), with teams working in the natural sciences, "natscs," as the reference group.

Sector is represented by four dummy variables: business sector, "bussector," government sector, "govsector," and other sector, "othsector," with teams working in the academic sector, "educsector," as the reference group.

Size of the home institution is represented by three dummy variables: small home institutions, "smallinst," mid-size institutions, "medinst, with teams affiliated with big institutions, "biginst," as the reference group[4].

Lastly, City-size is represented by three dummy variables: small city, "smallcity," mid-size city, "medcity," with teams located in big cities, "bigcity", as the reference group[5].

Appendix C shows descriptive statistics of the data used. As the table in the appendix shows, 39% of the teams studied collaborated internationally between 2003 and 2005, of which 21% hosted foreign researchers, and 25% worked with projects funded by foreign institutions. As for the characteristics of the teams, the data shows that most of the teams in Colombia work on issues in the humanities (24%) and in the natural sciences (23%), are affiliated with universities (90%), are hosted at large institutions (45%), and are located in large cities (75%).

A smaller sample of 672 teams selected randomly was used to account for the determinants of co-authoring with partners located overseas. This was necessary given the amount of work involved in attributing journal articles registered by the Web of Science and Scopus to the teams registered at Colciencias. Based on this sample, 17% of the teams co-publish research articles with foreign partners. Except for the fact that the teams working in the social sciences and the humanities were not included (due to the fact that they tend to publish more books or other materials than journal articles), the proportions related with the other characteristics analyzed were similar to those observed in the larger database.

In response to the characteristics of the dependent variables used (dummy variables), the analyses done were based on logistic regressions, where all conventional robustness checks were implemented as reported below.

In addition, in order to better understand collaborative behaviour, processes, econometric models, and results, 20 interviews were administered with experts and team members working in all the disciplines, organizational environments and sectors studied.

8. Findings

The following are the findings related with the choice of collaborating or not with international partners, the modalities chosen, the selection of partners, and the combinations between different types of partners and different types of collaboration modalities. Table 2 summarizes the results obtained.

The Choice of Collaborating Internationally

As Table 2 shows, larger teams, older team, teams with large numbers of doctorates, teams with many R&D projects active, and highly productive teams appear more likely to collaborate internationally than comparable teams of smaller size, with fewer years in existence, with fewer PhD members, fewer projects active and less productive.

Teams led by researchers able to write well in a second language, and teams led by someone who studied overseas in the past are more likely to collaborate than teams of similar characteristics led by someone without either capacities.

Teams working in the medical sciences, the social sciences or in the engineering are less likely to collaborate internationally than comparable teams working in the natural sciences.

Teams affiliated with large institutions are more likely to collaborate than comparable teams affiliated with small or mid-size institutions. And teams located in small cities are less likely to collaborate internationally than comparable teams located in big cities.

Contrary to what one would expect, and as a Wald Test of joint effects shows, the sector where the team works does not appear to significantly affect the probability of collaborating internationally. In fact, there is a 53% probability that the observed results could have occurred by chance. Therefore, we can confidently conclude that the hypothesis that the effects of the sector variables are simultaneously equal to zero cannot be rejected.

In particular, as Appendix D shows, the number of PhDs appears to be the variable with the greatest impact on the probability of collaborating internationally in Colombia, followed by the number of projects active, the past productivity of the team, and the characteristics of the team leader. In fact, a one standard deviation increase in the number of members with PhD (see column %StdX), increases team's odds of collaborating internationally by 75%, holding the other variables constant; and a one-unit increase in the number of members with PhD increases team's odds of collaborating by 29%, holding the other variables constant (see the "%" column).

A one standard deviation increase in the number of projects active in 2003, or in the number of projects reported, increased team's odds of collaborating internationally by 44% and 41% respectively; and while a one-unit increase in the number of projects active increased team's odds of collaborating internationally by 6%, an equivalent increase in productivity counts increased team's odds of collaborating internationally by 1%, holding all other variables constant.

Interestingly, the odds that a team led by someone who writes well in a language other than Spanish collaborates are 1.61 times as high as that of teams with leaders who do not write well in a second language, holding the other variables constant. Having leaders who are able to write well in a second language increases the probability of collaborating by 11.2 percentage points, holding the other variables constant at their means.

As expected, and as the table in the appendix shows, teams led by someone who studied overseas in the past are more likely to collaborate internationally than comparable teams led by someone who did not study overseas in the past. Holding the other variables constant, the odds that a team led by someone who studied overseas in the past collaborates are 1.57 as high as that of teams led by people who did not studied overseas in the past, and holding the other variables constant at their means, the former type of teams increases the probability of collaborating internationally by 10.6 percentage points[6].

This model predicted collaboration for 543 of the teams, of which 386 did collaborate and 157 did not. It predicted that 1346 did not collaborate, but 350 actually did. The sensitivity of the model is 52.5%: it correctly predicted 386 of the 736 who collaborated. Also, the model is quite specific: 86.4% of those who did not collaborate were not predicted to collaborate (996/1153); 66.9% of those who were predicted to collaborate actually did collaborate, and 74.6% of those who were predicted not to collaborate did actually not collaborate. More importantly, the model correctly classified 73.2% (386+996/1889), an improvement of about 12% compared to the null model (1153/1889=61.04%). By converting this to an adjusted count R2, we see that the number of errors in prediction drops from 736 to 507 (350+157), a decline of 31.1%.

In sum, based on the results obtained, team size, team age, team composition, leadership, productivity, discipline, institution of affiliation, and geographical location seem to affect the probability of collaborating internationally. In contrast, the sector where the team works is not significantly associated with the collaborative behaviour. No significant curvilinear effects were found.

The Choice of Collaboration Modalities

According to the data, the choice of hosting foreign funding depends mostly on the team's size, the number of PhDs, the characteristics of the team leader, the activities performed, the scientific discipline, and the size of the city where the team is located (see Table 2).

The choice of working with foreign funding depends on all the factors considered except team size and the size of the city where the team is located. This finding is confirmed by a Wald Test of the joint effects of the location variables.

More precisely, larger teams tend to host more foreign researchers than smaller teams of similar characteristics, but the size of the teams does not seem to affect the probability of working with foreign funding. Older teams tend to prefer working with foreign funding than younger teams, but team age is not associated with the choice of hosting foreign researchers. The number of PhDs is positively associated with both types of collaboration. Teams led by researchers able to write well in a second language or that studied overseas are more likely to collaborate internationally both through hosting foreign researchers and working with foreign funding than comparable teams. The number of projects active and the number of bibliographic products a team has is associated with the probability of working with foreign funding, but it is not significantly associated with hosting foreign researchers.

Teams working in the medical sciences, or in the engineering, are less likely to host foreign researchers than comparable teams working in the natural sciences. Teams working in the humanities are less likely to work with foreign funding than similar teams working in the natural sciences.

Teams working in the government sector or in the NGOs' sector are more likely to work with foreign funding than comparable teams affiliated with the academic sector. However, the sector where the team works does not seem to be associated with the probability of hosting foreign researchers. Teams affiliated with large institutions are more likely to work with foreign funding than comparable teams affiliated with small and mid-size institutions, but the size of the home institution does not seem to be significantly associated with the probability of hosting foreign researchers.

Finally, the size of the city where the team is located also seems to affect the choice of hosting foreign researcher as opposed to the choice of working with foreign funding. In fact, teams located in mid-size cities are less likely to host foreign researchers than comparable teams located in large cities.

The analysis of the factors affecting the choice of co-authoring with partners located overseas is done using the sample of 672 teams. In this case, the internal characteristics and the performance of the teams are excluded from the model as they were observed after the co-authorship took place (between 2001 and 2002). Leaving these variables would lead to problems of endogeneity due to reverse causality[7]. Similarly, the teams working on areas of the social sciences and the humanities were not included in the analyses as their main production (books, book chapters, non-peer reviewed articles, "grey literature", etc.) is not observable via Web of Science or Scopus.

Table 2: Determinants of International Research Collaboration

Variable	Internat. Res. Coll.	Foreign Researchers	Foreign Funding	Int. Co-Authorship in 2001-2	Int. Res. w/ North	Int. Res. w/ South	Researchers from North	Researchers from South	Funding from North	Funding from South
Team Size in 2003	0.026	0.048**	-0.008	-	0.013	0.028*	0.040**	0.046**	-0.007	-0.021
	(1.94)	(3.67)	(0.59)	-	(0.94)	(2.04)	(2.72)	(3.12)	(0.50)	(1.01)
Team Age in 2003	0.033**	0.006	0.028*	-	0.037**	-0.004	0.017	-0.025	0.030*	0.018
	(2.83)	(0.50)	(2.42)	-	(3.13)	(0.34)	(1.35)	(1.56)	(2.52)	(1.21)
Total PhDs in 2003	0.253**	0.187**	0.164**	-	0.267**	0.091*	0.206**	0.099*	0.191**	-0.011
	(6.14)	(5.08)	(4.29)	-	(6.54)	(2.40)	(5.08)	(2.33)	(4.93)	(0.24)
Leader Writes Oth Langua	0.466**	0.467**	0.467**	-	0.338**	0.493**	0.386*	0.520**	0.467**	0.313
	(3.94)	(3.46)	(3.39)	-	(2.63)	(3.25)	(2.30)	(2.91)	(3.27)	(1.33)
Leader Studied Overseas	0.453**	0.342**	0.395**	-	0.483**	0.096	0.375*	0.146	0.445**	0.146
	(3.96)	(2.67)	(3.00)	-	(3.90)	(0.68)	(2.37)	(0.88)	(3.27)	(0.67)
Tot. Proj. in 2003	0.054**	-0.018	0.065**	-	0.068**	0.002	-0.010	-0.015	0.066**	0.026
	(4.11)	(1.64)	(5.10)	-	(5.18)	(0.18)	(0.77)	(1.06)	(5.14)	(1.86)
Tot. Bib. Prods. by 2003	0.008**	0.000	0.011**	-	0.007**	0.008**	-0.001	0.002	0.009**	0.011**
	(3.81)	(0.29)	(5.64)	-	(3.50)	(4.72)	(0.43)	(1.24)	(4.94)	(5.52)

continued on next page

Table 2 continued

Variable	Internat. Res. Coll.	Foreign Researchers	Foreign Funding	Int. Co-Authorship in 2001-2	Int. Res. w/ North	Int. Res. w/ South	Researchers from North	Researchers from South	Funding from North	Funding from South
Agrosciences	-0.397	-0.482	-0.241	-1.050**	-0.567*	0.010	-0.875*	-0.285	-0.235	0.127
	(1.57)	(1.68)	(0.87)	(2.69)	(2.08)	(0.03)	(2.30)	(0.80)	(0.82)	(0.29)
Medical Sciences	-0.486*	-0.787**	0.028	-0.322	-0.419*	-0.380	-0.889**	-0.771**	0.052	0.168
	(2.45)	(3.46)	(0.13)	(1.25)	(2.03)	(1.58)	(3.24)	(2.58)	(0.24)	(0.51)
Social Sciences	-0.366*	-0.411*	-0.191	-	-0.376	-0.139	-0.542*	-0.397	-0.150	0.164
	(1.98)	(1.98)	(0.91)	-	(1.89)	(0.61)	(2.11)	(1.49)	(0.69)	(0.47)
Humanities	-0.176	0.076	-0.436*	-	-0.220	-0.069	0.087	-0.103	-0.355	-0.461
	(1.10)	(0.46)	(2.36)	-	(1.31)	(0.36)	(0.45)	(0.48)	(1.87)	(1.36)
Engineering	-0.579**	-0.711**	-0.258	-0.679**	-0.797**	-0.288	-1.266**	-0.353	-0.246	-0.225
	(3.03)	(3.28)	(1.24)	(2.59)	(3.84)	(1.24)	(4.16)	(1.35)	(1.15)	(0.62)
Other Sciences	-0.140	-0.286	0.332	-1.464	0.010	0.071	-0.079	-0.647	0.272	0.897*
	(0.47)	(0.91)	(1.06)	(1.93)	(0.03)	(0.21)	(0.23)	(1.44)	(0.84)	(2.20)
Business Sector	0.234	0.182	0.344	2.325**	0.270	0.288	0.268	0.330	0.263	0.572
	(0.65)	(0.48)	(0.83)	(3.78)	(0.71)	(0.70)	(0.59)	(0.69)	(0.62)	(0.90)

continued on next page

Table 2 continued

Variable	Internat. Res. Coll.	Foreign Researchers	Foreign Funding	Int. Co-Authorship in 2001-2	Int. Res. w/ North	Int. Res. w/ South	Researchers from North	Researchers from South	Funding from North	Funding from South
Government	0.083	-0.324	0.645*	2.154**	0.307	-0.048	-0.103	-0.406	0.623	0.722
	(0.28)	(0.90)	(2.01)	(4.66)	(0.99)	(0.13)	(0.24)	(0.84)	(1.91)	(1.45)
Other Sector	0.601	-0.104	1.687**	2.366*	1.051*	0.265	0.251	-0.229	1.761**	1.245
	(1.44)	(0.23)	(3.77)	(2.40)	(2.46)	(0.56)	(0.51)	(0.37)	(3.92)	(1.90)
Mid. Home Inst.	-0.297*	-0.263	-0.445**	-0.921**	-0.436**	-0.164	-0.460*	-0.072	-0.447**	-0.463
	(2.33)	(1.82)	(3.04)	(3.82)	(3.15)	(1.02)	(2.53)	(0.39)	(2.94)	(1.77)
Small Home Inst.	-0.341	-0.080	-0.762**	-2.917**	-0.400	-0.235	-0.092	-0.118	-0.656*	-0.810
	(1.73)	(0.37)	(3.05)	(5.19)	(1.85)	(0.92)	(0.34)	(0.41)	(2.57)	(1.80)
Small City	-1.100	-1.865	-0.162	-0.468	-0.653	-1.379	-1.231	-	-0.009	-0.073
	(1.94)	(1.82)	(0.28)	(0.59)	(1.15)	(1.34)	(1.19)	-	(0.02)	(0.07)
Midsize City	-0.235	-0.391*	-0.022	-0.403	-0.260	-0.141	-0.519*	-0.200	-0.088	0.049
	(1.68)	(2.34)	(0.14)	(1.54)	(1.69)	(0.79)	(2.34)	(0.96)	(0.52)	(0.18)
Constant	-1.820**	-1.958**	-2.427**	-0.392*	-2.146**	-2.435**	-2.499**	-2.541**	-2.648**	-3.492**
	(9.17)	(9.29)	(10.98)	(2.49)	(10.20)	(10.42)	(9.89)	(9.43)	(11.55)	(10.16)
Observations	1889	1889	1889	672	1889	1889	1889	1856	1889	1889
Pseudo R2	0.2020	0.1053	0.2225	0.2508	0.2249	0.0932	0.1317	0.0579	0.2263	0.1437
Absolute value of z statistics in parentheses										
* Significant at 5%; ** significant at 1%										

Hence, as shown in Table 2 above, teams working in the agricultural sciences or the engineering appear less likely to co-author with colleagues located overseas than comparable teams working in the natural sciences. Interestingly, teams working in the academic sector are less likely to co-author with colleagues located in foreign countries than comparable teams working in the business sector or in the government sector. This may suggest an important level of endogamy characteristic of the Colombian academic sector. Finally, teams affiliated with large institutions are more likely to co-author with partners located overseas than comparable teams affiliated with the small and midsize institutions. No significant effect of location is found. This is confirmed by a Wald Test of the joint effect of these variables not shown here.

The Choice of Partner

Based on the data, and as shown in Table 2, all the factors considered, except team size and team location, significantly affect team choice of collaborating with partners from the global North. In contrast, the choice of collaborating with partners from the global South seems to be associated with team size, the number of PhDs, the extent to which the team leader writes well in a second language, and team productivity only. The z-tests of the effects of individual variables and the Wald Tests of joint effects of the categorical variables confirm these findings.

The Choice of Combining Collaborative Activity and Partner

As the Table 2 shows, the choice of hosting foreign researchers from the North depends mostly on the size of the team, the number of doctorates the team has, the characteristics of the leader, whether the team works in the natural science as opposed to working in the agricultural sciences, the medical sciences, the social sciences or in the engineering; whether it is affiliated with a large institution and whether it is located in a big city. The choice of hosting researchers from the South also depends on the size of the team, the number of PhDs it has, whether the team leader writes well in a second language, or whether it works in the natural sciences as opposed to working in the medical science. Receiving funding from the northern countries is associated with team age, the number of doctorates the team has, the characteristics of the team's leader characteristics, the dynamism of the team, the sector, and the size of the home institution. Finally, the choice of working with projects funded by southern countries is associated with how productive the team is, and whether it works in the multidisciplinary sciences as opposed to working in the natural sciences only.

More precisely, and as discussed before, team size positively affects the choice of hosting foreign researchers. However, it is slightly more important for explaining the choice of hosting researchers from the south than for explaining the choice of hosting researchers from the north. The difference of the effects of each variable can be seen by comparing the z-statistics in each model.

The opposite is true regarding the effects of having PhDs in teams. As the number of PhD holder increases, the probability of hosting foreign researchers increases, but it raises more for hosting researchers from the north than for hosting foreign researchers from the south, holding the other variables constant.

Teams led by someone who writes well a second language positively affects the probability of hosting foreign researchers, but it increases it more for hosting researchers from the south than from the north, holding the other variables constant.

Teams led by someone who studied overseas appear more likely to host foreign researchers than teams not led by someone who studied overseas, but this is mostly because this factor affects the choice of hosting researchers from the north and not from the south.

Teams working in the natural sciences are more likely to host foreign researchers than comparable teams working in the medical sciences, the social sciences and the engineering. However, this is mostly due to its higher probability of engaging researchers from the north than for its probability of engaging researchers from the south, which is not statistically significant. By contrast, the odds of hosting foreign researchers are higher among the teams working in the natural sciences than among the teams working in the medical science. These differences are statistically significant regarding both types of partners. In this case, the difference in the odds is also higher regarding the choice of hosting researchers from the north than of hosting foreign researchers from the south.

Finally, the higher probability of hosting foreign researchers among teams affiliated with big institutions or located in large cities compared to that of teams affiliated with mid-size institutions or being located in mid-size cities responds mostly to the higher probabilities of the former types of teams to host researchers from the north.

As for the factors affecting the choice of working with foreign funding is concerned, team age appears to affect positively the choice of working with foreign funding, but it affects more the choice of working with funding from the north than of working with funding from the south, holding the other variables constant.

By contrast, although the effects of having PhDs in teams positively affects the choice of working with foreign funding, it seems to affect positively more the choice of funding from the north than from the south, holding the other variables constant.

The extent to which a team has a leader who is able to write well in a second language or studied overseas in the past is more important for explaining the choice of working with foreign funding from the north than for explaining the choice of working with funding from the south (whose effects are not statistically significant).

The number of projects active a team has is important for explaining the choice of foreign funding. However, the effect is greater for explaining the choice of working with funding from the north. In contrast, the number of S&T products a team has is more important for explaining the choice of funding from the south than from the north, although it is also important for explaining the choice of receiving funding from the north.

Teams working in the other sciences or in the multidisciplinary sciences are more likely to work with projects funded by southern countries than teams working in the natural sciences. They are also more likely to work with funding from the south than with funding from the north.

Teams affiliated with the NGOs' are more likely to work with foreign funding than comparable teams affiliated with the academy, mostly because the former are more likely to work with funding from the north.

Finally, teams affiliated with large institutions are more likely to work with foreign funding than comparable teams affiliated with small and midsize institutions. However, the main difference is due to their likelihood of working with funding from northern countries.

No significant effects were found regarding the location variables on the probability of working with funding of any origin.

9. Discussion and Conclusion

This research was inspired by the empirical and theoretical work attempting to contribute to the understanding of the effects or international research collaboration on local capabilities in developing countries, where recent research done by Ordonez 2008 found both negative and positive consequences on team building, productivity and research orientation in Colombia. The question addressed in this paper was then, what factors contribute to explain collaborative behaviour among research teams in developing countries?

The reader may find questionable the assumption that Colombian research teams are good proxies of the research community living in most developing countries. However, there are several reasons why this assumption may be considered plausible. First, research teams, and not individuals, are increasingly at the source of knowledge production, not only in developed but also in developing countries. Indeed, this is one of the consequences of the fact that the process of knowledge production requires more and more multidisciplinary perspectives, complex methods and data, which cannot be easily assured in individual research. This is the so-called Mode 2 of knowledge production portrayed by Gibbons *et al.* (1994) and followers, which also applies for research communities working in developing countries. Second, one of the distinctive characteristics of research teams in developing countries as compared to research teams in developed countries is their relative dependence on foreign sources of funding and information. This is a feature embedded in the "developing" concept, which other may prefer to call it otherwise to mean "poor" or "less wealthy" research communities who have to work with old equipment, scarce access to samples, information and protected intellectual rights, facing low salaries and social stigma, etc. The extremely low investment on R&D in these countries is a common denominator. Third, in these countries, international research collaboration is per se an indicator of research quality, that is, as an output indicator that reveals some degree of relevance and recognition in a highly competitive and asymmetric global arena regarding the S&T enterprise. Finally, there are no reasons to believe that team composition, scientific performance and willingness and propensity to collaborate internationally differ dramatically across developing countries.

Hence, based on the main findings of the research done using the 1889 research teams identified in Colombia, Table 3 summarizes the effects of the variables studied on the collaborative behaviour. It shows the positive, the negative, and the no net-effects (at the 0.05 level) for each variable based on the type of collaboration studied, the type of partner involved, and the preference for a specific combination of collaborative activity and partner's origin.

In particular, it shows that team characteristics, scientific field, sector, the characteristics of the home institution, and localization affects the probability of collaborating internationally, but that collaboration varies based on the modalities and type of partners.

Table 3: Summary: Determinants of International Research Collaboration in Colombia

Variable	IRC	Type of Collaboration			Type of Partner		Type of Collaboration and Partner			
		Foreign Researchers	Foreign Funding	Co-Authorship	North	South	Researchers from North	Researchers from South	Funding from North	Funding form South
Team size in 2003	+	+	No Sig	?	No Sig	+	+	+	No Sig	No Sig
Team Age in 2003	+	No Sig	+	?	+	No Sig	No Sig	No Sig	+	No Sig
Total PhDs in 2003	+	+	+	?	+	+	+	+	+	No Sig
Leader Writes in Other Lang.	+	+	+	?	+	+	+	+	+	No Sig
Leader Studied Overseas	+	+	+	?	+	No Sig	+	No Sig	+	No Sig
Tot. Proj. in 2003	+	No Sig	+	?	+	No Sig	No Sig	No Sig	+	No Sig
Tot. Bib. Prod by 2003	+	No Sig	+	?	+	+	No Sig	No Sig	+	+
Agro sciences	No Sig	No Sig	No Sig	-	-	No Sig	-	No Sig	No Sig	No Sig
Medical Sciences	-	-	No Sig	No Sig	-	No Sig	-	-	No Sig	No Sig
Social Sciences	-	-	No Sig	?	No Sig	No Sig	-	No Sig	No Sig	No Sig
Humanities	No Sig	No Sig	-	?	No Sig	No Sig	No Sig	No Sig	No Sig	No Sig
Engineering	-	-	No Sig	-	-	No Sig	-	No Sig	No Sig	No Sig
Other Sciences	No Sig	No Sig	No Sig	No Sig	No Sig	No Sig	No Sig	No Sig	No Sig	+
Business Sector	No Sig	No Sig	No Sig	+	No Sig	No Sig	No Sig	No Sig	No Sig	No Sig
Government	No Sig	No Sig	+	+	No Sig	No Sig	No Sig	No Sig	No Sig	No Sig
Other Sector	No Sig	No Sig	+	+	+	No Sig	No Sig	No Sig	+	No Sig
Small Home Inst.	No Sig	No Sig	-	-	No Sig	No Sig	No Sig	No Sig	-	No Sig
Mid. Home Inst.	-	No Sig	-	-	-	No Sig	-	No Sig	-	No Sig
Small City	-	No Sig	No Sig	No Sig	No Sig	No Sig	No Sig	No Sig	No Sig	No Sig
Midsize City	No Sig	-	No Sig	No Sig	No Sig	No Sig	-	No Sig	No Sig	No Sig

Team Characteristics and International Research Collaboration

According to the data, and as hypothesized, larger teams collaborate internationally more than comparable teams of smaller size. What was not expected, however, was that the underlying assumption supporting the hypothesis was wrong, as the attractiveness of those teams to host foreign researchers, particularly from southern countries, were higher as compared to their attractiveness to foreign funding, which appears not statistically significant. This raises the question How come that team size reveals important for attracting foreign researchers but it does not translate into more foreign funding? Perhaps if we could observe the hosting of foreign researchers on a period before we observe the funding by foreign institutions we could see a causal relationship (more foreign researchers leading to more foreign funding). This was not possible with the data available, however.

As hypothesized, team age positively affect the likelihood of collaborating internationally. However, what was not foreseen was that it affected particularly more for attracting foreign funding, particularly from northern countries, than for attracting foreign researchers. This is not surprising as team experience is an important criterion for granting resources, while this does not necessarily matter when deciding to work as an associate researcher. What is not clear is why funding from Northern countries seem to value more experience than funding from southern countries or alternatively, why older teams tend to prefer more funding from Northern countries than from Southern countries.

The numbers of PhD holders as well as the extent to which the team leader writes well in a second language are important predictors of international collaboration. This finding is consistent with the hypothesis. Moreover, the model interestingly reveals that these two factors do not matter for attracting funding from the South, that is, from peer communities with similar average level of education and of mastering of a second language.

As hypothesized, the extent to which the team leader studied overseas is important to explain international collaboration. However, the data also shows that this is particularly true when it comes to receiving foreign researchers or to acquiring foreign funding, both from northern countries, as compared with collaborating with partners from southern countries. This can be seen as a natural consequence of the fact that most scientists educated overseas have done their degree in northern countries.

Finally, past production and team dynamism (the number of projects active during the window of observation) appear as strong predictors of international collaboration. These findings support the hypothesis proposed in these respects. Moreover, the data shows that past production matters more for attracting foreign funding, both from northern and southern countries, than for attracting foreign researchers. This is consistent with the finding reported regarding team age. On the other hand, the number of projects active has similar effects, except that it does not seem to matter for attracting funding from southern countries.

Scientific Field and International Research Collaboration

Based on the analysis of the 1889 research teams studied, and contrary to the hypothesis, one can conclude that teams working in the agro sciences are equally likely to collaborate internationally than teams working in the natural sciences. More precisely, they even appear less likely to co-author with peers located overseas and to receive foreign researchers from the North than teams working in the natural sciences. This contradicts one of the assumptions made in support to one of the hypothesis as the teams working in the agriculture sciences were seen to have a relatively higher international exposure due to their relatively higher international recognition within the tropical agriculture research community[8].

The data also reveals that teams working in the medical sciences are less likely to collaborate internationally than teams of similar characteristics working in the natural sciences, and that, they are particularly less likely to attract foreign researchers, mostly from the global North. This is again surprising and contradicts the hypothesis proposed as tropical medicine is commonly portrayed as one of the strongest research area in the country due to its relative advantage derived from their geographical position.

According to the data, teams working in the social science are less likely to collaborate internationally than teams working in the natural sciences. This is consistent with the hypothesis proposed. However, it reveals that this is true, mostly because they are less likely to host foreign researchers from northern countries. Why is this so? Further exploration would be necessary.

Contrary to the teams working in the natural sciences, and consistent with the hypothesis, those working in the humanities are less likely to attract foreign funding. This finding suggests a lack of entrepreneurship characterizing these teams.

Teams working in engineering are less likely to collaborate internationally than similar teams working in the natural sciences. This is particularly true regarding the likelihood of hosting foreign researchers from the North, who might not see a comparative advantage on those teams, and of co-authoring with partners located overseas, perhaps because of their relative small exposure to the international arena.

Finally, teams working in other (multidisciplinary) sciences are equally international as compared with similar teams in the natural sciences.

However, they seem to be relatively more successful in attracting funding from southern countries.

Sector of Operation and International Research Collaboration

According to the data, and contrary to the hypothesis, teams working in the business sector are equally likely to collaborate internationally than teams of comparable characteristics working in the academic sector. Furthermore, and surprisingly, they appear more likely to co-author with partners located overseas than teams working in the academic sector. Once again, this finding opens up new questions and invites to propose speculative explanations. Does this support the claim that the internationalization of the economy has not affected local academy the same way it has affected the market of goods and services?

Teams working in the government sector are also more likely to co-author with peers located overseas than similar teams working in the academic sector, and even more likely to attract foreign funding. Similar pattern is found regarding the teams working in the non-for-profit sector, but they are particularly active when it comes to attracting funding from northern countries in particular. These findings deserve deeper exploration to better understand the causes and potential solutions to increase international exposure of university-based research teams in Colombia.

Characteristics of the Home Institution and International Research Collaboration

The data shows that teams hosted by small and mid-size institutions are less likely to co-author and to attract foreign funding as compared to teams of similar characteristics hosted by large institutions. This supports somewhat the hypothesis. However, it also reveals that these teams are particularly neglected by funding from the North, and in addition by foreign researchers from northern countries in the case of teams hosted by mid-size institutions only.

Localization and International Research Collaboration

Finally, according to the models studied, teams located in small cities tend to collaborate less than comparable teams located in large cities. This is consistent with the hypothesis proposed. However, the data also reveals that teams located in mid-size cities appear equally likely to collaborate internationally than similar teams located in big cities. But it shows that teams located in mi-size cities tend to attract less foreign researchers from the North than comparable teams located in large cities.

Discussion

One of the main finding of this research is that the number of doctorates a team has as well as the characteristics of its leader are the variables with the stronger explanatory power of team's propensity to collaborate internationally, all modalities considered. In fact, according to the data, for every additional team member with PhD team's odds of collaborating internationally increases by nearly 30%, holding the other variables constant. The odds that a team led by a researcher that writes well in a second language collaborates are 1.6 times as high as that of comparable teams with leaders who are not able to write well in a language other than Spanish. And, holding the other variables constant at their means, having leaders who studied overseas in the past increases team's probability of collaborating international by around 11 percentage points.

These findings, together with the findings by Ordonez 2008 in the sense that international research collaboration increases team productive capacity as well as the stock of local knowledge, are interesting in the sense that they remind us about the importance of policies oriented at creating a strong and competitive local science and technology human capital in developing countries. One composed by individuals highly trained, able to interact with world class scientific communities and to increase local S&T capabilities.

These goals imply the implementation of programs aiming at increasing the number of highly qualified beneficiaries of public and private grants who lack the resources necessary to pursue graduate studies both locally and overseas, to spend time as research associates in foreign laboratories, to attend international workshops and conferences, to perform cooperative research, to contract foreign researchers, to make internationally visible the research done domestically as well as to make domestically visible the research done internationally, to acquire linguistic skills, etc.

If the debate on whether or not to invest public money on the education and mobility of individuals was not a reiterative issue in these countries, these finding would have to be considered innocuous. However, this is not the case. The resources allocated in these activities are indeed meagre. Very often in Congress and in the media in these countries someone with a certain level of legitimacy raises arguments against having tax payers money invested on them.

As some of the fears relating to brain drain resulting from the implementation of some of these policies are in fact well grounded, the real policy challenge is to encourage both high levels of education and mobility as well as attractiveness to ensure retention, return, attraction or connection of those individuals with great potential to contribute to local development, including those supported as well as not supported with public funds.

Although the findings reported here fall short in offering guidelines in this direction, they fuel a healthy debate with the basic empirical data necessary. This is something that is strikingly missing. In any ways, the worst case scenario would be to do nothing to overcome the evident lack of competitiveness of local research teams in developing countries in a world increasingly integrated that battles for markets, space and recognition, and that has a great deal of solutions to offer to meet local needs as a result of its constant process of modernization and S&T progress.

The understanding of the determinants of international research collaboration and of the different ways it is conceived as well as of the choice of partners helps to better design public policies oriented at exploiting the benefits derived from collaborating internationally or at reducing the negative effects that may result from it.

Notes

1 People affiliated with the team producing certified research outputs or working as technicians are counted as part of the 'core' research team. Out of the 3342 teams registered in 2005, 1453 were excluded because they were either a) created the same year of registration, b) composed by only one member "active", that is, reporting certified research outputs done in 2003 or before, or c) did not report a research project active between 2003 and 2005. Following COLCIENCIAS' classification of products, certified research outputs include research articles, literature reviews, books, book chapters, software, technical pilots, technical projects, prototypes, industrial designs, technical norms, masters theses directed, and PhD dissertations directed. See Colciencias (2000a). Módulo de Cálculo para Escalafonamiento de Grupos y Centros de Investigación Científica y Tecnológica - 2000. Convocatoria Nacional para Grupos y Centros de Investigación Científica y Tecnológica 2000. Bogotá, D.C. Colombia: 20p.

2 The model used to account for the determinants of co-authoring did not include the characteristics of the research team as in this case co-authorship occurred before these variables were observed.

3 For the list of countries classified in each region see Appendix B.

4 The size of the institution of affiliation was calculated base on the total number of researchers affiliated with that institution.

5 The list of cities classified in each category can be found in the Appendix of Ordonez 2008.

6 Squared terms for team size, team age, total number of PhDs, total number of projects active and total number of bibliographic products were added to the model to see if there were curvilinear effects. In fact, according to one of the interviewees, "large teams sometimes experience free riding, that is, situations where when the team is too large, few people do the hard work while many get the merits. This situation ends by fatiguing those who do most of the work and affects internal cohesion. This lack of cohesion is sometimes reflected in the quality of the work done, and foreign institutions and foreign researchers perceive that tension." Another interviewee claimed that, "when there are too many PhDs in a team, there tend to be too many 'generals' and too few 'soldiers,' which ends by increasing transaction costs of any collaborative enterprise." The exploration of this new model shows that such claims are not supported by the data, except for the number of bibliographic products done, which increases team's odds of collaborating internationally but a decreasing rate. The top number of products at which this positive trend reverses is outside of our data range, however. In fact, holding the other variables constant, the probability of collaborating increases with every additional product but once the team reaches a total of 132 products the probability starts to fall at an increasing rate.

7 As an experiment, team characteristics and their performance were included into the model and the results showed that team age, the number of PhDs, and the production of the teams appeared positively (and statistically significantly) related to the probability of co-authoring with foreign partners. This seems plausible as discussed earlier.

8 In fact, Colombia hosts one of the few reknown international research centers dedicated to tropical agriculture: The "Centro Internacional de Agricultura Tropical" –CIAT.

References

Adams, J.D., Black, G.C., Clemmons, J.R. and Stephan, P.E. (2005), 'Scientific teams and institutional collaborations: evidence from US universities', 1981-1999, in *Research Policy*, 34(3): 259-285.

Allen, T. (1977), *Managing the flow of technology*, Boston, MA: MIT Press.

Beaver, D.D. (2004), 'Does collaborative research have greater epistemic authority?' in *Scientometrics*, 60(3): 399-408.

Beaver, D. D. and Rosen, R. (1979), 'Studies in Scientific Collaboration .2. scientific co-authorship: research productivity and visibility in the French scientific elite, 1799-1830', in *Scientometrics*, 1(2): 133-149.

Behrens, T. R. and Gray, D.O. (2001), 'Unintended consequences of cooperative research: impact of industry sponsorship on climate for academic freedom and other graduate student outcome', in *Research Policy*, 30(2): 179-199.

Bordons, M. and Gomez, I. (2000), *'Collaboration networks in science'*, Web of Knowledge - a Festschrift in Honour of Eugene Garfield. B. Cronin and H. B. Atkins. Medford, NJ.: Information Today Inc, 197-213.

Bozeman, B. and Corley, E. (2004), 'Scientists' collaboration strategies: implications for scientific and technical human capital', in *Research Policy*, 33(4): 599-616.

Bozeman, B. and Rogers, J.D. (2002), 'A churn model of scientific knowledge value: Internet researchers as a knowledge value collective', in *Research Policy*, 31(5): 769-794.

Burt, R. S. (2004), 'Structural holes and good ideas', in *American Journal of Sociology*, 110(2): 349-399.

Carayol, N. and Matt, M. (2004), 'Does research organization influence academic production? Laboratory level evidence from a large European university', in *Research Policy*, 33(8): 1081-1102.

Cohen, W.M. and Levinthal, D.A. (1990), 'Absorptive capacity: A new perspective on learning and innovation', in *Administrative Science Quarterly*, 35(1): 128-152.

Colciencias (2000), 'Módulo de Cálculo para Escalafonamiento de Grupos y Centros de Investigación Científica y Tecnológica -2000', *Convocatoria Nacional para Grupos y Centros de Investigación Científica y Tecnológica 2000*, Bogotá, D.C., Colombia: 20p.

Coleman, J. (1988), 'Social capital in the creation of human capital', in *American Journal of Sociology* 94(Supp.): S95-S120.

Crane, D. (1972), *'Invisible Colleges: diffusion of knowledge in scientific communities'*, Chicago, IL: The University of Chicago Press.

Cummings, J.N. and Kiesler, S. (2005), 'Collaborative research across disciplinary and organizational boundaries', in *Social Studies of Science*, 35(5): 703-722.

Diamond, A. M. (1985), 'The money value of citations to single-authored and multiple-authored articles', in *Scientometrics*, 8(5-6): 315-320.

Farrell, M. P. (2001), 'Collaborative circles: friendship dynamics and creative work', Chicago, IL: University of Chicago Press.

Florida, R. (1999), 'The role of the university: leveraging talent, not technology' in *Issues in Science & Technology*, 15(4): 67-73.

Forero-Pineda, C. and Jaramillo-Salazar, H. (2002), 'The access of researchers from developing countries to international science and technology', in *International Social Science Journal*, 54(1): 129-130.

Fox, M.F. and Faver, C.A. (1984), 'Independence and cooperation in research - the motivations and costs of collaboration', in *Journal of Higher Education*, 55(3): 347-359.

Frame, J.D. and Carpenter, M.P. (1979), 'International research collaboration', in *Social Studies of Science*, 9(4): 481-497.

Gelijns, A.C. and Their, S.O. (2002), 'Medical innovation and institutional interdependence: rethinking university-industry connections', in *Journal of the American Medical Association*, 287: 72-77.

George, G., Zahra, S.A., Wood, D. (2002), 'The effects of business-university alliances on innovative output and financial performance: a study of publicly traded biotechnology companies', in *Journal of Business Venturing*, 17(6): 577-609.

Basu, A. and Aggarwal, R. (2001), 'International collaboration in science in India and its impact on institutional performance' in *Scientometric*, 52(3): 379-394.

Basu, A. and Kumar, B.S.V. (2000), 'International collaboration in Indian scientific papers', in *Scientometrics*, 48(3): 381-402.

Bayona, C., Garcia-Marco, T. and Huerta, E. (2001), 'Firms' motivations for cooperative R&D: an empirical analysis of Spanish firms', in *Research Policy*, 30(8): 1289-1307.

Belderbos, R., Carree, M. and Lokshin, B. (2004), 'Cooperative R&D and firm performance', in *Research Policy*, 33(10): 1477-1492.

Chaparro, F., Jaramillo, H. and Quintero, V. (2004), 'The role of Diaspora in facilitating participation in global knowledge networks: lessons of the Red Caldas in Colombia', *Report prepared for the Knowledge for Development Program, The World Bank*, 25.

Frenken, K., Hölzl, W. and de Vor, F. (2005), 'The citation impact of research collaborations: the case of European biotechnology and applied microbiology (1988–2002)', in *Journal of Engineering and Technology Management*, 22(1-2): 9-30

Hagedoorn, J., Link, A.N. and Vonortas, N.S. (2000), 'Research partnerships', in *Research Policy*, 29(4-5): 567-586.

Georghiou, L. (1998), 'Global cooperation in research', in *Research Policy*, 27(6): 611-626.

Gibbons, M., Limoges, C., Nowotny, H., Schwartzman, S., Scott, P. and Trow, M. (1994), '*The new production of knowledge: the dynamics of science and research in contemporary societies*', Chapters 1-2, London: Sage Publications.

Glanzel, W. and Schubert, A. (2005), 'Domesticity and internationality in co-authorship, references and citations,' in *Scientometrics*, 65(3): 323-342.

Glänzel, W. and Schubert, A. (2004), 'Analyzing scientific networks through co-authorship', in Moed, H. Glänzel, W. and Dordrecht, *Handbook of quantitative science and technology research: the use of publication and patent statistics in studies on S&T Systems*, The Netherlands: Kluwer Academic Publishers.

Granovetter, M. (2005), 'The impact of social structure on economic outcomes', in *Journal of Economic Perspectives*, 19(1): 33-50.

Herbertz, H. (1995), 'Does it pay to cooperate - a bibliometric case-study in molecular-biology', in *Scientometrics*, 33(1): 117-122.

Katz, J. S. (1994), 'Geographical proximity and scientific collaboration', in *Scientometrics*, 31(1): 31-43.

Katz, J. S. and Hicks, D. (1997), 'How much is a collaboration worth? A calibrated bibliometric model', in *Scientometrics*, 40(3): 541-554.

Katz, J. S. and Martin, B.R. (1997), 'What is research collaboration?' in *Research Policy*, 26(1): 1-18.

Kleinman, D. (1998), 'Pervasive influence: intellectual property, industrial history, and university science', in *Science and Public Policy*: 25(2): 95-102.

Landry, R. and Amara, N. (1998), 'The impact of transaction costs on the institutional structuration of collaborative academic research' in *Research Policy*, 27(9): 901-913.

Landry, R., Amara, N. and Lamari, M. (2002), 'Does social capital determine innovation? to what extent?', in *Technological Forecasting and Social Change*, 69(7): 681-701.

Lee, S. (2004), 'Forein-born scientists in the United States -do they perform differently than native-born scientists?' *PhD Dissertation*, School of Public Policy, Atlanta, GA, Georgia Institute of Technology.

Lee, S. and Bozeman, B. (2005), 'The impact of research collaboration on scientific productivity', in *Social Studies of Science*, 35(5): 673-702.

Levine, J. M. and Moreland, R.L. (2004), 'Collaboration: the social context of theory development,' in *Personality and Social Psychology Review*, 8(2): 164-172.

Le Bas, C., Picard, F. and Suchecki, B. (1998), 'Innovation technologique, comportement de reseaux et performances: Une analyse sur donnees individuelles', in *Revue D'Economie Politique*, 108(5): 625–644.

Luukkonen, T., Persson, O. and Sivertsen, G. (1992), 'Understanding patterns of international scientific collaboration', in *Science, Technology and Human Values*, 17(1): 101-126

Landry, R., Traore, N. and Godin, B. (1996), 'An econometric analysis of the effect of collaboration on academic research productivity', in *Higher Education*, 32(3): 283-301.

Melin, G. (2004), 'Postdoc abroad: inherited scientific contacts or establishment of new networks?', in *Research Evaluation*, 13(2): 95-102.

NSF-NSB (2006), *Science and engineering indicators 2006*, National Science Board. Arlington, VA: National Science Foundation, Division of Science Resources Statistics.

NSF-NSB (2008), *Science and engineering indicators 2008*, National Science Board, Arlington, VA: National Science Foundation.

Narin, F., Stevens, K. and Whitlow, E.S. (1991), 'Scientific cooperation in Europe and the citation of multinationally authored papers', in *Scientometrics*, 21(3): 313-323.

Ordonez, G. (2005), 'The impact of research collaboration on the quality of the research outputs in Colombia', *Lecture at the Colloquium Harvard-MIT. Ciencia, Tecnología e Innovación en Colombia* 2005, Nov. 18-19.

Ordonez, G. (2008), 'International research collaboration, research team performance, and scientific and technological capabilities in Colombia - a bottom-up perspective', *PhD Dissertation in Public Policy.* Georgia Institute of Technology, Georgia State University. Atlanta.

Ordonez, G., Cozzens, S. and Garcia, M. (2010), 'International co-authorship and research team performance in Colombia', in *Review of Policy Research,* 27(4): 415-431.

Penner-Hahn, J. and Shaver, J.M. (2005), 'Does international research and development increase patent output? An analysis of Japanese pharmaceutical firms', in *Strategic Management Journal,* 26(2): 121-140.

Rigby, J. and Edler, J. (2005), 'Peering inside research networks: some observations on the effect of the intensity of collaboration on the variability of research quality', in *Research Policy,* 34(6): 784-794.

Rogers, J. D. and Bozeman, B. (2001), 'Knowledge value alliances: an alternative to the R&D project focus in evaluation', in *Science, Technology and Human Values,* 26(1): 23.

Sagasti, F. (2004), *Knowledge and innovation for development: the Sisyphus challenge of the 21st century,* Northampton, MA.: Edward Elgar.

Seibert, S. E., Kraimer, M.L. and Lindin, R.C. (2001), 'A social capital theory of career success', in *Academy of Management Journal,* 44(2): 219-237.

Shrum, W. (2005), 'Reagency of the Internet, or, how I became a guest for science', in *Social Studies of Science,* 35(5): 723-754.

Slaughter, S., Campbell, T., Holleman, M. and Morgan, E. (2002), 'The "traffic" in graduate students: graduate students as tokens of exchange between academe and industry', in *Science Technology and Human Values,* 27(2): 282-312.

Stephan, P. E. (2001), 'Educational implications of university-industry technology transfer', in *Journal of Technology Transfer,* 26: 199-205.

Tsai, W. P. and Ghoshal, S. (1998), 'Social capital and value creation: the role of intrafirm networks', in *Academy of Management Journal,* 41(4): 464-476.

Turner, L. and Mairesse, J. (2005), 'Individual productivity differences in public research: how important are non-individual determinants?' *An economic study of French physicists' publications and citations (1986-1997)*, Unpublished Manuscript. 35 p.

Uzzi, B. and Spiro, J. (2005), 'Collaboration and creativity: the small world problem', in *American Journal of Sociology*, 111(2): 447-504.

Wagner, C. S. and Leydesdorff, L. (2006), 'Measuring the globalization of knowledge networks', *Blue Sky Manuscript*, 12.

Wagner, C. S. (2005), 'Six case studies of international collaboration in science', in *Scientometrics*, 62(1): 3-26.

Wagner, C. S., I. Brahmakulam, Jackson, B., Wong, A. and Yoda, T. (2001), '*Science and Technology Collaboration: Building Capacities in Developing Countries*?' Santa Monica, CA: RAND.

Wagner, C. S. and L. Leydesdorff (2004), 'Network structures, self-organization and the growth of international collaboration in science', in *Amsterdam School of Communications Research*, 33.

Wagner, C. S. and Leydesdorff, L. (2005), 'Mapping the network of global science: comparing international co-authorships from 1990 to 2000', in *International Journal of Technology and Globalization*, 1(2): 185-207.

Wray, K. B. (2002), 'The epistemic significance of collaborative research', in *Philosophy of Science*, 69(1): 150-168.

APPENDICES

Appendix A: Sampling Strategy

Total Teams Registered in 2005 by Colciencias	3342
Teams Excluded (of which:)	1453
Teams created in 2005 (i)	6
Teams with less than 2 R/E active* by 2003 (ii)	919
Teams with no R&D projects active** btw 2003 and 2005 (iii)	1172
Teams used in the analysis of the larger sample	1889
Teams used in the analysis of the smaller sample***	672

Sums do not add up due to double counting of teams' attributes:

(i) This is justified as many teams may form only to be registered as such by Colciencias during the registration process

(ii) This is justified as there is no "team" of only one member

(iii) This is justified as there is no "research team" without at least one R&D project acting as their main common activity

* An active R/E is a Researcher or Engineer that reports research activities done in 2003 or before

** An active R&D project refers to Research and Development work reported as being in progress between 2003 and 2005

*** The smaller sample was created using the same criteria of the larger sample, includes teams created by March 2004 (to assure random selection), and excludes teams working in the social sciences or in the humanities

Appendix B: Classification of partner countries

Country	NORTH	SOUTH
Albania		X
Argelia		X
Argentina		X
Australia	X	
Austria	X	
Bahamas		X
Bangladesh		X
Belarus		X
Belgium	X	
Belize		X
Benin		X
Bermuda		X
Bolivia		X
Botswana		X
Brazil		X
Brunei		X
Bulgaria	X	
Burkina Faso		X
Cameroon		X
Canada	X	
Chad		X
Chile		X
China		X
Colombia		X
Costa Rica		X
Croatia		X
Cuba		X
Czech Republic	X	
Denmark	X	
Dominican Republic		X
Ecuador		X
Egypt		X
Ethiopia		X
Fiji		X
Finland	X	
France	X	
Gambia		X
Germany	X	
Ghana		X
Greece		X
Guadeloupe		X
Guatemala		X
Guyana		X
Honduras		X
Hong Kong		X
Hungary	X	
Iceland	X	
India		X
Indonesia		X
Iran		X
Iraq		X
Ireland	X	
Israel	X	
Italy	X	
Jamaica		X
Japan	X	
Kazakhstan		X
Kenya		X
Korea Dem. Rep.		X
Korea Rep.		X
Kuwait		X
Latvia		X
Lebanon		X
Lithuania	X	
Macedonia		X
Malagasy Republ		X
Malawi		X
Malaysia		X
Mali		X
Mauritius		X
Mexico		X
Moldova	X	
Mongolia		X
Morocco		X
Nepal		X
Netherlands	X	
New Caledonia		X
New Zealand	X	
Nicaragua		X
Nigeria		X
Norway	X	
Oman		X
Pakistan		X
Panama		X
Papua N Guinea		X
Paraguay		X
Peru		X
Philippines		X
Poland	X	
Portugal	X	
Puerto Rico		X
Rep of Georgia		X
Romania	X	
Russian Federation	X	
Saudi Arabia		X
Senegal		X
Serbia Montenegro		X
Singapore		X
Slovakia	X	
Slovenia		X
South Africa		X
Spain	X	
Sri Lanka		X
Sudan		X
Swaziland		X
Sweden	X	
Switzerland	X	
Syria		X
Taiwan		X
Tanzania		X
Thailand		X
Trinidad and Tobago		X
Tunisia		X
Turkey		X
Uganda		X
Ukraine	X	
United Kingdom	X	
United States	X	
Uruguay		X
Venda		X
Venezuela		X
Vietnam		X
W Ind Assoc St		X
Yugoslavia		X
Zambia		X
Zimbabwe		X

Appendix C: Descriptive Statistics

	Variable	Mean	Std. Dev.	Min	Max
Dependent Variables	IRC05	.3896241	.4877941	0	1
	ircpeople05	.2149285	.4108815	0	1
	ircproj05	.2588671	.4381285	0	1
	ircN05	.3128639	.4637822	0	1
	ircS05	.1604023	.367076	0	1
	peopN05	.1344627	.3412391	0	1
	peopS05	.1064055	.3084376	0	1
	projN05	.2382213	.426108	0	1
	projS05	.0629963	.2430206	0	1
Team Characteristics	Core03	7.258338	5.71711	2	74
	age03	6.904711	5.837255	0	68
	totphds03	1.455267	2.210634	0	47
	leadewrit~05	.5473796	.4978819	0	1
	leadstudo~05	.5542615	.4971786	0	1
	totprojec~03	5.75172	6.603742	0	70
	totbibprod03	30.34569	43.87513	0	458
Field	natscs	.2329275	.4228084	0	1
	agroscs	.0608788	.2391711	0	1
	medscs	.126522	.3325247	0	1
	social	.1614611	.3680531	0	1
	human	.2419269	.4283637	0	1
	engi	.1339333	.3406708	0	1
	othscs	.0423504	.2014407	0	1
Sector	educsector	.9052409	.2929595	0	1
	bussector	.0338804	.1809691	0	1
	govsector	.0386448	.1927979	0	1
	othsector	.0206458	.1422333	0	1
Characteristics of Home Institution	smallinst	.1678137	.3737997	0	1
	medinst	.3785071	.4851434	0	1
	biginst	.4536792	.4979816	0	1
Localization	smallcity	.0174696	.1310476	0	1
	medcity	.2191636	.4137893	0	1
	bigcity	.753838	.4308881	0	1

n = 1,889 teams

Appendix D: Determinants of international research collaboration: percentage change in odds

Internat. Res. Coll.	b	z	P>z	%	%StdX	SDofX
Team size in 2003	0.02745	2.034	0.042	2.8	17.0	5.7171
Team Age in 2003	0.03535	3.030	0.002	3.6	22.9	5.8373
Total PhDs in 2003	0.25248	6.146	0.000	28.7	74.7	2.2106
Leader Writes in Other Lang.	0.47462	4.023	0.000	60.7	26.7	0.4979
Leader Studied Overseas	0.44927	3.940	0.000	56.7	25.0	0.4972
Tot. Proj. in 2003	0.05508	4.203	0.000	5.7	43.9	6.6037
Tot. Bib. Prod by 2003	0.00777	3.846	0.000	0.8	40.6	43.8751
Agrosciences	-0.39975	-1.586	0.113	-33.0	-9.1	0.2392
Medical Sciences	-0.48066	-2.448	0.014	-38.2	-14.8	0.3325
Social Sciences	-0.38446	-2.088	0.037	-31.9	-13.2	0.3681
Humanities	-0.18291	-1.152	0.249	-16.7	-7.5	0.4284
Engineering	-0.59780	-3.143	0.002	-45.0	-18.4	0.3407
Other Sciences	-0.13717	-0.467	0.641	-12.8	-2.7	0.2014
Mid. Home Inst.	-0.28457	-2.263	0.024	-24.8	-12.9	0.4851
Small Home Inst.	-0.20575	-1.260	0.208	-18.6	-7.4	0.3738
Small City	-1.11583	-1.973	0.048	-67.2	-13.6	0.1310
Midsize City	-0.24056	-1.723	0.085	-21.4	-9.5	0.4138

b = raw coefficient
z = z-score for test of b=0
P>|z| = p-value for z-test
% = percent change in odds for unit increase in X
%StdX = Percent change in odds for SD increase in X
SDofX = Standard deviation of X

Acknowledgement

This research was partly funded by the National Science Foundation under Grant Number 0647126.

African Journal of Science, Technology,
Innovation and Development
Vol. 4, No. 2, 2012
pp. 69-91

Assessment of Technological Innovations in Selected Indigenous Oilfield Servicing Firms in Nigeria

Oluseye O. Jegede*, Abiodun A. Egbetokun**
& Willie O. Siyanbola***

Abstract

This study examined the types of technological innovations that had occurred in indigenous oilfield servicing sub-sector within the period 2001-2010, their intensities and evaluated the factors that influenced the capability of the firms in the sub-sector. The study used primary and secondary data sources. Sixty firms were sampled. Structured questionnaire were administered in the firms. This was supplemented with shop-floor observations and interviews. The questionnaires elicited information on the firms' innovation activities and the factors that influenced these. Sixty firms were purposefully selected. A total of 60 questionnaires were administered on heads of technical, finance and administration departments in the firms out of which 66.7% were returned and found suitable for analysis. Secondary data were sourced from the internet and other published sources. Organisational innovation was the most

* National Centre for Technology Management, Obafemi Awolowo University, Ile-Ife, Nigeria. Email: jegede.seye@yahoo.com

** National Centre for Technology Management, Obafemi Awolowo University, Ile-Ife, Nigeria. E-mail: egbetokunaaAgmail.com

*** National Centre for Technology Management, Obafemi Awolowo University, Ile-Ife, Nigeria, E-mail: williesiyanbola@yahoo.com

prevalent (65%), product and process innovations were implemented, respectively, by 15% and 28.2% of the firms. Specifically, product innovations in the sub-sector majorly involved introduction of new service; and process innovations were expressed as modification of existing processes. Innovation intensity was low. The important internal factors that accounted for the innovation performance included the skill of the workforce in the technical departments and extensive staff training. The important external factors included interaction with customers, competitors, suppliers of equipment and the industry association which had been a significant path of capability building. The study found that the overall innovation of the firms for innovations was mainly expressed in organisational changes; product and process innovations in the sub-sector were mainly incremental.

Keywords: Technological innovations, Oil servicing firms, Absorptive capacity, R&D, Technical training, Nigeria.

JEL Classification: O31; O34; O55.

1. Introduction

Nigeria is the 10th largest oil producer in the world, the third largest in Africa and the most prolific oil producer in Sub-Saharan Africa. The Nigerian economy is largely dependent on its oil sector which supplies 95% of its foreign exchange earnings. The upstream oil industry is the single most important sector in the economy. According to the 2008 BP Statistical Energy Survey, Nigeria had proved oil reserves of 36.22 billion barrels at the end of 2007 or 2.92 % of the world's reserves. The Nigerian government planned to expand its proven reserves to 40 billion barrels by 2010. Nigeria's wealth of oil makes it most attractive to the major oil-multinationals, most of which are represented in Nigeria, with the major foreign stakeholder being Shell. Nigeria produced an average of 2355.8 thousand barrels of crude oil per day in 2007, 2.92% of the world total and a change of -4.8 % compared to 2006 (BP Statistical Energy Survey, 2008).

According to the BP Statistical Energy Survey (2008), Nigeria had proved natural gas reserves of 5.29 trillion cubic metres, 2.98% of the world total. Due, mainly, to the lack of a gas infrastructure, 75% of associated gas is flared and 12% re-injected. Nigeria has set a target of zero flare by 2010 and is providing incentives for the production and use of gas. The government also planned to raise earnings from natural gas exports to 50 percent of oil revenues also by 2010. It has been reported in the BP Statistical Energy Survey (2008) that Nigeria had natural gas production of 34.97 billion cubic metres, 1.18% of the world total.

Nigeria's downstream oil industry is also a key sector including four refineries with a nameplate capacity of 438,750 bbl/d (BP Statistical Energy Survey, 2008). Problems such as fire, sabotage, poor management, lack of turnaround maintenance and corruption were responsible for. The refineries often operate at 40% of full capacity, if at all. This has resulted in shortages of refined product and the need to increase imports to meet domestic demand. Nigeria has a robust petrochemicals industry based on its substantial refining capacity and natural gas resources. The petrochemical industry is focused around the three centres of Kaduna, Warri and Eleme.

The business environment of the 21st century is proving to be very different from the past. This new competitive landscape has greater uncertainty, dynamism and volatility caused by increasing technological developments and the increasingly rapid diffusion of information and new technologies (Chesbrough, 2003; Hitt *et al.*, 2000; Drucker, 1999). This accounts for why some firms are able to implement and use advanced and appropriate technologies with relative ease while others struggle. The link between building local technological capacity and the ability to respond to challenges are usually brought about in the process of learning and co-operation between institutions. The spread of multinational corporation activity around the globe has benefited industries. The trend towards vertical disintegration of production activity in industrialised countries means that developing countries can now participate in the global economy by inserting themselves into international value chains. This is not easy though, as competition to host multinational oil companies' activity in developing countries is becoming tougher. Indeed, evidence shows that only a handful of indigenous oil firms have contributed to the productivity in the sector. Even-though, there is a level of Foreign Direct Investment (FDI) in Nigeria's oil and gas sector however, indigenous firms have not benefited from the internationalisation of production. According to Ozigbo (2008) the local content in the industry is still very low as over 60 percent of the work value in the oil and gas sector is carried out abroad.

Several studies have assessed the level of interaction among the various elements of Nigeria's National Innovation System (NIS) and analysed the factors influencing the generation and successful adoption or non-adoption of industrial innovation by Nigerian firms (Adjebeng-Asem, 1996; Oyewale, 2003; Oyebisi *et al.*, 1996; Oyelaran-Oyeyinka *et al.*, 1996). There is also a large body of evidence on the innovative characteristics of the manufacturing sector in Nigeria, particularly the small and medium enterprises (SMEs) (e.g. Abereijo *et al.* 2007; Oyelaran-Oyeyinka, 1997, 2001, 2002, 2005; Oyelaran-Oyeyinka *et al*, 2007; Oyelaran-Oyeyinka and Lal, 2006). In literature, there is very little attention given to the intensity of innovation in the indigenous oil and gas servicing firms that are providing services to the foreign oil and gas firms in Nigeria. Furthermore, the system approach was used in virtually all of the studies, which is good especially for the developing country context, but little attention is paid to sectoral influences on firm-level innovation capability. In addition, most studies have narrowly focused on either product or process innovations; not much has been said concerning other types of innovations. Indeed, there are not many detailed sub-sectoral studies that can be identified in the literature on innovation in Nigeria's indigenous oil and gas servicing firms.

In developing countries and regions, the process of industrial development involves the employment of extant technologies to overcome the wide gaps between them and the industrial forerunners (Oyelaran-Oyeyinka, 1998). Thus, to close the wide technological gap between the developed and the developing countries, the later need to adequately develop, deploy and update the existing technologies, as well as strengthen necessary technological capabilities and knowledge required for technological and innovative development. As noted by Oyelaran-Oyeyinka (2004), another strategy for reducing technological disparity between the developed and developing countries is how new technology is acquired and adapted. This is, through technological acquisition. Technology is a term used for not only physical devices but also encompasses ideas, procedures, know-how and social institutions involved in the technological processes; all of which are inseparable elements/factors in technological processes (Kemp, 1997).

Technology is a dynamic process which involves the introduction and diffusion of new technologies and as well the update and/or utilization of the existing technologies. The dynamism of technology determines or accounts for technological trajectories which are important factors in achieving social, economical and environmental goals at both local and global level. Hence, the mechanisms and driving forces of the technology changes, as well as characteristics and structure of both prevailing and emerging regimes (technologies) must be understood in order to conceive the actions necessary to stimulate the change in the required direction (Kemp, 1997).

Today, it has become apparent that the critical issue for industrial countries and firms is not the technology they have at present, but rather, how they learn to evaluate, adopt, and use the technology effectively to improve their products and services. What endow a competitive edge on a firm or a nation is what it knows, how it uses what it knows and how fast it can know something new (Prusak, 1996). With the pace of industrial transformation in developing countries, firms are experiencing a growing need for innovation to remain relevant in the market place (Kemp, 1997). Unfortunately, the absence of strong technological capability which contributes to sustainable competitiveness often impedes the firms from improving their innovations (Prusak, 1996).

In Nigeria and other developing countries, innovation is seen as a process of adoption, absorption and diffusion of traditional available technology (Lall, 1991). It is thus important for firms to develop the capability to exploit the locally available technology as a means of gaining competitive edge. This capability is embedded in the set of skills and competences which the firm possesses and/or can exploit to manage change (Oyelaran-Oyeyinka *et al.*, 1996). Innovation capability consists of the skills, knowledge, resources, creativity and attitude needed to continuously generate and translate ideas and change into marketable new or significantly improved devices, products, processes and services (Tidd, 2001). Innovation is very essential for the growth of firms and also for the firms to sustain competitive advantage (Souitaris, 2003; Hitt *et al.*, 1997; Tidd, 2001). Innovation has been strongly linked to economic growth (Tidd, 2001). As a nation's economic growth may be understood by a lay man as the nation's increasing capacity, to produce more and better goods and services to its population. Technological innovation is defined as the first commercial application of a new technology which occurs when a new or changed product is introduced to the market, or when a new or changed process is used in commercial production (Souitaris, 2003). The emergence of a new technology, which may take the form of a product, process or service, is a result of several activities spanning an appreciable length of time depending on the type of technology (Hitt *et al.*, 1997).

Industrialization has led to global competition among nations and firms which in turn has caused firms to innovate over time. A firm that intends to perform today and cope with the future must therefore incorporate innovation into its organizational routine. But this has not really been the case (Storey, 2000). Innovation in firms has been influenced more by economic development and the management culture rather than competition (OECD, 2005; Oyelaran-Oyeyinka *et al*, 1996). Owing to these, and some other reasons such as systemic weaknesses and weak research-industry interaction (Ilori *et al.*, 2000; Oyewale, 2005; Oyebisi *et al.*, 1996), a sharp contrast exists between firms in developing nations and the developed ones. Hence, innovation studies in technologically advanced countries cannot be correlated with innovation patterns in the third world countries.

Furthermore, the main factors promoting innovation in firms especially in the developing countries of the world is important for policy. In addition to innovation activities, a number of other factors may affect technological learning, capability and innovation (OECD, 2005). While there has been much study on the factors that influence firms' propensity to innovate, little of this has been in developing countries especially in Africa. This study is premised on the need to close this gap in development-relevant knowledge in Nigeria.

2. Research Questions

This study seeks to answer the following questions through empirical evidence:

- What types of technological innovation had occurred in the indigenous oil and gas servicing firms in Nigeria?
- How intense is innovation in this sub-sector?
- What are the specific factors that influence the capability of these firms to innovate?

3. Methodology

The main analytical concepts and the relationships in this study is based on established relationships in the literature on technological capabilities and represents a modification on the one applied by Romijn and Albaladejo (2002) in their study of the determinants of innovation capability in small high-tech firms in the United Kingdom (UK) and Egbetokun *et al,* (2007) in their study of the assessment of innovation capability in the cable manufacturing industry in Nigeria. Capabilities accumulate as a result of various internal and external inputs (Romijn and Albaladejo, 2002). Although Romijn and Albaladejo's (2002) results showed that not all of the inputs in the model are significantly related to innovation capability, they have all been included in this assessment for two main reasons. That is difference in industry and country contexts as well as the larger number of innovation types considered in this study.

This study focused on Nigeria's indigenous oil and gas servicing firms. The firms were purposefully selected. Data was collected from the firms through the use of a structured questionnaire. The questionnaires were administered on four departments identified as relevant to this study (Production, Engineering/Maintenance, Finance and Administration Departments). Sixty questionnaires were administered to the firms but only forty which were completed with accuracy was used in the analysis.

The questionnaire elicited information on the innovation strategies of the firm, its human resource, innovation rate and expenditure on R&D as well as the incidence of collaboration/joint activities with stakeholders within the Petroleum Innovation System (PIS). The questionnaire, which is for the Production Department and Engineering Department, covers the innovation and technological efforts of the firms; their sources of information for innovation as well as the nature of linkages and interactions in the industry.

Proxy variables of the firm's innovative performance as reflected in whether it has innovated and the type(s) of innovation it has undertaken (UNU-INTECH, 2004) were used in the study. To measure the technological innovation, this study considered four types of innovation as outlined:

- Product innovation was measured via three proxy variables, one of which is similar to those used in many previous studies (Romijn and Albaladejo, 2002). The first variable indicated whether or not the firm developed a new product during the reference period. The next two variables measured whether or not the firm introduced a new product to the market or modified an existing one.
- Process innovation was measured via three proxy variables indicating whether the firm developed, introduced a new process in its production activities or modified an existing one (Romijn and Albaladejo, 2002; UNU-INTECH, 2004).
- Organisational innovation was captured with four variables drawn from UNU-INTECH (2004): changes in quality controls; maintenance routines, waste management procedures and reverse engineered any product or process
- Diffusion-based innovation is considered to be unique in the sense that it is particularly important in the developing country context. This innovation type was measured through two simple binary variables: the acquisition of product licence and/or process licence. Whether or not a firm uses technology licensed from a foreign owned company or enters into a joint venture has been found to be important for firm growth.

UNU-INTECH (2004) noted that the propensity to innovate is related to:

- Location of the firm within or close to a major urban area;
- Proximity to sources of new knowledge and ease in participating in knowledge flows;
- Educational level of the Owner/CEO/Manager, especially a degree from a technical university or engineering programme that stimulates and facilitates problem solving;
- Global exposure through training, work or study abroad which opens opportunities for networking for knowledge flows and collaboration and creates an awareness of the utility to do so;
- Ownership structure of the firm, which influences the choice of products and processes as well as their subsequent modification or change. For instance, technology within a multinational group is often sourced from the foreign parent company and thus, the effect of being an affiliate of a foreign firm should be accounted for;

- The firm's sector, which provides a measure of the stimulus to innovation resulting from the higher R&D intensity of the sector and nature of competition within the sector;
- The size of the firm, which is related to its access to resources and opportunities for knowledge scanning to support a process of innovation. Among firms, small enterprises are better suited to carry out technological innovations due to their specific advantages of flexibility, concentration and internal communications ;
- Exports (as a percentage of sales) and whether this is rising as an indicator of the firm's competitive interests and abilities; and
- Habits and practices of innovation as reflected in having innovated in the past.

Five key areas of influence on an organisation's ability to innovate are generally identified in the body of literature which was reviewed for this study, and these can clearly be categorised, relative to the firm, into internal and external components. These influences relate to leadership, opportunistic behaviour, culture and change, learning, and networking and relationship building.

Internal Sources of Innovation Capability

- The professional background of the heads of Technical Departments was captured through three variables. The educational qualification was represented by multiple-choice measures of management, science and engineering and other academic degrees obtained. Prior work experience abroad was represented as the number of years that the heads of technical departments worked in any of small enterprises, large corporations, and university or related institutions. Prior training experience abroad in small enterprises, large corporations, and university or related institutions to current work were measured on a Likert scale.
- Human Resources of the firms were measured by variables representing the extent of organisational learning and the working proportion of R&D staff in total workforce was also considered (Romijn and Albaladejo, 2002).
- Investment effort was captured by variables representing innovation, R&D and training investment (Romijn and Albaladejo, 2002).

External Sources of Innovation Capability

- Networking and collaboration was captured by the incidence of contacts with external agents. For example, relationships with customers, suppliers, enterprises in related lines of business, financial institutions, universities, research institutions, training institutions, service providers and industry.

- Proximity advantages from networks measured the geographical proximity advantages associated with the above network interactions and these were measured by asking the respondents to indicate, whether or not a proximity advantage was attached to each of the interactions.
- Institutional support measured by whether or not firms had received financial support from government or other forms of support from other institutions such as trade associations. The information gathered was supplemented with additional information from published sources [e.g. Nigerian National Petroleum Corporation (NNPC), Department of Petroleum Resources (DPR)] and in-depth interviews, as well as field observations. Previously tested questionnaires such as the African template proposed by UNU-INTECH (2004), the revised questionnaire employed in the South African Innovation Survey 2001 (Oerlemans *et al.*, 2001) and the list of variables used by Romijn and Albaladejo (2002) and Egbetokun *et al.* (2007) in their studies on the determinants of innovation capability in UK SMEs and Nigeria cable manufacturing industry were consulted in designing the questionnaire for this study.

4. Results and Discussion

Types of Technological Innovations

The study considered the prevalence of different types of innovative activities in the sub-sector. Table one shows the statistics on the prevalence of each types of technological innovations found within the indigenous oilfield servicing sub-sector. It shows that not less than 30% of the firms had engaged in product, process and organisational innovations during the 2001–2010 periods. On the average, 29% of the firms were innovation-active during the reference period. This is lower than the innovation prevalence of 52.7%, in a study of small enterprises in the state of Karnataka, India (Bala-Subrahmanya, 2005) and also lowers than the innovation prevalence 72% of the firms in the manufacturing sector (NACETEM, 2010). Certain anomalies become obvious when one takes a closer look at the figures in Table 1.

Table 1: Showing the Types of Technological Innovation that had taken Place between 2001 and 2010

	Types of Technological Innovation	Yes (%)	Started but later abandoned (%)	No (%)
Product Innovation	Introduced new product	12.5	2.5	85
	Developed new product	2.6	5.1	92.3
	Improved existing product	5.1	0	94.9
Process Innovation	Introduced new process	12.8	5.1	82.1
	Developed new process	2.6	10.3	87.2
	Improved existing process	23.1	5.1	71.8
Organisational Innovation	Introduced quality Control	42.5	7.5	50
	Introduced maintenance routine	55	10	35
	Introduced waste management procedure	37.5	15	47.5
	Reverse engineered any product/process	10.3	28.2	61.5

Diffusion-Based Innovation

Of the total, 41% (16) of the firms developed/applied any new or modified versions of any of either product or process technology within the period 2001 and 2010. About 31% (5) firms developed the new or modified versions of product or process which they have a license on their own while 62.5% (10) of the firms developed or modified through partnership with the licensor.

The prevalence of organisational innovations was observed to be higher than that of all other innovation types. It was the only type of innovation that ranked high. This primarily suggests that organisational changes are at the heart of the innovation processes in the indigenous oilfield servicing sub-sector. These changes, like OECD (2005) argued, are typically expressed in business practices and workplace organisation that are new to the firm and occur as a result of strategic management decisions. The intensive prevalence of organisational innovation, alongside process innovation, within our developing country context is not surprising because organisational changes, very much like process innovations, are less risky and consume much less resources compared to other types of innovations. Concerning process innovation, Egbetokun *et al.* (2009) noted that changes in processes are less rigid, more responsive to 'shop-floor' serendipitous discoveries and may not generally require financial investments as much as product innovations.

The 41% incidence of diffusion-based innovation recorded in this study actually arose from product and process licences. This somewhat low figure is a true representation of the situation within the sub-sector. The firms in the industry are all SMEs that are mostly confronted by several resource constraints. It is therefore difficult for them to procure licences. Low levels of absorptive capacities may also explain this situation (Audretsch *et al*, 2005; Rosa and Mohnen, 2008). The firms that have been able to do this are those which are part of a Foreign-based corporation

Intensity of Technological Innovations

Training Expenditure

Table 2: Showing the Amount Range Expended on Staff Training within the Period 2007-2010

Amount (Million Naira)	2007 (%)	2008 (%)	2009 (%)	2010 (%)
Less than 1	66.7	50	35	30.5
Between 1 and 5	33.3	50	65	60.8
Between 5 and 10	Nil	Nil	Nil	8.7

The training expenditure of the firms is given in Table 2. Majority of the firms that engaged in staff training spent below a million naira per year but the trend became reversed as the years progressed (see Table 2)

Innovation Expenditure

Table 3: Showing the Budget Range Expended on Innovation within the Period 2007-2010

Amount (Million Naira)	2007 (%)	2008 (%)	2009 (%)	2010 (%)
Less than 1	55.5	50	50	41.7
Between 1 and 5	44.5	50	50	50
Between 5 and 10	Nil	Nil	Nil	8.3

The innovation expenditure of the firms is given in Table 3. Like the training expenditure, the innovation expenditure increased as the years progressed (see Table 3)

Internal Factors that Affect Innovation Capability of the Firms

The main internal sources of innovation capability evaluated in this study are the background of the head(s) of technical departments in the firm and the internal technological efforts of the firm (staff training and innovation expenditure).

Background of the head(s) of technical department(s)

11 out 40 have separate production and engineering departments while the remaining 29 have the production and engineering department as one single department.

Production department

52.5 % of the heads of production department have Higher National Diploma, while 20% have a Bachelors Degree, 22.5% have Masters Degree and 5% have Doctorate Degree. 80% of the heads of production department have degrees in Science or Engineering field while 20% have degrees in Management or Finance-related field. 7.5% of the heads of technical department went for training in other African countries 7.5% in Europe, 20% in Europe, 7.5% in South America, 15% in Asia and 5% in Australia at some point in time. 2.5% of the head of the production department obtained a degree in other African Countries, 15% obtained degree in Europe, and 2.5% obtained degree in United States, Canada or Mexico.

Engineering department

42.5% of the heads of engineering department have Higher National Diploma, while 30% have Bachelors Degree, 20% have Masters Degree and 7.5% have Doctorate Degree. 77.5% of the degree is in Finance-related field. 15% of the heads of engineering department went for training in other African Countries, 12.5% in Europe, 15% in United States, Canada or Mexico, 5% in South America, 12.5% in Asia and 2.5% in Australia at some point in time.10% of the heads of the engineering department obtained a degree in Europe, 2.5% in United States, Canada or Mexico while 2.5% of the heads of the engineering department had previously worked in other African Countries.

Internal Technological Factors

Training and technological learning

Table 4 shows the number of firms that had training (learnt some new technologies) within the period 2007 to 2010.

Table 4: Showing the Frequency of Training that took Place in the Firm within the Period 2007 to 2010

	2007	2008	2009	2010
Use of Information & Communication Technology	3 (7.5%)	4 (10%)	7 (17.5%)	7 (17.5%)
Repairs and Maintenance	1 (2.5%)	5 (12.5%)	12 (30%)	10 (25%)
Project Management	1 (2.5%)	2 (5%)	12 (30%)	14 (35%)
Technical Report Writing	0	1 (2.5%)	4 (10%)	2 (5%)
Industrial Safety	2 (5%)	4 (10%)	8 (210%)	8 (20%)

The fact that firms require an adequate stock of skilled manpower and the role played by firm-level investments in training in enhancing this pool has been established in the innovation literature (Romijn and Albaladejo, 2002; Amara *et al.*, 2008). More recent research has indeed proven that firms that continually invest in staff training tend to be more capable to innovate. For instance, Amara *et al.* (2008) found that Canadian manufacturing SMEs that carried out staff training activities were 1.92 times more likely to innovate than their counterparts who did not. The results in Table four showed that that the indigenous oilfield servicing firms in Nigeria were marginally active in this regard as all of the firms reported having implemented one or more staff training programmes within the period covered in this study

Research and development efforts

41% (16) of the firms developed/applied any new or modified versions of any of either product or process technology within the period 2001 and 2010. 31.2% (5) firms developed the new or modified versions of product or process which they have a license on their own while 62.5% (10) of the firms developed or modified through partnership with the licensor.

Research and development activities

37.5% of the firms are involved in research and development activities but 15.4% of the firms have separate research and development department. In 2007 and 2008, there were a total of twenty-four personnel working in the research and development department in five out of the forty firms that were selected for this study. In 2009, the number rose to thirty-seven and in 2010, six firms now have separate research and development department with a total number of forty-six personnel.

External Factors that Affect Innovation Capability of the Firms

Interactions within the petroleum nnovation system

The study considered networking and collaboration as well as the advantages that firms might derive from these when they are located close to the actors involved in these networks. Several previous studies (Meeus *et al.*, 1999a, 1999b; Romijn and Albaldejo, 2002) have highlighted the importance of a number of stakeholders within an innovation system that firms may network or collaborate with. Evidences exist in favour of customers, suppliers, industry associations, higher education and research institutions, among others as helpful sources of information for the firms' innovation activities.

Table 5 shows that the firms interacted more with Industry Association than with most other actors. Egbetokun *et al.* (2009) found that the most highly rated source of information for innovation were customers. Jaruzelski and Dehoff (2007) also showed that customers probably matter more than any stakeholder in innovation. Interaction with competitors and Training Institutions were also relatively intense as 65% of the sampled firms collaborated with each of these stakeholders during the period covered by this study.

All the firms are subcontracting for the Oil and Gas companies. 74.4% of the oil and gas servicing firms outsource to other oil and gas servicing firms.

Table 5: Intensity of the interactions between the elements of Nigeria's Petroleum National Innovation System

	(%)
Competitors	75.5
Customers	61.8
Suppliers	64.7
Associated Companies	40.6
Consulting and Marketing firms	21.9
Private Research Institutes	16.7
Public Research Institutes	13.3
Universities	36.4
Government Ministries	6.9
Financial Institutions	29
Training Institutions	67.6
Industry Association	92.1

In contrast with the general trend in the literature (e.g. Autant-Bernard and Massard, 2001; Keller, 2002; UNU-INTECH, 2004; Audretsch *et al.*, 2005; Rosa and Mohnen, 2008), the occurrence of proximity advantages from knowledge centres among the firms was very low except for the Training Institutions (see Table 5). This is in spite of the fact that all the firms are located in the same city with at least a university. Perhaps this is explained by the general economic paradigm that firms require a certain level of absorptive capacities (usually approximated by firms' proportion of R&D staff, engineers or scientists) to be able to assimilate scientific knowledge and to benefit optimally from partnerships with knowledge centres, especially universities (Cohen and Levinthal, 1990; Fontana *et al.*, 2006; Rosa and Mohnen, 2008). Although it was difficult to empirically evaluate the firms' absorptive capacity because data gathered on staff profiles were largely partial and unreliable, the information gathered from the interviews conducted pointed out that the absorptive capacities of the firms in the indigenous oilfield servicing sub-sector was quite low. For instance, in few of the firms, apart from the CEO and his heads of technical departments, every other staff had less than a university degree. Within the production department in those firms, nearly every worker was employed with secondary or vocational qualifications and then trained on the shop floor. In some firms, we found about 75% of employees having either secondary school or vocational qualifications. Proportion of engineers and scientists in firm's total workforce was 15% while the proportion of technicians was 10%.

Table 6: Advantages from the proximity between the elements of Nigeria's Petroleum National Innovation System

	(%)
Competitors	80.6
Customers	65.4
Suppliers	70.4
Associated Companies	40
Consulting and Marketing firms	13.6
Private Research Institutes	13.6
Public Research Institutes	18.2
Universities	38.5
Government Ministries	5
Financial Institutions	28
Training Institutions	69
Industry Association	94.3

On the other hand, majority of the firms admitted that close location to suppliers (70.4%), competitors (80.6%), customers (65.4%), training institutions (69%) and particularly industry associations (94.3%) had been very beneficial to them (see Table 6). This seems to suggest that it could have been easier for the firms to pursue and seize the advantages from being close to these actors since no considerable level of absorptive capacity is required. An implication that could be drawn from the foregoing discussion is that in facilitating industry-academic relations, both proximity and firm-level absorptive capacities are critical and require attention from all stakeholders.

Government Support

Previous studies have shown that major government S&T policies and programmes may have more impact on innovation than the activities and strategies of private enterprises (OECD, 2005). Thus, the role of government as an institution is critical for firm-level innovation. Such roles typically include the design and implementation of innovation-friendly policies, effective monitoring of these policies, procuring innovative products from domestic firms and creating a stable political and economic ambience, among others. 2.6% of the selected firms enjoyed support from the Nigerian government within the period 2001 to 2010 (see Table 7) while the remaining 97.4% did benefit an form of government support within the said period though 33.3% of the selected firms claim to be aware of some government policies that support innovation.

Perhaps even more striking is the fact that the firms have apparently not collaborated extensively with or gained serious proximity advantages from government organisation (public research institutes and government ministries). Only 6.9% of the firms have collaborated with government ministries and 5% indicated gaining proximity advantages from these, 13.3% have collaborated with public research institutes while 18.3% indicated gaining advantages from these. While the latter is understandable as the firms are not so closely located to the ministries, the dearth of collaborative activities with them seems to suggest that these institutions have not been adequately supportive.

Table 7: Advantages the Selected Firms have Benefited from Government

	R&D funding (%)	Training (%)	Subsidies (%)	Tax Rebate (%)	Technical Support (%)	Loans and Grants (%)
Not Important	7.5	5	0	0	2.5	10
Slightly Important	7.5	10	5	0	7.5	2.5
Important	0	0	7.5	17.5	5	5
Very Important	5	5	20	20	12.5	2.5

Table 7 reflects that the firms have not really benefited from government support and policies in the study period. There is need for government to formulated new policies that would support the growth of small and medium scale enterprises.

5. Conclusion

The results showed that these firms, which are mostly SMEs, demonstrated some level of innovation capabilities, albeit in an uneven manner. Although some product, process and diffusion-based innovation were found, organisational innovations were at the heart of the innovation activities of the firms. In addition, it was found that these firms operate within a weak Petroleum Innovation System (PIS). It is to be concluded from these that firms operating within such contexts are not necessarily innovation-inactive. However, they might not be able to engage in implementing product and process changes that require much knowledge and financial investments. Given the generally deficient state of the innovation influencers, it is not surprising that the firms were more capable to implement changes in organisation and processes than what they would do with their products and embodied knowledge from elsewhere.

The importance of firm-level investment in organisational learning is further brought to the fore by the findings. Firms are required to consciously make investments in developing a capable stock of human capital. When this happens within a network of strong institutions and a favourable economic ambience, a firm will definitely be much more capable for innovation. This is to say that while the firms make efforts to build capabilities, the success of their efforts depend directly on the supportiveness of the environmental context within which they operate. An importantly new knowledge advanced by this study is the specific role that industry associations could play in facilitating firm-level innovation capability. It has been indicated by the results that industry associations have a central role to play in facilitating firm-level innovation especially in the developing country context. Few earlier studies have identified such associations as important in the processes that lead to the build-up of firm-level capabilities and the knowledge available on the specific roles that they are capable of playing is still very sparse. Obviously, their roles now transcend mere activism and protection of rights but also involve covering resource deficiencies for member firms, helping member firms learn and creating access to innovation-friendly support.

The need for a strong innovation system is also indicated by the findings of this study. Firms were seen not to have received much support from knowledge and centres and even from government. Specifically, diffusion-based innovation was very low. The few firms that succeeded in doing this were those that on their own had significant external resource endowments by virtue of belonging to a global group or creating international ties. Most of the firms were largely unable to muster enough resources on their own to engage in activities that would give rise to that kind of innovation. Thus, stronger government-finance-research-industry linkages that would ease resource deficiencies are critical to firm-level innovativeness.

References

Abereijo, I. O., Ilori, M. O., Taiwo, K. A. and Adegbite, S. A. (2007), 'Assessment of the capabilities for innovation by small and medium industry in Nigeria', in *African Journal of Business Management*, 1(8): 209-217.

Adjebeng-Asem, S. (1996), 'Translating Technical Innovations into Entrepreneurship in Nigeria: Social and Policy Implications', In: Ogbu, O. M., Oyelaran-Oyeyinka, B. and Mlawa, H. M. (eds.), *Technology Policy and Practice in Africa*, Ontario: International Development Research Centre. Available at: http://www.idrc.ca/en/ev-30793-201-1-DO_TOPIC.html (Accessed: March, 2011).

Audretsch, D.B., Lehmann E.E. and Warning, S. (2005), 'University Spillovers and new Firm Location', in *Research Policy*, 34(7): 1113-1122.

Autant-Bernard, C. and Massard, N. (2001), 'The Geography of Knowledge Spillovers and Technological Proximity', In: Feldman, M. and Massard, N., *Institutions and Systems in the Geography of Innovation*, The Netherlands: Kluwer Academic Publishers Group.

Bala-Subrahmanya, M. H. (2005), 'Technological innovations in Indian small enterprises: dimensions, intensity and implications', in *International Journal Technology Management*, 30(1/2): 188-204.

B.P. Statistical Energy Survey (2008), Available at: http://www.mbendi.com/indy/oilg/af/ng/p0005.htm (Accessed: 17 January 2011).

Chesbrough, H. (2003), *Open Innovation: The new Imperative for creating and profiting form Technology*, Boston, MA: Harvard Business School publishers.

Cohen, W.M. and Levinthal, D.A. (1990), 'Absorptive Capacity: A New Perspective on Learning and Innovation', in *Administrative Science Quarterly* 35: 128-152.

Drucker, P. F. (1985), *Innovation and Entrepreneurship: Practice and Principles*, New York: Harper and Row Publishers.

Egbetokun, A. A., Siyanbola, W. O. and Adeniyi, A. A. (2007), 'Assessment of Innovation Capability in the Cable and Wire Manufacturing Industry in Nigeria: a case study approach', *Paper presented at the Micro Evidence on Innovation in developing Economies[MEIDE]*, UNU-MERIT, Maastricht, the Netherlands, May 31-June 1, 2007. Available at: http://www.merit.unu.edu/MEIDE/papers/2007/EGBETOKUN_SIYANBOLA_ADENIYI_Assessment%20of%20innovation%20capability...cable%20and%20wire%20manufacturing%20industry.pdf (Accessed: 11 January 2011).

Egbetokun, A.A., Siyanbola, W.O., Sanni, M., Olamade, O.O., Adeniyi, A.A. and Irefin, I.A. (2009), 'What drives innovation? Inferences from an industrywide survey in Nigeria', in *International Journal of Technology Management*, 45(1/2): 123-140.

Fontana, R., Geuna, A. and Matt, M. (2006), 'Factors affecting university-industry R&D projects: The importance of searching, screening and signalling', in *Research Policy*, 35(2): 309-323

Ilori, M.O., Oke, J. S. and Sanni, S. A. (2000), 'Management of new product development in selected food companies in Nigeria, in *Technovation*, 20(6): 333-342.

Jaruzelski, B. and Dehoff, K. (2007), 'The Customer Connection: The Global Innovation 1000', from *Strategy+Business*, Issue 49, Winter 2007,Winter, Booz & Company. Available at: http://www.urenio.org/wp-content/uploads/2009/01/global-innovation-1000-2007.pdf

Kemp (1997), *Imitation to Innovation: The Dynamics of Korea's Technological Learning*, Boston, MA.: Harvard Business School Press.

Keller, W. (2002), 'Geographic Localization of International Technology Diffusion', in *American Economic Review* 92(1): 120-142.

Lall, S., (1991), 'Human Resources, Technology and Industrial Development in Sub-Saharan Africa', In: Chhiber, A. and Stanely, F. (eds.), *Economic Reform in Sub-Saharan Africa*, Washington D.C.: World Bank.

Meeus, Marius T.H., Oerlemans, Leon A.G. and Van, D., and Jules, J.J. (1999a), 'Regional systems of innovation from within: An empirical specification of the relation between technological dynamics and interaction between multiple actors in a Dutch region', *Working Paper 99.1, ECIS*, Eindhoven Centre for Innovation Studies, The Netherlands.

Meeus, Marius T.H., Oerlemans, Leon A.G. and Hage, Jerald (1999b), 'Sectoral Patterns of Interactive Learning: An empirical exploration using an extended resource based model', *Working Paper 99.5, ECIS,* Eindhoven Centre for Innovation Studies, The Netherlands.

Oerlemans, L.A.G., Meeus, M.T.H. and Boekema, F.W.M. (1998), 'Learning innovation and proximity', *Working Paper 98/3, ECIS,* Eindhoven Centre for Innovation Studies, Eindhoven University of Technology, The Netherlands.

Organisation for Economic Cooperation and Development (OECD) (2005), 'Proposed guidelines for collecting and interpreting technological innovation data: Oslo Manual', 3rd edition, Paris: OECD.

Oyebisi, T.O., Ilori, M.O. and. Nassar, M.L. (1996), 'Industry-academic relations: an assessment of the linkages between a university and some enterprises in Nigeria', in *Technovation,* 16(4): 203-209.

Oyelaran-Oyeyinka, B. (1997), *NNEWI: An Emergent Industrial Cluster in Nigeria,* Ibadan Technopol Publishers.

Oyelaran-Oyeyinka, B. and Lal, K. (2006), *SMEs and New Technologies, Learning, E-Business and Development*, Basingstoke, UK: Palgrave Publishers.

Oyelaran-Oyeyinka, B. (2001), 'Networks and Linkages in African Manufacturing Cluster: A Nigerian Case Study', DP 2001-5, September, UNU-INTECH, Maastricht, The Netherlands

Oyelaran-Oyeyinka, B. (2002), 'Manufacturing Response in a National System of Innovation: Evidence from the Brewing Firms in Nigeria', *DP 2002-3,* April, UNU-INTECH, Maastricht, The Netherlands.

Oyelaran-Oyeyinka, B. (2004), 'Learning and Local Knowledge Institutions in African Industry', *DP 2004-2,* UNU-INTECH, Maastricht, The Netherlands.

Oyelaran-Oyeyinka, B., Laditan, G. O. A. and Esubiyi, A. O. (1996), 'Industrial innovation in Sub-Saharan Africa: the manufacturing sector in Nigeria', in *Research Policy* 25(7): 1081-1096.

Oyelaran-Oyeyinka, B. and Barclay, L. A. (2004), 'Human Capital and Systems of Innovation', in *African Development Review,* 6(1): 115-138.

Oyelaran-Oyeyinka, B. (2003), 'Innovation and Learning by Firms in Nigeria: The Role of Size, Skills and Ownership', in *International Journal of Business and Society,* 4(1): 1-22.

Oyelaran-Oyeyinka, B. (2003), 'Knowledge Networks and Technological Capabilities in African Clusters', in *Science, Technology and Society*, 8(1): 1-24.

Oyelaran-Oyeyinka, B. (2005), 'Inter-Firm Collaboration and Competitive Pressures: SME Footwear Clusters in Nigeria', in *Int. J. Technology and Globalization*, 1 (3/4): 343-360.

Oyelaran-Oyeyinka, B. (2006), 'Systems of Innovation and Underdevelopment: An Institutional Perspective', in *Science, Technology and Society*, 11(2): 239-269.

Oyelaran-Oyeyinka, B., Adelaja M. and Abiola, B., (2007), *SMEs Clusters in Nigeria: Institutions, Policies and Support Systems*, Ibadan: Booksellers Publishers.

Oyelaran-Oyeyinka, B. (1997), 'Technological Learning in African Industry: A study of Engineering Firms in Nigeria', in *Science and Public Policy*, 24(5): 309-318.

Oyewale, A. A. (2005), 'Addressing the research-industry linkage impasse in Nigeria: The critical issues and implementation strategies', *Paper presented at The 3rd Globelics International Conference*, Tshwane University of Technology, Pretoria, South Africa, 2005. Available at: www.globelics2005africa.org.za/papers/p0032/Globelics2005_Adesina%20Ayobami%20Oyewale.pdf (Accessed December 2, 2010).

Oyewale, A.A. (2003), 'Evaluation of the Interactions Among the Key Components of Science and Technology and Innovation System in Nigeria', *PhD Thesis*, Technology Planning and Development Unit, Faculty of Technology, Obafemi Awolowo University, Ile-Ife, Nigeria.

Ozigbo N. C. (2008), 'Technological Capacity Building in the Nigeria's Oil and Gas Industry', *Proceedings of the 19th Annual Conference of the International Information Management Association*, San Diego, California.

Prusak L. (1996), 'The knowledge advantage', in *Strategy and Leadership*, 24(March-April): 6-8.

Romijn, H. and Albaladejo, M. (2002), 'Determinants of innovation capability in small electronics and software firms in southeast England', in *Research Policy*, 31: 1053–1067

Rosa, J. and Mohnen, M. (2008), 'Knowledge Transfers between Canadian Business Enterprises and Universities: Does Distance Matter?' *UNU-MERIT Working Paper* # 2008-17. Available at: http://www.merit.unu.edu/publications/wppdf/2008/wp2008-017.pdf (Accessed March 21, 2011).

Storey, J. (2000), 'The management of innovation problem', in *International Journal of Innovation Management*, 4(3): 347-369.

Souitaris, V. (2003), 'Determinants of technological innovation: Current state of the art, modern research trends and future prospects', In: Shavinina L. V. (ed.), *The International Handbook on Innovation*, Oxford: Elsevier Science.

Tidd, J., Bessant, J., and Pavitt, K. (1998), 'Managing innovation: Integrating Technological, Market and Organizational Change', 2nd edition, Chichester, UK: John Wiley and Sons.

Tidd, J., Bessant, J., and Pavitt, K. (2005), 'Managing Innovation: Integrating Technological, Market, and Organizational Change', 3rd edition, Chichester, UK: John Wiley and Sons.

Tidd, J. (2001), 'Innovation Management in context: Environment, organization and performance', in *International of Mnangement Reviews Journal*, 3(3): 169-184.

United Nations University Institute for New Technologies (UNU-INTECH) (2004), 'Designing a Policy-Relevant Innovation Survey for NEPAD', mimeo: A Study prepared by UNU-INTECH, Maastricht, The Netherlands.

African Journal of Science, Technology,
Innovation and Development
Vol. 4, No. 2, 2012
pp. 92-108

A Guide for Enhancing Quality in Engineering Drawings: Preparation and Requirements

Zeundjua Tjiparuro*

Abstract

The quality of designed products is limited by the number of mistakes and errors in drawings. But, drawings can be very complex, especially those of large machines consisting of many parts and mechanisms. To check such drawings for accuracy and clarity, and be able to deliver error free drawings can be a daunting task. Procedures in most drawings manuals such as the NASA (1994) and *ISO 128-1* and standard drawing textbooks, besides assuming that drawings are of a kind, do not give a total approach to the enhancement of quality in engineering drawings. From 1997 to 2000, this author, working as design engineer recorded comments, for purposes of personal work improvement, made by his supervisor on drawings sent to him for approval. From 2005 to 2010, the author observed and recorded checking notes and comments made by other design engineers. These notes and comments were analysed and compared to procedures prescribed in drawing manuals and textbooks. It was established that the notes, manuals and textbook procedures could be categorised into three main classes: 1) general information; 2) shape, size and material description; and 3) clarity requirements. Moreover, further review of the extant drawings literature established that the literature fails to appreciate that different checking methods apply to different drawing scenario. Consequently, two distinct

* Rural Industries Promotions Company-Botswana, The Robert Kgasa Technical Building, Private Bag 11, Kanye, Botswana.
Email: zeundjua.tjiparuro@gmail.com

drawings scenario; Drawings-for-Prototyping and Drawings-for-Documentation, are presented. Lastly, it is observed that the introduction of computer controlled production equipment brings with it changes in drawings checking procedure and style, what in this paper is referred to as: technology induced drawing style.

Keywords: Engineering Drawings, Design Engineering, Drawings-for-Prototyping, Drawings-for-Documentation, Drawing Errors.

JEL Classification: O10; O20; O30; O55.

1. Introduction

Design ideas are often communicated from the design engineer to the machine shop technician, responsible for building the ideas, in a largely multi-view, orthographical and script format called working drawings or engineering drawings. And since drawings are not mere statements or illustrations, invariably, the designer prescribes everything, thus giving an order to the shop to execute the work as specified (Brown, 2000). To that end, engineering drawings must communicate unambiguously, the shape, material, finish, quantities, etc, of the individual components within the designed system, to the person making the product. A number of functions such as the costing of the technology, production plans and line inspections are heavily dependent and based on accurate and sufficient details supplied by the drawings. The consequences of errors and ambiguity in drawings are many. Functionality of the manufactured product could be curtailed. Premature product failure, budget over-runs, and missed schedules could occur. For vocations where margins of error should be kept to the lowest minimum, the consequences can be too ghastly to contemplate. It thus becomes absolutely important that information communicated by drawings is accurate and unambiguous to prevent the making of bad parts by the machine shop. This notwithstanding, errors and mistakes do occur. In fact, errors are impossible to eliminate (Magi, 2006; Hanifan, 2010).

It must be appreciated though, that engineering drawings require technical skills to decipher and understand. Accordingly, their review or checking for accuracy and quality should follow established protocols which every technical person responsible for drawings should understand. However, in most presentations, these protocols are rather not well organised for better intelligibility and systematic application. Hence, this paper sets forth to organize the necessary drawing requirements and in the process propose the minimum requirements required for the preparation of correct and sufficiently detailed engineering drawings for mechanical systems.

The rest of the paper is organized as follows. Literature will be reviewed followed by a presentation of the proposed methodologies for enhancing quality in engineering drawings. Discussions and conclusions are then made.

2. Literature Review

Time was when design was in a state of transition, from old to new. Part of this transition saw the emergence of engineering drawings as a significant shift from, what Wolfgang Konig was later to call, *'Designing-in-the-Material'* to what Christopher Jones had earlier referred to as *'Design-by-Drawing'* (Konig, 2007; Jones, 1970). This transition brought about a demarcation between a designer and a manufacturer, and with it the attendant problems of insufficient details or errors in drawings for them to be of use to the machine shop. In response, remedies were promulgated. Of particular importance to this study was the emergence of Taylorism, an efficiency movement of the late nineteenth century whose effect in engineering design, especially in Germany, led to the establishment of production planning departments, with the key responsibility of examination of the appropriateness of drawings for manufacturing (Konig, 2007). However isolated it may seem, for reasons to be returned to shortly in this paper, it nevertheless marked a significant step towards the recognition of the centrality and importance of enhancing quality in engineering drawings.

In spite of this immense importance recognised above, about a century ago, checking of engineering drawings is a completely neglected activity, perhaps one taken for granted compared to the mathematical fields of design such as finite element analysis. In 1977, Eugene Ferguson (1977: 834), bemoaning the attention that non-verbal thinking was getting in the engineering curriculum wrote:

> ...science, when applied to engineering, is analytical, and in engineering curricula analytical courses have proliferated at the expense of courses attempting to teach design. Nonverbal thinking ... involves perceptions ... [and] because perceptive processes are not assumed to entail hard thinking ... [are]... considered inferior to verbal or mathematical thought.

Ferguson concluded that:

> ...courses in design, which in a strongly analytical engineering curriculum provide one of the few remaining links to the complexities of the real world, may be the next to go, so low is their status among engineering courses. [However], when they [go], we can expect to witness an increasing number of silly but costly errors [to] occur in advanced engineering systems...

By non-verbal thinking, as also noted by (Belofsky, 1991), Ferguson referred to engineering drawings. Thus in this conclusion, Ferguson must have had in mind the checking of drawings. In fact, drawing standards, as we know them today, viewed against the history of engineering drawings, are a recent development (Weisberg, 2008).

Similar negligence has also been recognised in land planning, another form of design representation. For example, Brent Ryan (2011: 309) argued that:

> While plans are arguably planners' most important product, important corollaries of this creative process, plan interpretation and interpretation of planning ideas contained in plans, are less often examined. Planners may read plans frequently, but the understanding or interpretation of plan content seems to be treated by the profession as something that is either too obvious or too unimportant to require explicit discussion.

Scholarly literature on guidelines for enhancing quality drawings is almost non-existent. In fact if it were not for the work of Kenji, Akio and Minoru (1997), the subject would have no single scholarly publication to its name. The three Japanese co-authors did a study in which they sought to automate the process of checking students' drawing assignments. The motivation for their work was on the realisation that detailed checking of students' drawing assignments, manually, was a tedious task due to their numbers. Their method therefore involved displaying in white lines, on a monitor, the correct model drawings (their answer model) to overlap the students' drawings displayed in red-lines. Differences between the displays were able to be easily and quickly checked to determine the correctness or otherwise of the students' work. It may be said that the same tediousness that Kenji, Akio and Minoru experienced for students work is certainly bigger in the industry as most industrial designs run into at least hundreds of parts that need checking. Thus if there is any area that is in need of review for better methods of delivering accurate and sufficiently detailed drawings, that area is the industry.

Magi (2006), on the other hand reviewed the causes of errors in engineering systems and categorised these into errors due to lack of knowledge and errors due to carelessness. Magi further differentiated between essential and unessential mistakes. Magi then ask the question: *'Is it an essential error to ignore requirements of a standard…for example ISO 5457?'* Of relevance to the checking of engineering drawings, and cited by Magi, is whether ignoring the standard on the specification of title block sizes and dimensions is an essential error. On this, Magi concludes by opining that what is essential in the title block is only the scale and format, while some of the requirements are taken care of by modern computer aided design (CAD) systems (Magi, 2006: 387-388). Lastly, reference should be made to the extant literature on the checking of mechanisms and systems for *assimilability* and *dis-assimilability*. This is one area which is highly developed and of late has been done with the help of computer software such as virtual reality, CAD or the computer aided three-dimensional interactive application known as CATIA. Among such works are: Gomes and Zachmann (1999); Chen and Cai (2003); Clark and Paasch (1996); Tjiparuro and Thompson (2006a, 2006b) to mention a few. The above works are classical cases of the ubiquitous use of drawings and models as *'[media] for experiment and change'* (Baynes, 2005: 10).

Be that as it may, the ability of CAD to spot errors in drawings is yet to be fully acknowledged in literature. In fact, according to some publications, CAD has failed to impress as *'errors [appearing] on drawings today are the same as they always have been, except now CAD and modeling have added new dimensions of problems. A little like constipation and diarrhea. The old days were like constipation, really hard and slow, but CAD is like diarrhea, fast and everywhere'* (Hanifan 2010: 5). The secret weapon that such publications fail to notice is Excitech CAD Checker, a software application that allows users to check CAD drawings against pre-set standards print out an error report and assist in correcting them (Lion, 2004). This is not only unknown, but against the grain, as the data on the computer is known to go nowhere compared to the paper drawing that receives everyone's attention (Hanifan, 2010). Notwithstanding this paucity in literature, various drawing handbooks, textbooks and drawing manuals have successfully filled in the gap by compiling chains of features that should characterise acceptable drawings in formats almost akin to shopping lists. Not only does this reflect poorly on the profession of engineering drawing, but they tend to give an impression that drawings are always similar and are checked exactly the same way. Far from it, drawings are different and their checking depends on the stage of the product being depicted in the development process. To that end, this paper undertakes, firstly, to succinctly classify drawings checking methods. It then establishes the appropriate checking procedures at different stages of the design process. Using literature, notes and empirical observations, the study further established if the introduction of new production methods led to changes in drawings checking procedure. Accordingly, these questions guided the study:

Question 1: Into what categories can the drawings practices reported in the extant research be classified?

Question 2: What practices are appropriate for what stage of drawings?

Question 3: What practices became obsolete due to the introduction of new production methods?

3. Methodology

Part of this work is based largely on the extant literature and its review. To that end, integrative literature review approach is used. The approach is used as a comprehensive method of interrogating extant literature in order to provide new insights. According to the oft-quoted Torraco (2005: 356), integrative literature review '*...is a distinctive form of research that generates new knowledge about the topic being reviewed. ... [It] reviews, critiques, and synthesizes representative literature on a topic in an integrated way such that new frameworks and perspectives on the topic are generated.*' Accordingly, the lists of parameters given in various manuals and drawing textbooks were gathered, categorized and used to formulate a comprehensive understanding of the underlying principles.

Moreover, this study used observations, notes and comments recorded during the drawings checking practices of a machines design company in Botswana. These empirical observations were used not only to compare the theory against literature but to also enrich our understanding of these multivariate drawing checking practices. The company is a leading research and development centre in the country and a leader in sorghum milling technology in the Southern African region.

The above reviews were analysed according to the main steps explained below and illustrated in Figure 1 (A) as per Tjiparuro and Thompson (2004). Figure 1 (B) is a further illustration.

Step 1: Exploration of literature. Lists of drawing best practices from empirical records as well as in the extant literature were compiled.

Step 2: Union and Intersection. The union and intersection of the lists were undertaken, to group the practises. Some practices grouped easily (in the intersection). Others not so easily and had to be suspended. The suspended parameters were reviewed further as follows. In the case of synonymous terms, the practice most frequently encountered in drawings checking discourse was adopted in the final classification. This was meant to weed out colloquialism and preserve the technical content of the subject. However, if terms were equally used in literature, they were all adopted. In the third approach, where antonymous terms were encountered, terms that convey positive attributes were adopted unless both terms occurred equally in the literature

Step 3: Reconciliation. In this step, two approaches were used: (1) If the suspended parameters were mutually exclusive (i.e. their concepts were different from the others) then there were added to the core set as new practices. (2) However, if the practices overlapped with others, their proper locations were determined.

Figure 1: Exploration and Reconciliation of Literature

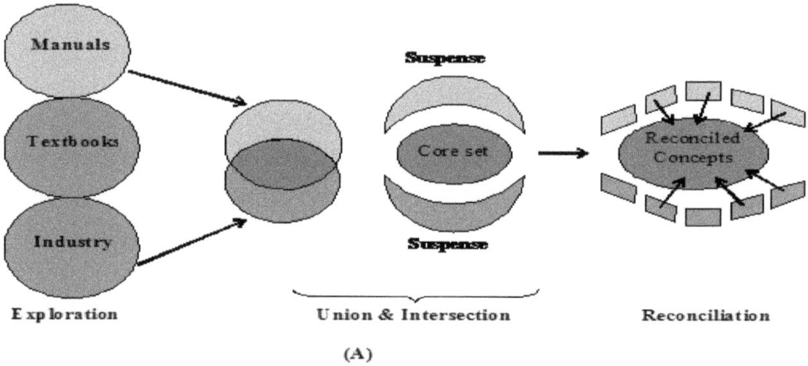

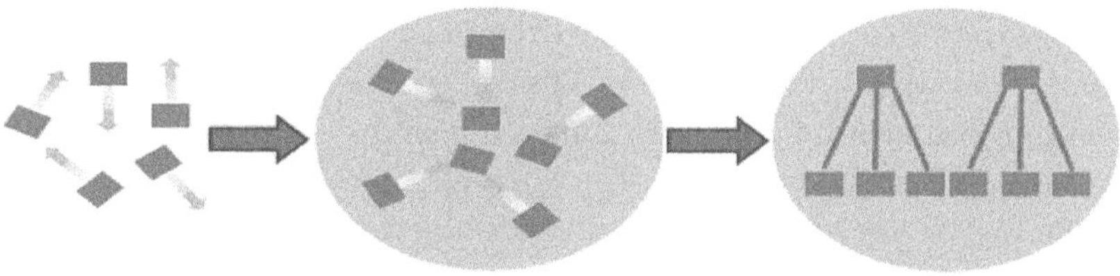

(B) Adapted from: Robbins and Coulter, 2007

4. Findings

The following texts, books and manuals were consulted: Magi (2006); Jolhe (2008); Simmons *et al.* (2009); NASA (1994); and ISO 128). Drawing checking practices given in these sources were organised as per the methodology explained above. Empirical notes from the design office (whose sample is given in Figure 2) were also organised. And as can be noted from the sample, some notes are in prose while others can best be described as explanation-seeking markings on the drawings. Figure 3 gives the summarised categories into which drawings checking schemes can be classified. According to the classification, three main functions are served by drawings checking methods, namely, 1) general standard information; 2) size, shape and material description, and 3) clarity. The lists under each category may not necessarily be exhaustive, and was meant to be, but sufficient to illustrate the point. However, the meanings of these categories are presented in the next subsections.

General Standard Information

Under this category falls all the information normally provided on the drawing sheet without applying to a specific part, sometimes called title block information, though in this paper, this description is not favoured as the title block is but a component of the general information. General standard information also contains general notes that apply to the entire drawing, some of which may contain such exempting statements as: *unless otherwise stated*. A good part of this information as can be seen in Figure 2 has nothing much to do with the actual description of the product being fabricated. As noted by Magi (2006) some of this information does not constitute an essential error if ignored except the drawing main scale and the projection used and such information can easily be taken care of by modern CAD systems. Perhaps, this is one area where Kenji, Akio and Minoru's (1997) overlapping style can be used. A template may be printed on a transparency and whenever a draughtsman submits drawings, the checker can overlap it over what has to be checked and quickly pick up inconsistencies.

Shape, Size and Material Description

This is the vital information needed for the fabrication of the components. It defines the components as they should be made and checking becomes absolutely necessary. The checker should commit enough time to go through the drawings in detail.

Clarity

Subsumed under this heading are all the techniques necessary to present information in a clear and unambiguous manner. The purpose is to ensure that interpretation of the drawings would be done in the same way. It confers to drawings their universality dimension. There certainly isn't a better way to illustrate this than by citing James Brown's Design Plans, Working Drawings and National Style. Brown relates that, at the height of Nazism aggression in 1940, Britain desperately needed replacement of their carriers which were sinking at the hands of Germany U-Boats, and thus engaged American ship builders, only for work to halt because the English supplied drawings did not make sense to the makers and had to be redrafted to American national style (Brown, 2000).

Figure 2: Collated Checking Notes

1. Tolerance specs of part X not matching part Y
2. Dimensions insufficient to mark from a blank,
3. Don't use angles, dimension from a datum surface
4. Give your dimension from centre to centre, is called design intent
5. Show development
6. Incomplete material specs-which nylon? Use catalogue or check Central Stores for suppliers specs.
7. Shaft diameter larger than the hub (Part 25)
8. Don't dimension from hidden detail/show section view
9. Dimension lines crossing
10. Dimension extension lines too heavy/please reset line types
11. Swap views-third angle projection
12. Over-dimensioned
13. Don't hatch bolts
14. Hatching not properly varied
15. Part 24 not identified in the assembly
16. Member 1, Member 2, etc., part names not descriptive, try: Upper Long Vertical Member, Lower Long Vertical Member
17. Parts too crowded, use more drawing sheets
18. Get appropriate technology number from drawing clerk
19. Is this triangulation correct? Try it on a paper model
20. Part will be difficult to dismantle once assembled

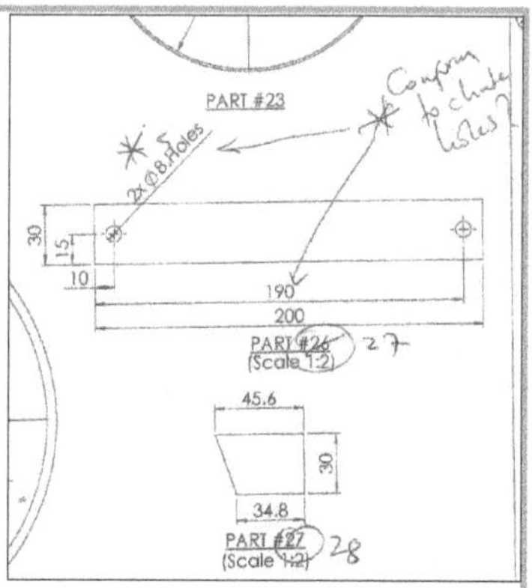

Sample from the Fodder Processor (Checker Unknown)

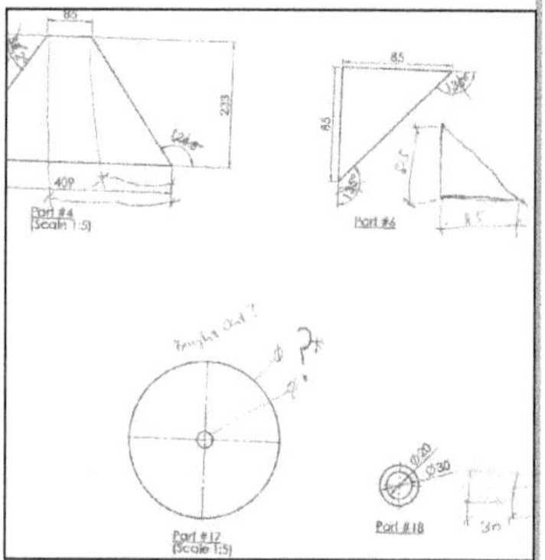
Sample from the Modular Tractor Drawn Planter (Checker Unknown)

Figure 3: Drawing Checking Methods Classification

GENERAL STANDARD INFORMATION	SHAPE, SIZE AND MATERIAL DESCRIPTION	CLARITY
1. Drawing Sheet: Size, Layout, Margins, & Border Lines 2. Title Block Position (bottom right hand corner) 3. Title of Drawing 4. Company Name (or Client of the Drawing) 5. Boxes for Designer and Draughtsman to sign. 6. Projection Used (1st or 3rd Angle). 7. Drawing Main Scale 8. Revision Table (detailing history of the revisions to date). 9. General linear dimensions and tolerances, such statements as: *All Dimensions in "mm" unless otherwise state*	1. Material specifications 2. General Dimensions and Tolerances (GD&T): i. Dimensions of Parts and applicable Tolerances ii. Dimensions to enable the cutting of the part from a blank	1. Identification Number of each individual part 2. Part Name 3. Quantity Required to complete assembly 4. When the parts list is very large a separate drawing sheet may be used for the parts list alone 5. Methods to reveal hidden details and their Rules (Section views, cutaways, exploded views, etc.) 6. Dimensioning Rules (e.g. dimensions not too far removed from part, dimensions outside the drawing, avoid dimensioning from hidden edges, etc.)

5. Checking Drawings

From the foregoing it is obvious that drawing errors could arise from multifarious sources; such as shape, size, and material description, to functionality problems. To that end, handling of such errors should certainly require a systematic approach. Organisation of drawing information should be a good starting point in bringing about a systematic approach to enhance quality in engineering drawings. As noted so far in this paper, enhancing quality in engineering drawings is about three main considerations:

1. Is the general information given accurate, sufficient and clear to be understood?
2. Are the size and shape dimensions given, accurate, sufficient and clear to produce the system/product?
3. Are the two aspects above given in an intelligible and unambiguous way to enable interpretation by a competent person?

How a competent person goes about establishing these main considerations may not necessarily be a matter for prescriptive templates as most engineering manuals and textbooks tend to do. Rather, the main consideration should be that the underlying principles to look for are understood and known. Once these underlying principles are understood, the competent professional should be able to consult relevant sources for best practices. However, as noted so far in this paper, extant literature has not noted or addressed the differences that exist in the checking of drawings at different stages of the product development process.

For new to the market products, there are generally two fundamental levels at which the checking of drawings occur. Firstly drawings are checked before the production of a prototype (*drawings-for-prototyping*). This is the most difficult stage where most mistakes are made, as there is normally no sample against which to compare the drawings. The second stage is when drawings are checked against a sample or prototype for final documentation of the product (*drawings-for-documentation*). On comparative basis, this is the easiest checking stage. It happens either after a successful performance of the product or purely for purposes of archiving what has so far been achieved in the development process of the product. Therefore on the basis of the above, drawing checking process should, of necessity, be divided into two stages, namely, Drawings-for-Prototyping and Drawings-for-Documentation. The procedure for ensuring quality in both categories is not exactly the same though the underlying requirements (e.g. accuracy, sufficiency and clarity) may be similar. This is discussed further below.

Drawings-for-Prototyping

Drawings-for-prototyping are produced in order to initialise first production of an untested product. These drawings are a crystallisation of the embedded images in the minds of the design team, a significant step towards the physical embodiment of the final product. In much the same way that Joseph Whitworth's *'truly professional drawing office'* in the 1840s was meant to *'keep pace with the innovative ideas flowing from his mind'* (Brown, 2000: 203). In this particular case, compared to any other situation, engineering drawings serve as a *language* which *engineers* use to communicate their design ideas. These first drawings should communicate in unambiguous and precise way information about the shape and size of the product to be made. Issues of shape identification and interpretation become very crucial.

In most cases, this task is performed by the design team, invariably, consisting of a design engineer and a technician. The design engineer working with the technician sanctions the production of drawings in CAD paying attention to the agreed conceptual layout. In this situation, the technician performs the role of a CAD operator or draughtsman. The engineer should then check the drawings against the agreed product layout. As the engineer checks the drawings, the following questions become imperative and form part of the fundamental checklist or pass criteria for the documentation.

1. Is the general drawing information correct and accurate?
2. Is the presentation, orientation and views correct?
3. Would the details given facilitate marking off of the part from a blank?
4. Are the features specified constructible or *manufacturable,* in respect of the capability of the machine shop?

Drawings-for-Documentation

Sample drawings or drawings for documentation, in this paper refer, to drawings of a product that has been manufactured before and therefore benefits most significantly from the field data gathered. Instances where components could not fit for various reasons would have been captured and provided as feedback in the modifications of the drawings. To that effect, in addition to the process specified above for prototype drawings which would have been cleared by this stage, the system of checking sample drawing should ask the following fundamental questions:

1. Do the drawings match the sample? This is because checking drawings at this stage is more than desktop. Not only should sufficient time be allowed to ensure that adequate dimensional descriptions have been provided to enable marking off of the parts; but the machine also has to be dismantled to access all parts including deeply located components. Each bit and piece is then checked against the drawings to ensure that all parameters that define the component have been captured. It must however, be noted that the dismantling may not be necessarily destructive, involving cutting up of permanent joints, but should be so thorough as to enable the documentation of components as designed. Physical measurements of parts as a form of checking drawings is not fully appreciated, let alone mentioned, in the existing drawing manuals and textbooks.
2. Can these drawings *reproduce* another sample or a clone of the existing sample to the same quality level or better? In drawing documentation, this is another very important step that doesn't seem to have received any attention at all. In this particular instance, drawings are released to the machine shop for fabrication of a new sample. It is not uncommon to unearth a lot of drawings errors and mistakes in the process. It is the drawings corrected after this process that now become the official drawings for future production of the product's replicas. In this way, drawing errors and mistakes would have been reduced significantly, though may not have been eliminated completely.

Technology Induced Drawing Style

In the company under review, some checking practices which used to be regular before acquisition of computer controlled production machinery disappeared once the company acquired those machines. Notable among this was the practice of *'marking from a blank'* (item 2 in Figure 2). Machine shop engineers went mute on this requirement as manual *'marking off'* of components was automated and taken over by computer controlled plasma cutters. More surprisingly, even when the requirement was made by the design engineers, draughtsmen protested and found it to be unnecessary. This shift is illustrated in Figure 4 and Figure 5 in which two drawings of almost identical components are shown. Figure 4 is from a double row tractor planter whose drawings were handled by the author in 2000. The style and manner of dimensioning of the component was such that the piece could be accurately marked off from a blank sheet. However, this style was found not to be necessary for Figure 5, from a Morama bean cracker, whose design was also handled by the author in 2012. In this particular style, dimensions provided are such as to enable checking of the processed piece for conformity to specifications. This is indeed a classic case of technology introducing a different drawing culture and style.

It was also observed that production aiding tools, such as templates, jigs, and fixtures, though absolutely necessary to enhance production efficiency, have tended to diminish the essence of checking drawings. Technologies that the company has been producing for a long time using such production tools produced errors once drawings were used. Of course this are mostly the old drawings produced manually on the drawing table and did not benefit from the 'drawing-for-documentation' checking process already discussed in this paper.

Figure 4: Chute (double row tractor planter)

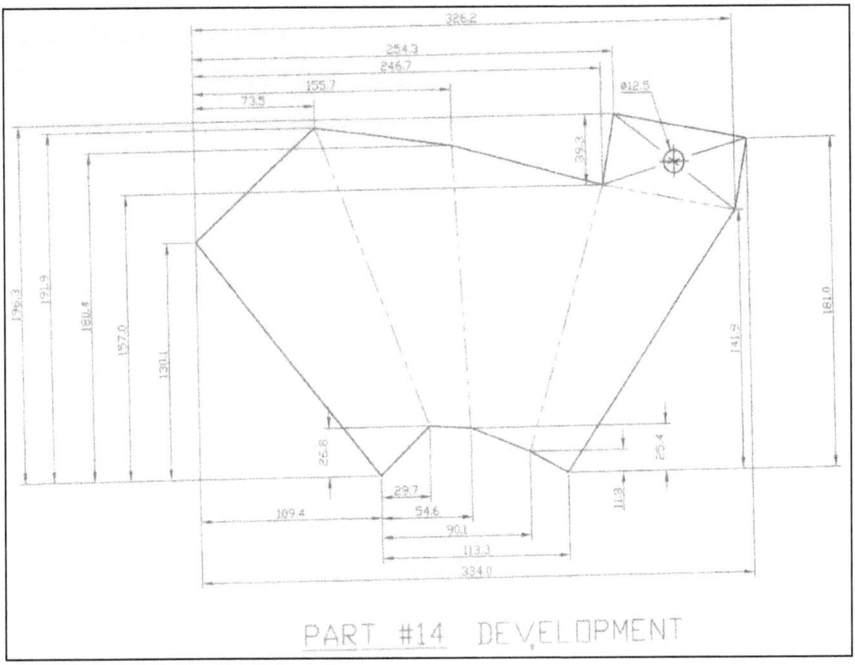

Figure 5: Chute (Morama bean cracker)

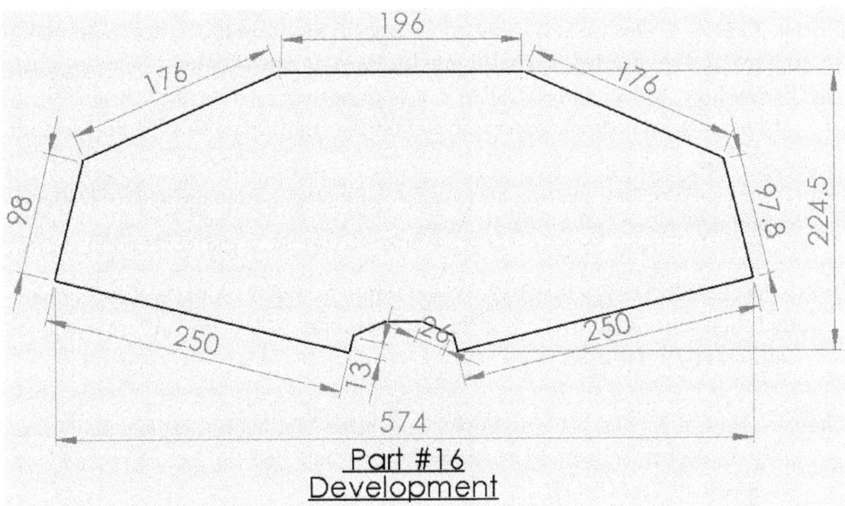

6. Conclusions

In this paper, drawings checking parameters have been collated and categorised. Three classes, namely, general standard information, shape, size and material description as well as clarity have been given. These categories define the underlying concepts necessary for enhancing quality in engineering drawings. The paper has also brought to the fore the difference between two main stages of product development; prototyping and sample documentation, that call for different approaches in the checking of their drawings. Most importantly, two main approaches, sample cannibalisation and production, have been identified as fundamental approaches towards the reduction of drawing errors and mistakes. In addition, an experience has been shared whereby acquisition of new production technology brought with it a new drawing culture and style.

Finally, this paper must be understood as part of the grand scheme of emphasising the importance of manual drawing for the enhancement of drawing skills as amongst others proposed by (McLaren, 2008). In his seminal paper, McLaren decried the poor standards of CAD drawings produced by engineering and design students as result of lack of understanding of basic geometric construction and the conventions of drafting skills due to over-exposure to CAD.

References

Baynes, K. (2005), 'Design and Democracy: Speculations on the radical potential of design, design practice and design education, Warwickshire, UK: Design and Technology Association (DATA) & Loughborough University. Available at: http://www.data.org.uk/generaldocs/dater/Design%20and%20Democracy.pdf.

Belofsky, H. (1991), 'Engineering Drawing-A Universal Language in Two Dialects', in *Technology and Culture*, 32(1): 23-46.

Brown, J.K. (2000), 'Design Plans, Working Drawings and National Styles: Engineering Practice in Great Britain and the United States, 1775-1945', in *Technology and Culture*, 41(2): 195-238.

Chen, L. and Cai, J. (2003), 'Using Vector Projection Method to evaluate maintainability of mechanical system in design review', in *Reliability Engineering and System Safety*, 81(2): 147-154.

Clark, G.E. and Paasch R.K. (1996), 'Diagnostic modelling and diagnosability evaluation of mechanical systems', *Journal of Mechanical Design*, 118(3): 425-431.

Ferguson, E.S. (1977), 'The Mind's Eye: Nonverbal Thought in Technology', in *Science,* 197(4306): 827-836.

Gomes De Sá A. and Zachmann, G. (1999), 'Virtual reality as a tool for verification of assembly and maintenance processes', in *Computers & Graphics,* 23(3): 389-403.

Hanifan, R. (2010), *Reduce Your Engineering Drawings Errors: Preventing the Most Common Mistakes,* Momentum Press.

ISO 128-1 (2003), *Technical drawing-General principles of presentation.*

Jolhe, D. A. (2008), *Engineering Drawing,* Noida, India: Tata McGraw-Hill.

Jones C.J. (1970), *Design Methods,* New York and Chichester: John Wiley.

Kenji, I., Takimoto, A. and Morita, M. (1997), 'A Study on the Checking Method of Machine Drawings by a Personal Computer', in *Memoirs of the Faculty of Engineering, Yamaguchi University,* 47(2): 349-357.

Konig, W. (2007), *Design and Engineering,* In: Jones, G. and Zeitlin, J (eds.), *The Oxford Handbook of Business History,* Oxford: Oxford University Press.

Lion, R. (2004), 'CAD Checker: Simplifying the burden of CAD', in *Excitech Computers Limited: Design Productivity Journal,* 3(3): 53-58

Magi, R. (2006), 'Engineering education and errors', In: Elleithy, K. and Others (eds.), *Advances in computer, information, systems sciences, and engineering,* Proceedings of IETA 2005, TeNe 2005 and EIAE 2005, Springer: 387-391.

McLaren, S.V. (2008), 'Exploring perceptions and attitudes towards teaching and learning manual technical drawing in a digital age', in *International Journal of Technology and Design Education,* 18(2): 167-188.

NASA (1994), *Engineering drawing standards manual by Greenbelt, Maryland.* Available at: http://mscweb.gsfc.nasa.gov/543web/files/GSFC-X-673-64-1F.pdf (Accessed: November 2011).

Robbins, S. and Coulter, M. (2007), *Management,* 9th Edition, London: Prentice Hall.

Ryan, B. D. (2011), 'Reading Through a Plan', in *Journal of the American Planning Association,* 77(4): 309-327

Simmons, C. H., Maguire, D. E., and Phelps, N. (2009), *Manual of Engineering Drawing: Technical Product Specification and documentation to British and International Standards*, Butterworth-Heinemann.

Tjiparuro, Z. and Thompson, G. (2004), Review of maintainability design principles and their application to conceptual design', Proceedings of the Institution of Mechanical Engineers - Part E, *Journal of Process Mechanical Engineering*, 218(2): 103-113.

Tjiparuro, Z. and Thompson, G. (2005), *Maintainability and Reliability Analysis in CAD and Virtual Environment*, unpublished Ph.D. Thesis, The University of Manchester, UK.

Tjiparuro, Z. and Thompson, G. (2006a), 'Reliability Analysis Methods for Mechanical Assemblies during Conceptual Design using CAD', in *Maintenance & Asset Management*, 218(1): 12-18.

Tjiparuro, Z. and Thompson, G. (2006b), 'Maintenance Training using CAD and a Virtual Reality Environment', in *Maintenance & Asset Management*, 218(4): 20-26.

Torraco, R. J. (2005), 'Writing integrative literature reviews: Guidelines and examples', in *Human Resource Development Review*, 4: 356-367.

Weisberg, D.E. (2008), 'A Brief Overview of the History of CAD', Available: http://cadhistory.net/contents.html (accessed Nov., 2011).

African Journal of Science, Technology, Innovation and Development
Vol. 4, No. 2, 2012
pp. 109-129

Financial Lending and Investment in Sustainable Small-Scale Agribusiness in Sub-Saharan Africa: A Review of Carbon Sequestration and Welfare Benefits

Benjamin Olatunbosun*

Abstract

Expansion of operations by rural financial and non-financial institutions in developing countries has prompted the enactment of regulations and emphasis on risk management by national supervisors. However, lending to smallholders especially sustainable framers and financial investment in small-scale climate mitigation and adaptation agriculture has not seen substantially increased. The impact of financial institutions on anti-climate-change agricultural practices and sustainable development has been advocated by a number of researchers. This study examines ways of using the opportunities provided by climate-change to reverse existing disconnect between smallholders and small-scale agribusinesses and financial institutions. Using available literature on sub-Saharan banking, climate change investment and economic development, this paper explores support mechanism for investing in climate-friendly agriculture and the possible integration of mitigation payment into Credit risk management. The collaboration between financial institutions and smallholders is an appropriate foundation for relationship building which will ease credit constraints, improve information asymmetry and increase agricultural investment.

* Bergische University of Wuppertal (BUW), Technical University of Munich (TUM), Germany. Email: emmanuel.benjamin@tum.de

Keywords: Sustainable agriculture, Small-Scale Agribusiness, Microfinance, Agribusiness investment, Sub-Saharan Africa, Certified Emission Reduction (CER)

JEL Classification: O13; O16; O19.

1. Introduction

Agricultural growth plays a critical role in eradicating poverty especially in low-income countries. In developing countries, especially sub-Saharan Africa, apart from generating a substantial level of revenue, the sector contributes ca. 32 per cent to Gross Domestic Product (GDP) (Christiaensen and Demery, 2007). About 75 per cent of the work-force in low income countries in sub-Saharan Africa is engaged in agriculture with largely small-scale farming of between 0.5 and 2 hectares of land (The World Bank, 2007). In promoting agricultural growth, it is essential to increase factors of production and productivity (labor – L, capital – K and total factor productivity – A) in a sustainable manner as this ensures food and energy security. The ability to alleviate poverty depends to a large extent on the availability of finance as both urban and rural business activities must have access to regular and adequate capital as well as resource management knowledge to function (Balkenhol, 1991). Finance and Capital to rural small-scale agribusiness requires well-defined and stable financial institutions as the investment and individual wealth or asset of rural smallholders are quite digress and the absence of these institutions may lead to a plunge in capital stock during economic downturn (Gonzalez-Vega and Graham, 1995).

The composition of rural financial institutions has evolved from Micro Finance Institutions (MFIs), money lenders and Non-Governmental Organizations (NGOs) to include commercial banks due to the gap in the access to wide range of credit (Randhawa and Gallardo, 2003; Cull *et al.*, 2008). The prime objective of micro finance remains the ability to providing financial services to low-income households, micro, small and medium size firms at affordable rate to support economic growth while utilizing appropriate methodology that guarantees financial soundness and enhance consumer livelihood. Sub-Saharan pre-regulatory eras of micro finance in the 1980s were characterized by structural disorganization, high default rate and lack of financial discipline. In order to foster a stable financial environment international and national prudential organs have stipulated guidelines or regulations which financial institutions specifically deposit-taking organizations have to abide by (Amha, 2001). As financial and non-financial institutions in the sub-Saharan Africa regions are increasing regional operations, it is important that these institutions also adhere to international standards such as the Basel accord. Stakeholders and depositors protection as well as monitoring and measuring of risk is a vital component these guidelines (Lafourcade *et al.*, 2005). loans to off-farm enterprise has shown remarkable success due to reduced vulnerability, stable income and group guarantee, however, micro financing of agriculture is not as profitable as conventional lending with collateral or collateral substitute (Cull *et al.*, 2008).

An array of literatures identifies credit constraints as one of the major problems confronting development of agriculture not only in developing countries but on a global scale. Factors ranging from information asymmetry, moral hazard, contract enforcement, high rate of interest and farm debt, under-developed financial institution to high transaction cost may be responsible for limited credit allocation. In the 1970s, 15 per cent of farmers had access to institutional credit in Latin America and 5 per cent Africa (Gonzalez-Vega, 1993; Gonzalez-Vega and Graham, 1995). The issue of land tenure system has compounded to the woes of agricultural financing because lack of proper definition of right to land deprives usage as collateral while the absence of stable income arising from risk associate with agriculture (weather, price volatility, poor infrastructure) means no physical collateral. The direct effect of climate change on the banking operations can be due to severe weather threat or indirectly due to regulatory compliance or change in societal preference. Financial institutions in rural areas can, however, seize business opportunities to provide services and develop financial techniques that foster climate mitigation and adaptation through emission trading and advisory services (Furrer *et al.*, 2009).

Africa will be one of the most vulnerable regions to the effect of climate change, due to projected decrease in precipitation and increase in temperature and population as well as decline in GDP (Schneider *et al.*, 2007). Therefore there is a need to shift attention to what can be done not only to adapt but also to mitigate its negative in order to ensure food security for the growing population. Investment in adaptation and mitigation of harmful climate change (including agriculture – carbon sink) requires an estimated investment of over US$1 trillion per annum with 86 per cent anticipated to come from the private sector, such as financial institutions, directed to developing countries. Although the private sector seems discouraged by carbon market situation, there are certain investments that are starting to emerge (Jones and Hiller, 2010). Climate smart agriculture can be propelled by smallholders and may provide sustainable investment potential of ca. US$1 trillion over the next 4 decades which has been projected for sub-Saharan Africa (Branca, 2011). There are signs of strong interest in investing in sustainability amongst financial investors on a global scale. A study by the Rockefeller foundation found that 69 per cent of financial advisory perceived sustainable investment as an avenue for growth. However, only

38 per cent actively participated in international micro-finance engaged in sustainable development while over 80 per cent were not engaged and 43 per cent were either doubtful or uninterested (Conway and Stevens, 2012).

This paper seeks to establish how financial institutions engaged in microfinance can benefit directly from agricultural sustainability through climate investment or indirectly through a targeted lending with climate-backed- security, which may lead to rural development and solid financial environment. There are indications that there is need to emerge with new innovative approaches to be countered the old problems relating to credit constraint experienced by the poor at the hands of financial institutions. Specifically, this study aims to establish a benchmark that can be used for further research into climate financing.

This paper proceeds by investigating the financial sector servicing the rural low-income farmers and changes in operations and compliance in order to facilitate a stable financial environment. The following section reviews the lending behaviour of financial and non-financial organisations towards smallholders and their participation in investments relating to environmental protection and development. The fourth section outlines possible benefits of sustainability to credit institutions and how this can be an integral part of their operation in line with international standards. The formulation of policies which may help prompt sustainable lending and investment are the focus of the fifth section. The paper then draws a conclusion from the relevant research materials and information gathered on the topic.

2. Trends in Sub-Saharan Rural Credit Institutions

Some authors have questioned if the existence of banks in the conventional definition, in this modern times, are relevant as banks continue to engage in off-balance sheet rather than deposit taking and loan disbursement, become less dependent on core business and are exploring core competences. It is also argued on the one hand that the involvement of other non-banking organization in banking activities is undermining the *traditional banks* which are causing banks to *shrink* (Llewellyn, 1999). On the other hand financial service provided to rural smallholders in sub-Saharan African by institutions is not wide-spread as the market it is both limited and under-served thus the financial sector has continued to see growth in size and operations. A substantial number of microfinance institutions in Africa have been able to post impressive growth without compromising portfolio quality, even as competition intensifies (Fernando, 2008). There are several changes that have taken place in the financing of rural poor. However, this paper would rather focus on 4 of these namely:

- Institutional expansion and profitability
- Deposit
- Regulation (Risk Management)
- Technology

Institutional Expansion and Profitability

The low entry requirement for the establishment of financial institution in Sub-Saharan Africa in the 1970s and 1980s propelled the growth of local banks and non-bank financial institutions (NBFI). This period also witnessed the setting-up of government backed developmental banks, intended for the urban and rural entrepreneurs, which proved to be inefficient, despite the decline in the number of financial institutions in the 1990s due to bank failures, commercial and other financial institutions has witnessed a revival and a more stable financial environment (Brownbridge, 1998; Steel and Andah, 2003). There has been an increase in the number of sub-Saharan financial institutions in Africa operating beyond national borders in accordance to international standards (Verhoef, 2005). However, the profit efficiency of banks in Africa is argued to be in smaller size banks than in big financial institution therefore casting doubt over the development of the continent´s financial sector through the establishment of mega banks (Kiyota, 2009). This may be in line with studies which show that more unconventional financial institutions, especially non-governmental organizations (NGOs), are shifting away from non-profit towards for-profit while increasing in the number of financial institutions represented by small entity in remote areas (Campion and White, 2001; Mix 2010). The fear that a for-profit approach by micro finance will result in high market profit as well as the neglect of the poor has not materialized, instead there may be an increase in diversification in the operations by microfinance institutions in different directs (Charitonenko and Campion, 2003). This may not have a negative effect as it enables these institutions to explore new innovative ideas in financing the efficient amongst the poor. The influx of a number of commercial bank into microfinance may, to a large extent, reshape the financial landscape. The economy of scale and scope from non-microfinance activities of these institutions may be used to further develop the microfinance sector.

Deposit

Asia microfinance is a prime example of how saving (deposit) can help strengthen the productivity and increased investment, the microfinance in sub-Saharan Africa has also helped increase the number of bank account and saving holders in addition to those provided by other institutions

(WSBI, 2008). On the contrary, commercial banking in Africa has rather witnessed a steady movement of asset by the wealthy to off-shore location rather than deposit to local financial institutions, which may explain the low rate of saving (The World Bank, 2006). Microfinance comprising non-bank financial institution, credit unions and financial cooperatives and a small number of NGOs reached an estimated 9 million depositors with a total volume of US$2.1 billion. The number of depositors in 2010 increased to 10.2 million clients (MIX, 2008). This trend in depositors growth is in line with a general consensus that the poor will deposit part of savings in the presence of an adequately and stable financial environment (Wisniwski, 1998). In order to protect the depositors' institutions engaged in deposit-taking are guided by standards such as those recommended in Basel´s core principle for effective banking supervision (e.g. Principles 2 – permissible activities; 3 – licensing Criteria; 6 – capital adequacy; 7 – risk management procedure; 8 – credit risk, etc) (BIS, 2010).

Regulation (Risk Management)

The number of regulated sub-Saharan microfinance institutions including those operated by commercial banks in 2003 was 71, while 92 institutions were unregulated (Lafourcade *et al*, 2005). The laissez-faire approach to enacting financial regulation may not necessarily be an appropriate generalization (Arun and Murinde, 2005). In Ghana, legislation and regulation for rural and micro financial institutions are creating appropriate level of new entries and providing opportunities while improving performance. The regulator of microfinance in Ghana complies with international standards (BASEL), which focus on reserve requirements which are then changed according to a classification system based on loan recovery performance (Steel and Andah, 2003). Microfinance providers in most African countries do not only have to register but are expected to adhere to the procedures for compliance with capital adequacy and solvency requirements for deposit-taking and other institutions, these prudential rules described above as well as risk concentration limits (on single borrowers), liquidity limits, have been found to exist in other countries such as Tanzania, Benin and Guinea (Basu *et al.*, 2004). Stringent regulatory and supervision has also helped improve the microfinance in Uganda with a capital adequacy level well above the minimum requirement (UCB, 2010). Although the banking and non-banking sector in Sub-Saharan Africa has made progress in generating profit over the years, the environment in which they operate is risky due to weak legal institution and low enforcement. This high risk is argued as the driver behind high returns (Flamini *et al.*, 2009)

Technology

Technological advancement has been instrumental in advancing and increasing financial services to rural dweller. For instance, mobile phones have been fully integrated into the financial operation through retail payment and checking price updates in the last decades (Porteous, 2006). The use of technology in microfinance in rural areas ranging from Automated Teller Machines (ATMs) or Point of Sales (POS), Interactive voice response (IVR) technology, Phone -Internet banking, Personal digital assistant (PDA), Management information system (MIS) to Credit scoring have proven to reduce not only operating cost but also aid risk assessment (Hishigsuren, 2006). Mobile phones are gaining popularity and are used by households to remit money to family and friends in remote Sub-Saharan, leading to synergy between banks and mobile operators in countries like Kenya. It was argued that mobile banking may be more favoured in the rural areas in a number of countries if it connects to financial institutions (Comninos *et al.*, 2008). On the operational front, the need to report to supervisors as well as keep track of business dates, develop methodology for calculating interest and lending/saving has increased the use of information and communication technology (ICT). To this end certain software over the years has been developed to specifically cater for microfinance taking their unique features into consideration (Augsburg and Schmidt, 2011).

3. Credit Institution's Agricultural Lending and Sustainable Investment in Sub-Saharan Africa

Credit constraint is a major problem confronting the development of sustainable agriculture (Feder and Umali, 1993; Fernandez-Cornejo and McBride, 2002; Ahmad, 2005). Studies have shown that by providing credit to smallholders, adoption of new technology (e.g. hybrid maize) is encouraged and the ability of smallholders to bear risk increases (Diagne *et al*, 2009). All studies found that a credit constraint had a negative impact on the adoption of agricultural innovation, which ultimately might lead to limited agricultural growth and development and increased poverty. A number of rural smallholders source their savings for funds (when and if available) or from family and friends or other sources such as rich people or money lenders in the community who usually charge above market interest rates. There is doubt that such a situation will help promote sustainable agricultural development. Smallholders in Kenya have expressed their dismay at the credit situation they are facing, insisting that it was the main cause of low agriculture productivity. There is limited data available on lending from microfinance to small scale agriculture for in sub-Saharan Africa. It is, however, estimated that less than 10 per cent of total lending by commercial financial institutions in sub-Saharan Africa goes to agriculture with large scale farmers as core benefactors (Mhlanga, 2010). Figure 1 provides an overview of the lending pattern of commercial banks to agriculture in a number of selected sub-Saharan African countries between 1995 and 2008. The graph shows that lending in a number of selected sub-Saharan countries has experienced modest growth with some cases of slight decline.

Figure 1: Value of commercial Bank lending to the agricultural sector of selected countries in Africa 1995 -2008 (USD million)

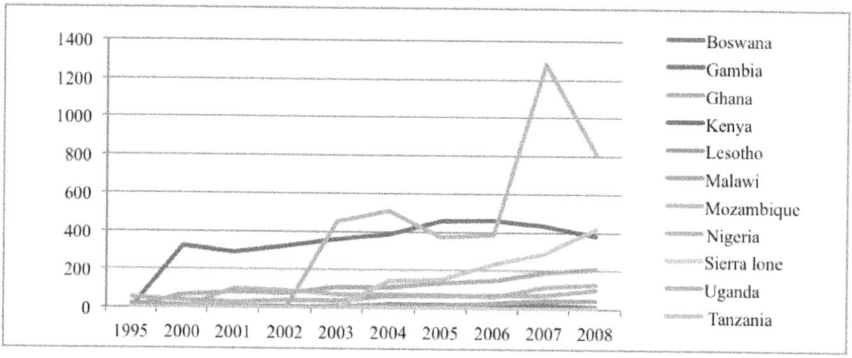

Source: Authors calculation using the data of Mhlanga (2010)

Although microfinance institutions (MFIs) have helped facilitate credit to the rural smallholders by adopting a different approach based on business's cash flow evaluation or income as eligible collateral substitute, its impact has not been widespread (Salami et al., 2010). Co-operatives in rural areas have also helped spread agricultural credit. This is because information complied on respective members by the organization is useful not only in the loan assessment process but also repayment due to peer pressure. Furthermore, financial institutions do not have to engage in high infrastructure costs like in the case of institutional set-up (Admasu and Paul, 2010). Financial institutions can thus reduce transaction costs by aligning operations to those of the co-operatives.

Eighty three percent of enterprises and firms in sub-Saharan Africa were obliged to provide a form of security or deposit before they were granted loans by financial institutions (The World Bank, 2006). One major reason deterring commercial and for-profit financial institutions from disbursing credit to sub-Saharan Africa (smallholders) or small-scale agriculture is the lack of proper collateral and their documentation (Beck *et al.*, 2009). Sub-Saharan African agricultural production is characterized by a disproportionately large fraction of agricultural output which is in the hands of smallholder farmers. The average land holding is about one to three hectares, thus agricultural asset (farmlands) is available in rural areas, a number of smallholders however lease or rent farmlands for cultivation (Ogunlela and Mukhtar, 2009). Collateral plays a major role in credit risk and capital requirement of an agriculture portfolio (Katchova and Barry, 2005). Credit risk variables such the probability of default (PD) and capital adequacy's value-at-risk (VaR) have collateral evaluation as an integral element (Katchova and Barry, 2005). PD estimates the probability that an individual farmer will not be able to meet his/her obligation, in other words, the likelihood that the farmer's asset will fall below the farmer's debt. Value-at-risk (VaR) estimate probability distribution of credit losses conditional on portfolio composition (Thonabauer and Nosslinger, 2004). If the asset valuation of the rural smallholders at the initial period is perceived to be zero, default already occurs as at the time that the smallholder applied for the loan. This method of modelling credit risk does marginalize small-scale agribusiness and/or smallholders due to the high risk and even higher capital requirements that the commercial banks would face in the event of lack of collateral. However, the conventional method of modelling agriculture risk and lending may be discriminatory toward sustainable agriculture which offers stable income eligible as collateral apart from the conventional farmland.

The difficulty project investors face, especially in developing countries, in balancing profitability with the needs of people NGOs etc. can be tackled by increasing local participation, long-term interests of projects, fair and competitive long-term price and uniform conservative environmental standard as well as contributing to peace and stability (Wagner, 2004). Financing of projects which are developed to be socially and environmentally sustainable is a way financial institutions can and are contributing to sustainable agriculture and development. The Environmental Social Governance (ESG) factor which remains an indicator for sustainable investments, amongst others investment decision-making, may however not be quantitative but rather qualitative in nature (Bassen and Kovacs, 2008). Financial institutions in Nigeria and South Africa are working to improve their ESG in terms of lending and investment under the Equator Principles (a comprehensive set of environmental and social guidelines for the financing of projects over US$50 million) although progress has been slow (UNEP, 2007a). The joint venture between Diamond bank (Nigeria), the international financial corporation (IFC) and shell petroleum, were only ecosystem friendly efficient businesses profit from an investment fund of ca. US$1.5 million and Nedbank's Green Trust (South Africa) with US$770,000 in fund which focuses mainly on agribusiness are examples of how financial institutions are improving their ESG (UNEP, 2004). The total socially responsible investment fund for South Africa is estimated to be ca. US$1.4 billion. Although microfinance investment vehicles (MIVs) are promoting the use of ESG, enough is not being done across sub-Saharan Africa (CGAP, 2010a). With MIV concentrated in Eastern Europe and Central Asia (43 per cent), allocated investment to Africa (6 per cent) is quite minimal presumably due to the risks involved (CGAP, 2010b).

4. Sustainable Agriculture Opportunities for Sub-Saharan Credit Institutions

Climate change due to the emission of greenhouse gases (GHGs) primarily carbon dioxide (CO_2) and other gases such as methane (CH_4) and nitrous oxide (N_2O) are a global threat. Agricultural is a contributor to GHGs, fertilizer usage, burning and felling burning of trees, land use change and animal dung releases CO_2 and N_2O. Activities such as afforestation and reforestation, the management of forest, soil, livestock, manure and land, sustainable biofuel production, energy efficiencies and biodiversity mitigates GHGs emissions (Seeberg-Elverfeldt, 2010). Sustainable agriculture practices provide a solution to climate change since it has the ability to store and capture CO_2. Certain rural smallholders and small-scale agribusinesses are therefore able to mitigation climate change by engaging in afforestation (reforestation). Carbon capture and storage is economically viable due to the ability to trade each ton of sequestrated carbon as an entity on the secondary market similar to those on the stock exchange. *"Taungya"* is an example of sustainable small-scale agroforestry practice; *Taungya* is the combined cultivation of timber trees and horticultural crops (Harrison, 2009). Others nitrogen fixing trees with energy potential such as *Calliandra* and *Sesbania sesban*, Jatropha curcus and Pongamia pinnata can be used in small-scale agroforestry with diverse benefits (Rossi and Lambrou, 2009). A variety of small-scale sustainable agroforestry by smallholders can be beneficial not only in the adaptation and mitigation of climate change, but could help improve food and energy security if well propagated (Seeberg-Elverfeldt, 2010).

There is need to explore not only the direct benefits small-scale agroforestry may provide to smallholders such as yield improvement and increased productivity, but also the indirect benefit such as capital formation and increase welfare which may have positive impact on banks loans or agroforestry projects decision-making. This paper elaborates on Jatropha agroforestry, whereby an estimated 120,000 hectares is being cultivated in Africa by both corporate and small-scale farmers, Asia and Latin America have 760,000 and 20,000 hectares respectively (Brittaine and Lutaladio, 2010). The Jatropha tree has a high level of toxicity and is also invasive nature. Its oil production varies between 400 and 2,200 litres per hectares (Sielhorst *et al.*,

2008). Although Jatropha seed has been in use in sub-Saharan Africa for ca. 50 years, predominantly in the making of soap and lighting, its socio-economic evaluation has being limited. Another aspect that has received less attention apart from the indigenous use is the carbon sequestrated through its cultivation in small-scale agroforestry (Hellings *at el.*, 2012). It is argued that promoting carbon sink either through the Kyoto protocol or voluntary market provides a promising avenue to address the north-south equity issues, while noting that the conservation practices is beneficial to small-holders depending on the practice and household endowment (Tschakert, 2004). It is important to point out that the study above also emphasizes the need to assist smallholders financially, technically etc. in their pursuit of sustainability. To illustrate capture and storage (environmental service), a 3 hectares small-scale agroforestry with Jatropha may range from between 1100 and 2500 trees depending on density (Benge, 2006). Small-scale cultivation of Jatropha on marginal land or wasteland compared to large scale cultivation, although characterized by non-optimal growth, may be socio-economically viable. The sequestration potential of the small-scale cultivation is estimated to be 5.5 t CO2 ha^{-1} $year^{-1}$ (Abhilash *et al.*, 2010). The carbon sequestrated is a mitigation measure which is eligible for compensation in the form of carbon credit. the possible annual revenue from trading the sequestration mention above in 2007 on the clean development mechanism (CDM = US$11 → CO_2e) and voluntary market (VCS = US$12.5 → CO_2e) is equivalent to US$60 and US$68.75 respectively while estimated cost of carbon market participation of a micro-scale *project* (< 5000 ton CO_2/yr) for potential investor is ca. US$65,000 for the CDM and ca. US$25,000 for the VCS which includes negotiation, project approval, project monitoring, verification, and insurance costs (Green Markets International, 2007; Lipper at el., 2011; De Pinto *at el.*, 2010). Jatropha medicated soap production due to the simple local production techniques is observed in sub-Saharan Africa to be highly profitable and provides additional revenue to low-income earners (Eijck, 2007). The amount of soap derived from 13 litres of Jatropha oil, given an estimated five working hours, is 4.7k g (Henning, 2004). Seed cake residue which is a by-product of soap production serves as an organic fertilizer, applying this type of fertilizer on farmland is a way to generate carbon credit because it does not contribute to the release of N_2O (Brittaine and Lutaladio, 2010).

Model A

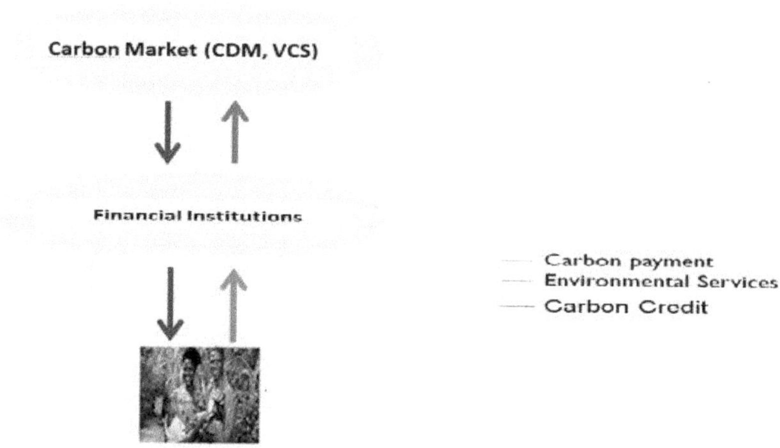

Source: Author

Carbon trading presents a win-win situation for both carbon buyers and sellers especially for sustainable smallholders in developing countries (The World Bank, 2011a). Some literatures out on how to create a broker between the demand and the supply of carbon certificates via emission trading championed by financial institutions are reviewed and models of climate-agricultural based investments and lending are introduce hereafter."Carbon trading partners are to be linked by an investment vehicle with adequate financial capital willing to dedicate substantial capital to the project" (Perez *et al.*, 2007). "Accumulating and storing carbon may also yield higher returns whereby these returns may come with a lag or delay, if this is the case farmers may require a positive financial incentive, such as a loan, to be encouraged to bear the fixed and variable costs of adopting and maintaining conservation practices" (Antle and Diagana, 2003). The argument of the authors is that the carbon market can act as the financier of sustainability if stable financial institutions are in place.

Microfinance institutions can reduce credit risk and promote sustainability improving on their ESG factor if there are able to target rural climate certified smallholders. The voluntary certification process for smallholders, although still in its infancy, is starting to gain recognition as conservation practices have not only resulted in stable income through improved yield but also carbon revenues (The World Bank, 2011b). The database of verified carbon standards puts the number of agriculture, forestry and land use related project observed in countries such as Kenya, Tanzania, Uganda,

South Africa, Mali and Madagascar with active participation from NGOs at 11 (VCS, 2012). Since the support for the inclusion of social and environmental risk in credit risk analysis of African banks is on the increase, smallholder carbon credit inclusion in risk calculation may lead to more lending (UNEP, 2007b). Carbon credit on one hand may to some extent improve smallholders asset base making them less riskier as far as calculation of the probability of default is concern and on the other hand may help free up capital which would otherwise be tied to capital adequacy.

Model B

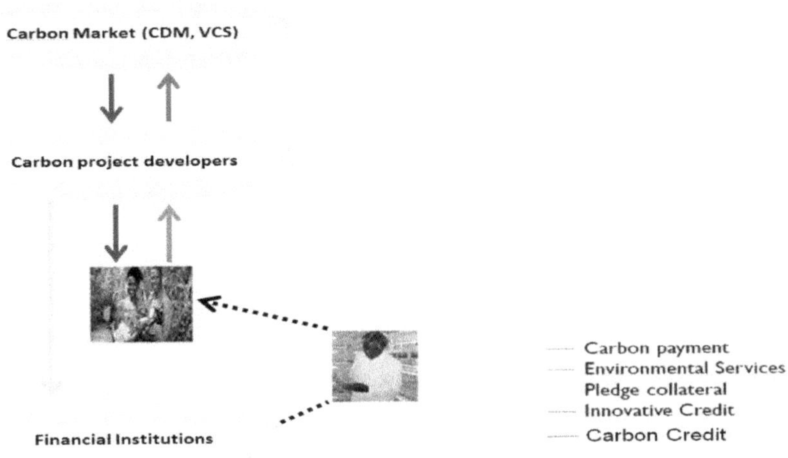

Source: Author

5. Policy Implication

The policies on (small-scale) agriculture drafted by Africa governments and international organization and donors which seeks the development of agricultural research, technology dissemination and adoption to sustain long-term productivity growth and national poverty reduction have not adequately addressed the agriculture and rural development (UKFG, 2012). Theoretically, where there is efficiency in small scale agriculture, government intervention in agriculture should be minimal rather market forces should prevail, thus the focus of policy interventions should be to offer an enabling economic environment for market-led development (Daio, 2007). The author further argues that the existence of institutional and market failures, ultimately leading to poverty trap, would however not permit such hands–off approach. Diversifying the income of poor smallholders in

developing countries are slim, effective policies which may help broaden this opportunity have to be formulated. This formulation should give rise to innovative institutional arrangements between the public and private sector which guarantees the growth of both sectors.

The existence of a equator principle for financial institution to foster development based on the framework of international finance corporation performance standards on social and environmental sustainability and on the world bank group environmental, health, and safety guidelines should pave way for a sub-Saharan Africa version directed at microfinance institutions (EP, 2011). The limited number of financial institutions from sub-Saharan Africa, namely six, who are signatory to the equator principle mainly from South Africa and Nigeria signals a need by the governments and national regulators to push for a bottom-up approach.

6. Conclusion

The problems confronting sub-Saharan agriculture and a move towards a sustainable agriculture are complex and far reaching. As the demand for and the prices of food and fossil fuel continue to surge, with Africa being the most vulnerable, concerns about sustainability and climate change are genuine. In order to ensure sustainable food and energy security, agriculture development in a sustainable manner has to be the main focus. With the food versus fuel and poverty elevation debate heating up in sun-Saharan Africa, a possible solution amongst others is in sustainable small-scale agroforestry with energy potential. The guidelines of international climate consensus such as the CDM and voluntary carbon markets are continuously amended to accommodate rural sustainable smallholders in developing countries. The eligibility for carbon credit certificate due to sustainable farming and resulting trading on carbon market means smallholders are recipient of stable long-term income. The active participation of financial and non-bank financial institutions on the carbon projects may provide climate financing capacity building and a base for the asset valuation of these local smallholders in credit risk management process. The opportunities that climate mitigation instruments presents can be used to reverse the trend of credit constraints due to lack of collateral (farm asset or stable income). A number of issues however need further investigation, such as the actual cost and revenue as well as risks of climate financing and sustainable lending through accurate case studies.

References

Abhilash, P. C., Srivastava, P., Jamil, S. and Singh, N. (2010), 'Revisited Jatropha curcas as an oil plant of multiple benefits: critical research needs and prospects for the future,' in *Environmental Science and Pollution Research* 18:127–131

Admasu, A. and I. Paul (2010), 'Assessment on the mechanism and challenges of small scale agricultural credit from commercial banks in Ethiopia: the case of Adaá liben woreda Ethiopia,' in *Journal of Sustainable Development in Africa,* 12(3): 323 – 304.

Ahmed, A. (2005), 'The impact of finance and funding on technology adoption,' in *Journal of African Development,* 7 (1): 20-41.

Ahma, W. (2001) *'Revisiting the Regulatory and Supervision Framework of the Microfinance Industry in Ethiopia;'* Norway: Drylands Coordination Group / Noragric.

Antle, J. M. and B. Diagana. (2003), 'Creating Incentives for the adoption of sustainable agriculture practices in developing countries: The role of soil carbon sequestration,' in *American Journal of Agricultural Economics,* 85(5): 1178–1184.

Arun, T. and Murinde, V. (2010), 'Microfinance regulation and social protection,' *Paper presented at the Conference Experiences and lessons from social protection programmes across the developing world: what role for the EU,* 17-18 June, Paris, France.

Augsburg, B., Schmidt, J.P. and Krishnaswamy K. (2011), 'Free and open source software for microfinance: increasing efficiency and extending benefits to the poor,' In Ashta, A. (ed.), *Advanced Technologies for Microfinance: Solutions and* Challenges, Hershey, PA: IGI Global.

Balkenhol, B. (1991), 'Savings, Credit, and the Poor: What Has the ILO to Do with the Financial Sector,' in *International Labour Review,* 130(5-6): 645-655.

Bassen, A., and Kovacs, A., (2008), 'Environmental, social and governance key performance indicators from a capital market perspective,' in *The Journal for Business, Economics and Ethics,* 9(2): 182-192.

Basu, A., Blavyand, R. and Yulek, M. (2004), 'Microfinance in Africa: Experience and Lessons from Selected African Countries,' in *International Monetary Fund (IMF), Working Paper,* 174: 1 – 24.

Benge, M. (2006), 'Assessment of the potential of Jatropha curcas, (biodiesel tree) for energy production and other uses in developing countries;' *Ascension Publishing,* 20 August 2001. Available at: http://www.ascension-publishing.com/BIZ/jatropha.pdf.

Beck, T., Fuchs, M. and Uy, M. (2009), 'Finance in Africa: Achievements and Challenges,' in *The World Bank Policy Research Working Paper,* 5020: 31 – 47.

BIS (2010), *Microfinance activities and core principle for effective banking supervision,* Basel: Bank for international settlement (BIS) communication.

Branca, G., Tennigkeit, T., Mann, W., and Lipper, L. (2011), *Identifying Opportunities for Climate-Smart Agriculture Investments in Africa,* Rome: Food and Agriculture Organization of the United Nation and World Bank.

Brittaine, R., and Lutaladio N. (2010), *Jatropha: A Smallholder Bioenergy Crop: The Potential for Pro-Poor Development,* Rome: United Nations.

Brownbridge, M. (1998), 'The Causes of Financial Distress in Local Banks in Africa and implication for prudential Policy,' in *United Nations Conference on Trade and Development,* 132: 1– 40.

Campion, A. and White, V. (2001), 'NGO Transformation,' *microfinancegateway,* June 9. Available at: http://www.microfinancegateway.org/gm/document-1.9.28745/19230_N_073.pdf.

Charitonenko, S. and Campion, A. (2003), 'Expanding Commercial Micro Finance in Rural Areas: Constraints and Opportunities;' *Chemonics,* June 9. Available at: www.basis.wisc.edu/live/rfc/cs_05a.pdf

CGAP (2010a), 'CGAP Awards Recognize Three Microfinance Investors for Social Commitment,' *CGAP,* June 9. Available at: http://www.cgap.org/p/site/c/template.rc/1.26.14337/.

CGAP (2010b), MIV Survey Report Market Data and Peer Group Analysis, *CGAP,* June 9. Available at: http://www.cgap.org/gm/document-1.9.47373/CGAP_2010_MIV_Survey_Report.pdf.

Christiaensen, L.J. and Demery L. (2007), *'Down to Earth: Agriculture and Poverty Reduction in Africa,'* Washington D.C.: The World Bank.

Comninos, A., Esselaar, S., Ndiwalana, A. and Stork, C. (2008), 'M-banking the Unbanked,' in *Research ICT Africa* 1(4): 1 – 20.

Conway, J. and Stevens, A. (2012), 'Industry Survey of Financial Advisors on Sustainable and Impact Investing' gatewaytoimpact.org, June 9. Available at: http://www.gatewaystoimpact.org/images/ gatewaystoimpact.pdf.

Cull, R., Demirgüç-Kunt, A. and Morduch, J. (2008), *Microfinance Meets the Market*, New York: The World bank.

De Pinto, A., Magalhaes, M. and Ringler, C. (2010), 'Potential of Carbon Markets for Small Farmers: A Literature Review,' in *IFPRI Discussion Paper*, 1004:1–36.

Diagne, A., Simtowe, F. and Zelle, M. (2009), 'The impact of credit constraints on the adoption of hybrid maize in Malawi,' in *Review of Agricultural and Environmental Studies - Revue d'Etudes en Agriculture et Environnement*, 90(1): 5-22.

Eijck, V. J. (2007), *Transition towards Jatropha biofuels in Tanzania? An analysis with Strategic Niche Management,'* Leiden: African Studies Centre.

EP (2011), 'Members and Reporting, Equator Principle,' June 9. Available at: http://www.equator-principles.com/index.php/members-reporting.

Feder, G. and Umali, D.L. (1993), 'The Adoption of Agricultural Innovations: A Review,' in *Technological Forecasting and Social Change*, (43): 215-239.

Fernandez-Cornejo, J. and McBride, W.D. (2002), 'Adoption of Bioengineered Crops,' in *agriculture economic report No. 810*, Washington, D.C: U.S. department of agriculture.

Fernando, N.A. (2008), 'Managing Microfinance Risks: Some Observations and Suggestions,' in *Asian Journal of Agriculture and Development*, 4(2): 1-22.

Flamini, V., McDonald, C. and Schumacher L. (2009), 'The Determinants of Commercial Bank Profitability in Sub-Saharan Africa,' in *IMF Working Paper*, 09(15): 1-32.

Furrer, B., Hoffmann, V. and Swoboda, M. (2009), 'Banking and Climate Change:Opportunities and Risks An Analysis of Climate Strategies in more than 100 banks worldwide', *ETH Zurich and SAM*, June 9. Available at: http://ec.europa.eu/enterprise/policies/sustainable-business/corporate-social-responsibility/reporting-disclosure/swedish-presidency/files/surveys_and_reports/banking_and_climate_ change-_sam_group_en.pdf.

Gonzalez-Vega, C. (1993), 'From Policies, to Technologies, to Organizations: The Evolution of the Ohio State University Vision of Rural Financial Markets,' *Economics and Sociology Occasional Paper No. 2062*, Columbus, Ohio: The Ohio State University.

Gonzalez-Vega, C. and Graham, D.H. (1995), 'State – Owned agricultural Development Banks: Lessons and Opportunities,' *Economics and Sociology Occasional Paper No. 2245*, Columbus, Ohio: The Ohio State University.

Green Markets International (2007), 'The Voluntary Carbon Market: Status and Potential to Advance Sustainable Energy Activities', *Greenmarkets*, June 9. Available at: http://www.green-markets.org/Downloads/vCarbon.pdf.

Harrison, S.R., Jesusco, J., Sevare, M. and Mangaoang, E. (2009), *Agroforestry farming practices of smallholders in Leyte and implications for agroforestry systems design*, Queensland: The University of Queensland.

Hellings, B.F., Romijn, H.A. and Franken, Y.J. (2012), 'Carbon storage in Jatropha curcas trees in Northern Tanzania,' in *Fuels from Agriculture in Communal Technology (FACT)*, (1): 1–25.

Henning, R.K. (2004), 'Jatropha curcas in Africa: Assessment of the impact of the dissemination of "the Jatropha System" on the ecology of the rural area and the social and economic situation of the rural population (target group) in selected countries in Africa,' *GFU*, June 9. Available at: http://www.underutilized-species.org/documents/publications/jatropha_curcas_africa.pdf.

Hishigsuren, G. (2006), 'Information and Communication Technology and Microfinance: Options for Mongolia,' in *ADB Institute Discussion Paper*, (42):1–33.

Jones, W.A. and Hiller, T.B. (2010), 'Achieving Scale in Investment Global Risk and Opportunity from Climate Change', *UK's First Climate Change Risk Assessment (CCRA)*, June 9. Available at: http://www.foresight.gov.uk/index.asp.

Katchova, A. and Barry, P. (2005), 'Credit Risk Models and Agricultural Lending,' in *American Journal of Agricultural Economics*, 87(1): 194-205.

Kiyota, H. (2009), 'Efficiency of Commercial Banks in Sub-Saharan Africa: A Comparative Analysis of Domestic and Foreign Banks,' *Paper presented at the CSAE Conference*, 22 - 24 March, University of Oxford, UK.

Lafourcade, A., Isern, J., Mwangi, P. and Brown M. (2005), 'Overview of the Outreach and Financial Performance of Microfinance Institutions in Africa', *Microfinance Information eXchange (MIX)*, Nov. 10. Available at: http://www.rural financenetwork.org/pubs/MIX%20Africa_Data_Study.pdf.

Lipper, L., Neves, B., Wilkes, A., Tennigkeit, T., Gerber, P., Henderson, B., Branca, G. and Mann, W. (2011), *Climate Change Mitigation Finance for Smallholder Agriculture: A guide book to harvesting soil carbon sequestration benefits,* Rome: Food and Agriculture Organization of the United Nations.

Mhlanga, N. (2010), '*Private sector agribusiness investment in sub-Saharan,*' Rome: Food and Agricultural Organization of the United Nations.

MIX (2008), 'Sub-Saharan Africa Microfinance Analysis and Benchmarking Report,' *Microfinance Information eXchange (MIX),*' June 9. Available at: http://www.themix.org/sites/default/files/2008%20Africa%20Microfinance%20Analysis%20and%20Benchmarking%20Report%20-%20English.pdf.

MIX (2010), 'Sub-Saharan Africa Microfinance Analysis and Benchmarking Report,' *Microfinance Information eXchange (MIX),*' June 9. Available at: http://www.themix.org/sites/default/files/096_MIX_Africa%20Report_05-05-2011.pdf.

Ogunlela, Y. and Mukhtar, A. (2009), 'Gender Issues in Agriculture and Rural Development in Nigeria: The Role of Women,' in *Humanity and Social Sciences Journal,* 4(1): 19-30.

Perez, C., Roncoli, C., Neely C. and Steiner J.L. (2007), 'Can carbon sequestration markets benefit low-income producers in semi-arid Africa? Potentials and challenges,' in *Agricultural Systems,* (94): 2-12.

Porteous, D. (2006), *The Enabling Environment for Mobile Banking in Africa,* Boston: Department for international development.

Randhawa, B. and Gallardo, J. (2003), 'Microfinance Regulation in Tanzania: Implications for Development and Performance of the Industry', in *Africa Region Working Paper Series,* (51): 1-48

Rossi, A. and Lambrou, Y. (2009), *Making sustainable biofuel work for smallholder farmers and rural households: issues and perspectives,* Rome: FAO.

Salami, A. Kamara, B. and Brixiova Z. (2010) '*Smallholder Agriculture in East Africa: Trends, Constraints and Opportunities,*' Tunis: African development bank (ADB).

Schneider, S.H., S. Semenov, A. Patwardhan, I. Burton, C.H.D. Magadza, M. Oppenheimer, A.B. Pittock, A. Rahman, J.B. Smith, A. Suarez and F. Yamin, (2007), 'Assessing key vulnerabilities and the risk from climate change', In: *Climate Change 2007: Impacts, Adaptation and Vulnerability*, Contribution of Working Group II to the Fourth Assessment Report of the Intergovernmental Panel on Climate Change, M.L. Parry, O.F. Canziani, J.P. Palutikof, P.J. van der Linden and C.E. Hanson (eds.), Cambridge University Press, Cambridge, UK, 779-810.

Seeberg-Elverfeldt, C. (2010),'Carbon finance possibilities for Agriculture, Forestry and Other Land Use Projects in a Smallholder Context,' in *Environmental and natural resources management working paper 34*. Rome: United Nations.

Sielhorst, S., Molenaar J. W. and Offermans D. (2008), 'Biofuels in Africa An assessment of risks and benefits for African wetlands,' *Wetlands international*, June 9. Available at: http://www.wetlands.org/LinkClick.aspx?fileticket=vPIIvbwvqTs%3D&tabid=56.

Steel, W.F. and Andah, D.O. (2003), 'Rural and microfinance regulation in Ghana: Implications for development and performance of the industry,' *World Bank Africa Regional Working paper Series No. 49*, Washington, D.C.: The World Bank.

The World Bank (2006), *Africa Region: Making Finance Work for Africa*, Washington D.C.: The World Bank.

The World Bank (2007), *World Bank Assistance to Agriculture in Sub-Saharan Africa: an IEG review*, Washington, D.C.: The World Bank.

The World Bank (2011a), 'First African Emission Reductions Purchase Agreement For Soil Carbon Signed in The Hague' *Press Release No: 2011 /165/SDN*, June 9. Available at: http://web.worldbank.org/WBSITE/EXTERNAL/NEWS/0content MDK:22753334~pagePK:34370~piPK:34424~theSitePK:4607,00.html.

The World Bank (2011b), 'Triple Win of Climate-Smart Agriculture put into Practice,' June 9. Available at: http://web.worldbank.org/WBSITE/EXTERNAL/TOPICS/EXTSDNET/0contentMDK:22842518~menuPK:64885113~pagePK:7278667~piPK:64911824~theSitePK:5929282,00.html.

Thonabauer, G. and Nosslinger B. (2004), *Rating Models and Validation: Guidelines on Credit Risk Management*, Vienna: Oesterreichische Nationalbank.

Tschakert, P. (2004), 'Carbon for farmers: Assessing the potential for soil carbon sequestration in the old peanut basin of Senegal,' in *Climatic Change*, 67(2-3): 273–290.

UCB (2010), 'Uganda's Experience in Regulating Microfinance Deposit-taking Institutions,' *Paper presented at the Microfinance Regulation – Who Benefits? Conference*, 15 - 17 March, Dhaka, Bangladesh.

UNEP (2004), *Sustainability Banking in Africa,* Nairobi: The United Nations Environment Program Finance Initiative.

UNEP (2007a), 'Africa's Banks Starting to Rise to Challenge of Wider Environmental, Social and Governance Concerns,' *UNEP News Release 2007/22,* June 9. Available at:
http://www.unep.org/Documents.Multilingual/Default.Print.asp?DocumentID=512&ArticleID=5613&l=en.

UNEP (2007b), *Banking on Value: A New Approach to Credit Risk in Africa,* South Africa: United Nations Environment Program Finance Initiative (UNEP FI) and African Task Force (ATF).

UKFG (2012), 'More Aid for African Agriculture Policy implications for small-scale farmers,' *UK Food Group,* June 9. Available at: http://www.ukfg.org.uk/docs/More_Aid_for_African_Agriculture_MAIN_REPORT.pdf.

VCS (2012), 'The VCS Project Database,' *Voluntary carbon standard,* June 9, Available at: http://www.vcsprojectdatabase.org/.

Verhoef, G. (2005), 'Globalization, concentration and regulation: Trends in the globalization of South African banking, 1990-2005,' *University of Johannesburg,* June 9. Available at: http://ehsanz.econ.usyd.edu.au/papers/Verhoef.pdf.

Wagner, D. (2004), *Investing in Stability: Conflict Risk, Environmental Challenges, and the Bottom Line,* United Nations Environment Program and International Institute for Sustainable Development.

Wisniwski, S. (1998), 'Savings in the Context of Microfinance –Lessons Learned from Six Deposit-Taking Institutions,' *Paper presented at the Interamerican Microenterprise forum,* 26-28 March Mexico-City, Mexico.

WSBI (2008) Microfinance services by savings banks in Africa: The sleeping giants have started moving, but where are they going? *World savings banks and institute,* June 9. Available at: http://www.wsbi.org/uploadedFiles/Publications_and_Research_%28WSBI_only%29/microfinance%20leadership%20of%20WSBI%20African%20members%20GB%20screenview5.pdf.

African Journal of Science, Technology,
Innovation and Development
Vol. 4, No. 2, 2012
pp. 130-149

Rural Development Initiatives Under the Military and Civilian Regimes in Nigeria: A Comparative Analysis

Nseabasi S. Akpan*

Abstract

Nigeria's post-independence governance structure has been characterized by frequent military intervention beginning from January 15, 1966 when the first military coup disrupted the First Republic civilian government. Given the oscillation between the military and civilian regimes, this paper attempts a comparative review of rural development practices as a way of measuring the differences between the military and civilian governance. The review observes that rural development in Nigeria was relatively better focused during the military regime than what is obtainable under the civilian democracy. However, long years of military rule characterized by frequent regime changes made it impossible to set standard and build effective rural development institutions. Given that long years of military rule had inhibited whatever progress that would have been achieved in rural development, the paper argues that the emerging democratic regimes have not shown significant political commitment for improvement because of excessive politicization of development plans, fragmented and uncoordinated planning, poor implementation practices, a lack of continuity in policies and, corruption among several other problems. The paper observes that post-military rural development practice is not significantly different from the practice under the military especially when viewed against its narrow policy contents and focus. Given these observations, the paper argues for a much

* Department of Sociology and Anthropology, University of Uyo, Nigeria.
Email: akpan.nseabasi@ymail.com

broader conceptualization of rural development beyond agricultural development and improvement of living standard to incorporate a broad range of social opportunities to improve the general capabilities of the rural areas.

Keywords: Rural development, Military dictatorship, Civilian democracy, Rural Policy, Nigeria.

JEL Classification: O10; O20; O30; O55.

1. Introduction

Rural development as a concept has no clear and comprehensive definition. Ploeg *et al.* (2000) had argued that the notion of rural development emerged through socio-political struggles and debate. Once, it was part of the discussions that is associated with agriculture and countryside. In such context, Ward and Hite (1998) linked rural areas with 'remoteness' often characterized with single, central market-such as the marketplaces for the outputs of small, agricultural producers in past centuries. This notion is also related to Hite's (1997) argument that rural be understood as a point on a Thunen plain, characterized by 'remoteness' from the main centre. Ploeg *et al.* (2000) reported studies that show that while some see rural development as a process that will end with the final expropriation of farmers, others regard it as a force that will revitalize agriculture (the authors cited Broaekhuizen *et al.*, 1997).

A survey of literature has shown that the concept of rural development has evolved over the five decades ranging from community development, green revolution, integrated rural development to increased attention to sustainable livelihoods and poverty reduction (Ashley and Maxwell, 2001; Ploeg *et al.*, 2000; Ward and Hite, 1998; Maxwell and Heber-Percy, 2001). Ashley and Maxwell (2001), for instance, observed that the evolution of mainstream policy on rural development is located on two axes-representing the balance between productive sectors and social sectors, and between state and market. For instance, in the 1960s the Green Revolution was associated with large-scale state investment in infrastructure, research, and support for adoption of new technology. In the 1970s, budget priorities shifted somewhat to the social investments required by integrated rural development programmes. In the 1980s came the structural adjustment where public sector institutions were trimmed and budgets cut, while the 1990s witnessed an upsurge of interest in poverty reduction.

The above analyses show that the notion of rural development changes depending on the dominant context. But in terms of basic meaning, the general consensus is that rural development refers to the process of improving the quality of life and economic wellbeing of the people living in relatively isolated and sparsely populated areas. In African context, rural development has historically centred on the exploitation of land-intensive natural resources such as agriculture and forestry. However, globalization and expansion in urban settlements have tended to de-emphasize rural agriculture and resource extraction due to the rise in the phenomenon of rural tourism and recreation as new avenues of rural development. How has this trend been translated in the general conceptualization and practice of rural development in Nigeria at post-independence?

This paper attempts a comparative analysis of rural development practice in Nigeria within the context of military dictatorship and civilian democracy. To help in achieving such comparison, the paper is organized into sections. The next section, following this introduction, gives the general overview of the post-independence governance structure as well as the general socio-economic background of Nigeria with particular reference to rural areas. The third section discusses the various rural development plans over the years of military and civilian governance to see how rural development have been conceptualized and translated into practical impact. The fourth section discusses key distinguishing highlights of rural development practices between the military and civilian regimes in a comparative manner as a way of gaining a better insight on approaches, distinguishing features, best practices and impacts associated with each governance contexts. The fifth section highlights the summary of findings as well as drawing some conclusions.

2. Nigeria: Post-Independence Governance Structure and Socio-economic Background

Post-Independence Governance Structure

Nigeria's post-independence governance structure has been characterized by frequent military intervention beginning from January 15, 1966 when the first military coup disrupted the First Republic government led by Alhaji Tafawa Balewa. The pioneer coupists which was led by Major General J. T. U. Ironsi was immediately replaced in another set of military coup led by Lieutenant Colonel Yakubu Gowon on July 29, 1966. Shortly, the government of Gowon was confronted with the outbreak of a civil war in 1967 as a result of the secessionist bid of the then Lieutenant Colonel O. Ojukwu. Gowon used his tenure to fight for a united Nigeria which ultimately materialized in a ceasefire in 1970. The Gowon military administration lasted upto 1975 and was replaced by another military regime led by Mutala Muhammed, who himself, was assassinated in July 29, 1976. Mutala

Muhammed's assassination brought in Olusegun Obasanjo in 1976 which lasted up to 1979.

Beginning from 1979, the Obasanjo's military administration led Nigerians in a brief return to democracy when power was transferred to civilian regime led by Alhaji Shehu Shagari. The military coup of 1984 led by General Muhammadu Buhari overthrew the Shehu Shagari civilian regime and, Buhari's regime did not last as it was overthrown in 1985 by General Ibrahim Babangida. Babangida made effort to return Nigeria to a democratic system in 1992 through a democratic election which was later annulled in a manner that generated serious crisis among the populace. The consequent crisis and violent agitation arising from the June 12, 1993 election prompted the setting up of an interim civilian regime which was led by Ernest Shonekan in 1993. That regime was later overthrown same year by the military coup that was led by General Sani Abacha. The death of Sani Abacha in 1998 automatically ushered in a new military leader led by Abdulsalami Abubakar.

Nigeria attained democratic governance in 1999 when it elected Olusegun Obasanjo as the new democratic president. This brought to an end almost 33 years of military rule (from 1966-1999) excluding the short-lived second republic (1979-1983). Obasanjo had survived two democratic tenures (1999-2003 and 2003-2007) before handing over to another civilian administration that was led by Alhaji Umaru Yar' Adua in 2007. Yar' Adua died on May 5, 2010 paving way for Dr. Goodluck Jonathan (his former vice president) to be sworn in on May 6, 2010 as the substantive President of Nigeria. Goodluck Jonathan secured a fresh democratic tenure in 2011 and was sworn-in on May 29, 2011 to serve a four-year term which will end in 2015.

General Socio-economic Background

A great majority of Nigeria's population resides in the rural areas. For instance, the 1963 Census recorded 80.7% of the national population as rural residents. By 1985, the proportion had slightly gone down to 70.13% and was estimated that a further drop to 69% in the proportion was expected in the 1990s (Muoghalu, 1992). In 2005, it was estimated that 53% of the Nigerian populace resides in the rural areas and in 2011, the world Bank reports recorded 51.6% of Nigeria's rural population. The general consensus seems to be that the rural areas in Nigeria are very heavily populated. Agriculture is the mainstay of the economy, contributing about 45 per cent of GDP. The agriculture sector employs about two-thirds of the country's total labour force and provides a livelihood for about 90 per cent of the rural population. Nigeria is the world's largest producer of cassava, yam and cowpea – all staple foods in sub-Saharan Africa. It is also a major producer of fish. Yet it is a food-deficit nation and imports large amounts of grain, livestock products and fish. Apart from serving as the agricultural base for the country, the rural areas constitute the major sources of capital formation as well as huge markets for domestic products (Olatunbosun, 1975; Abdu and Marshall, 1990; Olayiwola and Adeleye, 2005). Indeed, the rural areas are involved in primary economic activities that are important in sustaining the entire Nigerian economic system.

Despite Nigeria's plentiful agricultural resources and oil wealth, poverty is widespread in the country and has increased since the late 1990s. Over 70 per cent of Nigerians are now classified as poor, and 35 per cent of them live in absolute poverty (IFAD, 2011). Poverty is especially severe in rural areas, where up to 80 per cent of the population lives below the poverty line and social services and infrastructures are limited. The country's poor rural women and men depend on agriculture for food and income. About 90 per cent of Nigeria's food is produced by small-scale farmers who depend on rainfall rather than irrigation systems. Surveys show that 44 per cent of male farmers and 72 per cent of female farmers across the country cultivate less than 1 hectare of land per household (IFAD, 2011). This implies that Women play a major role in the production, processing and marketing of food crops.

Rural infrastructure in Nigeria has long been neglected. Investments in health, education and water supply have been focused largely in the cities. As a result, the rural population has extremely limited access to services such as schools and health centres, and about half of the population lacks access to safe drinking water. The productivity of the rural population is also hindered by ill health caused by HIV/AIDS, tuberculosis and malaria. Neglect of rural infrastructure affects the profitability of agricultural production.

Despite the fundamental contributions to the national economy, the rural areas are not attractive to live in given the general absence of basic infrastructure (potable water, roads, electricity, healthcare systems, and financial institutions, among several others) and poor quality of life occasioned by persistent poverty. Attempts at solving the rural development challenges had been the concern of the governments over the years. Several programmes such as Operation Feed the Nation (OFN); the National Accelerated Food Production Programme (NAFPP) and the Directorate for Food, Roads and Rural Infrastructure (DFRRI), National Economic Empowerment and Development Strategy (NEEDS), among others, have been utilized in developing the rural areas most especially at post-independence era. What were the contents of such programmes and how did they respond to the diverse needs and development challenges in the rural areas? The next section discusses the various versions of public infrastructural commitments to rural development in Nigeria since independence.

Post-Independence Rural Development Practice in Nigeria

Post-independence rural development strategies in Nigeria were articulated under the various national development plans namely, the first national development plan (1962-1968); second national development plan (1970-1974); the third national development plan (1975-1980); the fourth national development plan (1985-1990).

The major objective of Nigeria's first national development plan was to maintain and, if possible, to surpass the average of 4% per year of its gross domestic product at constant prices. To realize the aim, government planned a yearly investment of approximately 15% of Nigeria's gross national product. Given that agriculture is the mainstay of Nigeria's rural economy, policy attention and governmental investment in it were seen as direct and indirect avenues of developing the rural areas. Using agriculture to develop the rural areas was, therefore, at the top of Nigeria's first national development plan. According to Saheed (2010), interest in rural development owed much to a number of events which had their origin in the colonial heritage and the unanticipated oil boom of the seventies. These include massive rural-urban drift, declining productivity in agriculture, increasing food imports, growing unemployment and the widening gap in welfare terms between the urban and rural areas. Despite this policy effort at developing agriculture, and by implication the rural areas, the first development policy was more of an extended colonial policy and practice of exploitation. Abass (1993) argues that under the first national development plan period, peasant farmers were further squeezed to produce cash crops, at the expense of the subsistence crops, for export. The plan itself did not articulate any clear statement or policy on rural infrastructural development. Rather, emphasis was placed on encouraging the cultivation of agricultural produce for export purpose, without strengthening the real agricultural base of the country by providing necessary infrastructures such as good road network, electricity, agricultural processing facilities and water, among several others.

The second national development plan (1970-1974) came as a post-civil war development initiative. It was also during this plan period that Nigeria had the 'phenomenon of oil boom'. Fundamentally, the plan was aimed at: a) building a united, strong and self-reliant nation; b) building a great and dynamic economy; c) building a just and egalitarian society; d) building a land of bright and full opportunities and; e) building a free and democratic society. The plan placed high priority on reducing the level of inequality among the social classes and between urban and rural areas. One important feature of the second national development plan as observed by Marcellus (2009) was its democratic content, having emerged from a participatory process that involved stakeholders at every level of governance. Although its primary focus was not about rural development, the plan's intention of building a just and egalitarian society suggested holistic development whereby every segment of the Nigerian space and population were to be covered. These ideals were not realized principally owing to the phenomenon of 'oil boom', which ended up undermining every efforts and commitment at mobilizing material and human resources for the achievement of the primal objective of building an egalitarian and self-reliant society. 'Oil boom' soon translated into struggle for 'oil rents' which led to massive corruption at every levels of governance. Huge spending and import of food characterized the state activity while agriculture that served as the mainstay of the economy was relegated to the background. Given the relationship of agriculture with rural development in Nigeria, government massive dependence on oil revenue during this period meant that all policies on rural development could no longer be on the agenda of government.

In the third national development plan (1975-1980), rural development was revisited based on government conviction that such investment will contribute in closing the yawning gap between the demand for food and the supply capacity of the home-based industries. Consequently, government developed interest in modernizing agriculture and introducing new initiatives to strengthen the agricultural and food base of the nation. Although the objectives of the plan looked similar to those of the second national development plan, there was a significant and radical approach as the plan emphasized the need to reduce regional disparities in order to foster national unity through the adoption of integrated rural development. Increased budgetary allocation was provided to fund diverse and interrelated rural development programmes including rural electrification scheme; the establishment of Agricultural Development Projects (ADPs); the establishment of nine River Basin Development Authorities (RBDAs); the construction of small dams and boreholes for rural water supply and the clearing of feeder roads for the evacuation of agricultural produce; the supply of electricity to rural areas from large irrigation dams; commitment of resources to large scale mechanized state farming enterprises; the introduction of Operation Feed the Nation (OFN) campaign and the Green Revolution and; public efforts at land reforms through the Land Use Act of 1978.

From the first to the third national development plans, there was observable progressive budgetary improvement to enhance agricultural productivity. Olorunfemi and Adesina (1998) reported increasing financial allocation for agricultural development as follows: first national development plan had a total financial allocation of #30,835,000; second national development plan was allocated a total amount of #71,447,000; while the third national development plan had the highest allocation of #2,201,373,000 for agricultural development. Investment in rural agricultural sector is one component that could catalyze substantive improvement in individual capabilities. However, such lopsided development interest was not enough for transforming rural areas without corresponding investment in rural infrastructures such as roads, electricity and healthcare, among several others.

The Fourth National Development Plan (1980-1985) came with several distinguishing features and potentials. First, it was formulated by a civilian government under a new constitution based on the presidential system of government. Second, it was the first plan in which the local government authorities were allowed to participate fully in rural development (FGN, 1981). The plan emphasized among other things the need for balanced development of the different sectors of the economy as well as the various geographical areas of the country. It emphasized the importance of rural infrastructural development as a vehicle for enhancing the quality of rural life. The period saw improved budgetary allocation to the eleven River Basin Development Authorities (RBDAs) whose functions include among other things, the construction of boreholes, dams, feeder roads and jetties. In this case the RBDAs was, to a large extent, empowered to develop the rural areas by opening up feeder roads, drilling boreholes and wells, building farm service centres and earth dams. This period saw increasing participation of all levels of governments in rural development activities especially in the areas of roads construction, healthcare services, and electricity services, water supply etc. According to Filani (1993: 250): 'the 1981-1985 national development plan marked a turning point in rural development efforts in Nigeria because it was the first to recognize the rural sector as a priority area. It made provision for integrated approach to rural development, focusing on rural infrastructure as well as institutional and administrative apparatus to facilitate rapid development of the country's agricultural potential'. The author observed that increase of 12% specific allocation to agriculture and rural development over 5% in the 1962-1968 plan represented significant political commitment to rural development practice.

The post-Fourth plan period (1986-1998) witnessed some general policies and programmes that produced massive impact in the rural areas. Key and prominent programmes and policies included the Structural Adjustment Programme[1] (SAP) and the vision 2010. The structural adjustment programme, for instance, witnessed the establishment of the Directorate for Food, Roads and Rural Infrastructure (DFRRI) in 1985 for the purpose of providing rural infrastructures in the country-side. The laws establishing the Directorate was promulgated under decree number four of 1987. The core of the Directorate's programme was to promote productive activities. Besides, the Directorate recognized the provision of rural infrastructure such as feeder roads, water, electricity and housing as essential for the enhancement of the quality of life in the rural areas.

The plan for the implementation of DFRRI programme was organized into two phases. In phase one, the target was to provide water for 250 communities in each of the states of the federation, to construct 90,000 km of feeder roads, and to promote rural housing, health and agriculture. To facilitate industrial growth, and improve the attractiveness of the rural environment, the Directorate planned to commence its rural electrification programme in the second phase starting in June 1987. In pursuit of its objectives, DFRRI also planned to co-operate with organizations like Nigerian Building and Road Research Institute (NBRRI) as well as Rural Water Supply and Sanitation programme (RUWATSAN). The Directorate for Food, Roads and Rural Infrastructures (DFRRI) was not to be involved in direct implementation of the programmes. Rather, for the purpose of the programme implementation, the Directorate used as its main agents, the states and the local governments, to execute its programmes. The funds for the programme of the Directorate were made available directly to each state government who then saw to its disbursement to the local governments. The local governments in the federation were constituted into rural development committees. These committees comprised of the local government officials and the rural communities. The Vision 2010 was framed under the then General Sani Abacha. The Vision 2010 Committee made large scale recommendations for rural transformation. The recommendations emphasized on massive rural infrastructural intervention on the one hand, and agricultural transformation on the other hand (Vision 2010, 1997). Under the rural infrastructural development, the framework of the RBDAs were to be used in building small and large scale dams, irrigation channels, boreholes, dykes, flood and erosion projects, among others. The policy orientation was laid out in the National Rolling Plan (1996-1998, vol. 1). According to Mustapha and Meagher (2000), other important agencies such as Agricultural Development Programmes (ADPs), National Agricultural Land Development Authority (NALDA) and Federal Department of Agriculture (FDA) were to be utilized to develop hectares of farmlands, produce tonnes of seedlings and rehabilitate rural roads, among several others. The Vision 2010 could not survive following the death of the then General Sani Abacha. On the whole, this period witnessed radical and more holistic intentions towards the development of rural areas.

Subsequent efforts at rural development came in the light of Nigeria's democratic experiment (1999-to date). A four-year development plan was initially articulated (1999-2003) with the objective of pursuing a strong, virile and broad-based economy that is highly competitive, responsive to incentives, private sector-led, diversified, market-oriented and open, but based on internal momentum for its growth (Marcellus, 2009 and Donli, 2004). Emphasis on private sector-led growth did not carry sufficient message for rural development. As the prospect of achieving the intended objective of the plan did not materialize, a re-think was therefore necessary. When the ruling party (the People's Democratic Party-PDP) got re-elected in 2003, they came up with a new programme namely, the National Economic Empowerment and Development Strategy (NEEDS: 2003-2007). NEEDS was quite comprehensive and ambitious, as it was not only duplicated at all levels of governments (State Economic Empowerment and Development Strategy-SEEDS; and Local Economic Empowerment and Development Strategy-LEEDS), it incorporated the private sector, non-governmental organization and the general public in pursuits of its developmental goals. As a framework for poverty reduction and for the stimulation of economic growth, NEEDS' key objective was to facilitate a broad-based market oriented economy that will involve active participation of the private sector, with the main source of economic empowerment coming from the generation of gainful employment opportunities as well as the provision of social safety nets for vulnerable groups. By attempting to empower the rural populace, NEEDS had a substantive vision of eliminating rural poverty and promoting the development of the rural space. Given a run-down of the various rural development plans in Nigeria, the next section attempts a comparative analysis of rural development practices under the military and civilian rule regimes as a way of gaining better insights on approaches, best practices and impacts.

3. Military Context and Civilian Democracy in Rural Development Practice: A Comparison

Rural development practice at post-independence Nigeria has been influenced by two broad regime episodes namely, the military system and civilian democracy. What were the major characteristics and approaches and what form of impacts were produced?

The first (1962-1968), second (1970-1974), third (1975-1980), fourth (1980-1985), post-fourth (1986-1998) development plans were all framed and implemented by the military. The military has ruled Nigeria from 1966 to 1999, with a brief interlude between 1979 and 1982. The brief democratic interlude had no clear development plan for rural Nigeria. Post-military rule beginning from 1999 came with a number of development documents namely, the Poverty Alleviation Programme (PAP, 1999-2000); National Poverty Eradication Programme (NAPEP) and National Economic Empowerment and Development Strategy (NEEDS, 2003-2007). Under the military system, rural development practices were mostly conceptualized around agricultural development clearly envisaged in the number of 'development plan specific agricultural programmes' such as increased investment of about 15% of the country's gross domestic product in the agricultural sector (1962-1968); River Basin Development Authorities (RBDAs), Agricultural Development Projects (ADPs), Operation Feed the Nation (OFN) and land use reforms (1975-1980 plan period). Improved conceptualization of rural development came under the military directed fourth national development plan (1980-1985) whereby rural agricultural development was planned alongside the provision of essential rural infrastructures such as feeder roads, boreholes, dams. This is when the idea of using the River Basin Development Authorities (RBDAs) for integrated development of the rural areas received high policy priority. The RBDAs concept was followed by the post-fourth development plan (1986-1998) which brought some radical approaches to rural development through the agency of the Directorate for Food, Roads and Rural Infrastructures (DFFRI).

While the military system gradually progressed from agriculturally centred conceptualization of rural development, the democratic governments beginning from 1999 conceptualized rural development around economic empowerment of the rural populace. This can be seen in the light of the Poverty Alleviation Programme (PAP), National Economic Empowerment and Development Strategies (NEEDS) with state and local parallels. Interestingly, agricultural development has been de-emphasized while youth employment, rural infrastructures and the development and conservation of natural resources took the centre stage of policy governance, at least on paper. Based on some studies and reports, rural development practice under this period has not been significantly different from previous public programmes in terms of political commitment and implementation practices. These have consistently led to poor results. For instance, Bambale (2011) reported that NEEDS failed as an empowerment programme in eliminating poverty and improving the basic infrastructures with direct link to poverty reduction in the rural areas. This was statistically substantiated by the UN Human Development Index report which showed an increase in poverty in Nigeria from 34.0 percent to 38.8 percent during the periods of NEEDS (UNDP, 2009). Marcellus (2009) specifically observed that while Nigeria's wealth rose within the period of NEEDS owing to better petroleum oil prices and substantial debt relief by Paris club, the average Nigerian especially in the rural areas remained disproportionately very poor quite contrary to some official figures from the Central Bank of Nigeria (the author cited CBN, 2005: 76). On the other hand, Osagie (2007:29) saw poor leadership and a lack of proper coordination as responsible for failed public programmes (as in NEEDS). As a neo-liberal oriented development strategy, NEEDS could not have been the appropriate development strategy for a country whose citizens are still struggling for some basic infrastructures which the State alone can provide.

How focused and feasible were the various development plans in Nigeria could best be evaluated by looking at the respective plan scope and target output. One key problem that confronted national development plans under the military rule had much to do with the challenge of regime stability and continuity. Regime instability always rendered rural development plans and policies short-lived and replaced by subsequent ones as a result of regime change. While this specific problem applied to the military system, the practice of democratic governance has not built on the lessons of the past as most rural development programmes seemed more associated with particular regimes and would soon disappear with regime change. Rural development initiatives often carry excessive politicization while their survival most often depends on regime longevity. Taking example of Vision 2010 of the Sani Abacha regime, Aluko (2006) observed that in spite of the best ideas and intentions encapsulated in the reform agenda, the subsequent regime led by Olusegun Obasanjo terminated the plan because of sheer hatred for Abacha. He went on to observe that Obasanjo's tenure elongation programme was explicitly premised on guaranteeing the survival of his vision 2020 plan.

Most rural development plans under the military seemed better focused in terms of contents and implementation practices. Emphasis on agriculture was important entry point given its importance in guaranteeing food security, sustaining massive employment opportunities, contributing to foreign exchange earnings, and as a framework for the development of other physical and social infrastructures in the rural areas. Abba and others (cited in Abdu and Marshall, 1990) had noted the role of agriculture as Nigeria's main industry as far as employment was concern with over 65% of the population being dependent on it for livelihood. As early as 1964, Liman (cited in Abdu and Marshall, 1990) had reported a 70% of GDP contribution from the agricultural sector to Nigerian economy.

Under the military era, numerous agriculturally based programmes including the River Basin Development Authorities (RBDAs), Operation Feed the Nation (OFN), Green Revolution and Agricultural Development Projects (ADPs) carried some useful impact on economic, social and physical infrastructures. The River Basin Development Authorities (RBDAs) of 1976, and further amended in 1987 and the Directorate for Food, Road and Rural Infrastructures (DFFRI) established in 1985 represented progressive improvements in rural development under the military system. DFFRI, for instance, was set up to pursue the following programmes:

- the organization and mobilization of the local people to enhance or facilitate closer interaction between the government and the people. In addition the local communities were asked to form unions or associations for the purpose of providing common facilities for themselves;
- the provision of rural infrastructures such as rural feeder roads, rural water and sanitation, rural housing and electrification;
- the promotion of productive activities such as food and agriculture, rural industrialization and technology;
- the promotion of other extracurricular activities such as socio-cultural and recreational programmes, intra and inter community cohesion activities.

Other complementary agencies include the establishment of the National Directorate for Employment (NDE), Better Life Programme for rural women/dwellers, peoples'/community banks and the Directorate of Mass Mobilization for Social Justice and Economic Recovery (MAMSER). According to Filani (1993), by the late 1980s and early 1990s, there was some improvement in the conception of what constituted rural development. In this case, rural development at policy and practice levels was conceived in a way that transcended mere agricultural development to incorporate the development and expansion of rural infrastructures, emphasize on poverty alleviation and socio-economic empowerment of the rural inhabitants. The concept of integrated river basin development was, therefore, strengthened as a way of using the resources of the river basin for the comprehensive development of the basin areas. In essence, it can be argued that rural development practice under the military had clearly outlined agenda as opposed to the civilian regimes whose programmes were bereft of well-articulated and focused plans for rural development.

Citizenship participation and input in any policy formulation and implementation processes is very crucial since the outcome of such arrangements is bound up with popular views and inputs. This is the most important element of a democratic system as opposed to dictatorial arrangements. Every development plan in Nigeria beginning from post-independence revolves around an individual or a group of individuals in governments and public offices. The normal top-down communications were the dominant practice under the military where the federal government passes its development packages to states and local governments for implementation at the local levels. The River Basin Development Authority initiated and consolidated by the military and inherited by the civilian governments, still retain its uniform mandate and objectives of rural development in total disregard of the huge environmental, socio-economic and physical diversities of the various regions of Nigeria. Akpabio (2010), in this particular case of the River Basin Development Authorities, had argued that most public policies and programmes in Nigeria hardly succeed because of utter disregard for local socio-ecological circumstances of operation. This argument applies to all other agricultural and rural development policies and programmes under the military regime except the second development plan (1970-1974). The uniqueness and participatory character of the second development plan could be appreciated against the backdrop of the circumstances of the post-civil war where the need for rehabilitation, and building a united and egalitarian society necessitated interest and subsequent engagement of relevant stakeholders. Such context of participatory governance and development soon could not be sustained given subsequent military intervention. In this case, all other subsequent development plans claimed participation, though falsely, at inter-governmental levels, which in reality amounted to mere directives and communication of what to implement at the state and local government levels.

Fundamentally, the emergence of democratic governance beginning from 1999 was to offer the best opportunity for participatory rural development at every level. For one, the constitution of Nigeria guarantees, in principle, some levels of autonomy to state and local authorities. Second, the power of democratic election and political informational debates offer remarkable political incentives of participatory development at every levels of governance. However, these standards have not yet been internalized in the Nigerian political space. Every known rural development programme beginning from 1999 hardly reflect the true perspectives of the diverse stakeholders and voices. Rural development programmes and policies are still driven by individuals and select few in public offices as was common practice during military dictatorship. This equally accounts for why rural development programmes hardly outlive regime change. Much could be blamed on the nature of Nigeria's institutional arrangements. The military were not able to create enabling institutional environment for participatory governance given that power revolved around individuals and groups within the military hierarchy. When Nigeria started experiencing democratic governance, the needed institutional foundation for democratic and participatory governance was already not nurtured. The implication is that individuals and leaders still cultivate enormous power and influence over the machinery of government, to the extent that corruption, nepotism and poor leadership have combined not only to corrupt public development processes, but also serve to inhibit the proper functioning of public policies and plans that are meant for rural development.

4. Summary and Concluding Remarks

Rural development efforts in Nigeria have not been successful in general. The reasons for this could be located in wider contexts of long years of military intervention, poor understanding and synchronization of development plans with local realities, absence of effective development planning institutional capacity, and the problem of institutionalized corruption, among others.

Clearly, rural development practice in Nigeria has, for the past five decades, been driven by the military government. During the more than 33 years of military intervention, various regime-specific development plans were utilized with short-lived implementation span occasioned by frequent regime change. Rural development programmes came and went with regime change. Agricultural development dominated almost all the rural development documents and practices under the military until the late 1980s when attention started focusing on other aspects of social, physical and economic infrastructures. This was possible within the framework of River Basin Development Authorities (RBDAs) and the Directorate for Food, Roads and rural Infrastructures (DFFRI). The evolution of rural development practice from agricultural to a much broader outlook in the 1980s was understandable from the background of Nigeria's colonial experience which imposed some learning necessities on the post-colonial military rulers. The colonial exploitative relations with local resources still dominated the mind-set of the post-colonial leaders to the extent that rural areas were seen from the perspectives of serving the ends of not only supplying basic food needs of the urban areas but contributing to foreign exchange earnings through basic raw material exports. Consequently, infrastructural development for the rural areas was mostly based on critical elements that only could enhance the goal of food and raw materials production. Unending exploitation replaced the real needs for socio-economic and infrastructural developments in the rural areas. The late 1980s witnessed improved governmental commitment to rural development when integrated and holistic approaches were utilized. In summary, the period before the late 1980s could be said to represent the learning period for the emerging military rulers after the country's independence. However, frequent military intervention made it impossible for such learning phase to be strengthened. This probably contributed to why rural development could not practically be detached from agricultural exploitation. Given the lack of professional understanding and skills in political governance, one could hardly expect much profound and better approach to rural development under the military system.

If the military had not done much in transforming the rural areas, the emergence of democratic governance beginning from 1999 would serve to correct whatever deficiencies that were related to the military system of rural development. However, this seems not to be the case as rural development policies and practices still have the imprint of short-lived lifespan and fragmented programmes, which come and disappear with a specific regime. While this problem has been explained in relation to weak institutional arrangements, the phenomenon of corruption among public officials and elite groups often ensures that important public policy and rural development agenda of governments do not get directly to the intended beneficiaries by way of unduly influencing project distribution, kickbacks, ethnic and patronage politics, contract inflation and poor job execution. Although rural development practice in Nigeria have been recognized at various institutional levels (Ministries of Agriculture, Rural Development, Water Resources, etc.), absence of proper coordination has resulted in many challenges of inefficiency and inter-agency competition. Many of the agencies directly or indirectly in charge of rural development choose to pursue disparate and politically-motivated interests manifesting in a waste of public resources and funds on parallel and most often unrelated projects. Absence of strict and focused institutional arrangements also explains why rural development policies and plans rarely survive regime change as discussions in the paper have clearly illustrated. These problems can only be addressed with strong and well-coordinated institutional arrangements at various levels of governance, in addition to professional and participatory engagements in rural project plan initiatives and implementation practices. Hopes of addressing these problems under the present democratic environment are already not very encouraging as most of the rural development practices under the democratic governance hardly have clear focus. Some plans carry many ambitious and overlapping objectives while actual implementation is often, in most cases, not related to local needs and realities. Politicization of development benefits and absence of professionalism in planning and implementation have conspired to render most rural development plans very ineffective most especially during the present democratic experiment.

Although some of the rural development plans of economic empowerment and poverty alleviation embodied in the post-military rural development approach are useful for the improvement of standard of living of the rural populace, the paper argues that policies and programmes should be targeted more at expanding social opportunities of the rural populace through massive public investment in education, healthcare, social security and physical infrastructures. Taking this approach will not only contribute in improving the quality of life of the rural populace, it will be helpful in expanding their basic capabilities for development

Notes

1 The structural adjustment programme which was conceived to stimulate domestic production processes carried the following objectives: a) to restructure and diversify the productive base of the economy in order to reduce dependency on the oil sector and on imports; b) to achieve fiscal and balance of payments viability over the period; c) to lay the basis for a sustainable non-inflationary growth; d) to reduce the dominance of unproductive investment in the public sector, improve that sector's efficiency and enhance the growth and potential of the private sector (Phillips, 1987). The key policies designed to achieve these objectives were: i) strengthening of the hitherto strong and relevant demand management policies; ii) adoption of measures to stimulate domestic production and broaden the supply base of the economy; c) the setting up of a second-tier foreign exchange market (SFEM), as a mechanism of realistic exchange rate and consequently, the alteration of relative prices to enhance efficiency in resource allocation, and to promote domestic-based production and non-oil exports; d) further rationalization and restructuring of tariffs in order to aid industrial diversification; e) the liberalization of the external trade and payments system-dismantling of price, trade and exchange controls; f) the elimination of price controls and commodity boards; g) the decontrol of interest rates; and h) the rationalization and restructuring of public sector enterprises and overhauling of the public sector administrative structure.

References

Abass, I.M. (1993), 'The challenge of rural development strategies in a deregulated economy', paper prepared for a national seminar on rural development-doing more less developing rural resources in a deregulated economy-organized by New Nigerian Newspapers Limited in collaboration with Arthur Green consultants held at Shiroro Hotel Minna, Niger State from 10th-12th February.

Abdu, M.S. and Marshall R. (1990), 'Agriculture and development policy: a critical review of Nigerian experience in the period up to 1985', in *Journal of Rural Studies*, 6(3): 311-323.

Aderonmu, J.A. (2007), 'Poverty eradication in rural Nigeria: the role of local government', *Paper presented at a Conference on empowerment of rural people*, Charity Centre for Advancement and Rural Development, 6-7 December, Jos, Nigeria.

Aluko, S. (2006), 'Abacha's vision 2010 Blueprint reviewed', #airaland Forum, Tuesday, 09 May 2006.

Akpabio, E.M. (2010), *Integrated Water Resources Management in Nigeria: Local factors and institutional challenges*, Germany: Lap Lambert Academic Publishing.

Ashley, C. and Maxwell, S. (2001), 'Rethinking rural development', in *Development Review,* 19(4): 395-425.

Bambale, A. J. (2011), 'National economic empowerment and development strategy and poverty reduction in Nigeria: a critique', in *Economics and Finance Review* 1(1): 15-24.

CBN (2005), 'Microfinance policy: Regulatory and supervisory framework for Nigeria', Abuja, Nigeria.

Donli, J.G. (2004), 'An overview of Nigeria's economic reforms', in *NDIC Quarterly,* 1(4): 62-82.

FGN (1981), *Fourth National Development Plan (1981-85),* Lagos: Federal Republic of Nigeria (FGN).

Filani, M.O. (1993), 'Transport and rural development in Nigeria', in *Journal of Transport Geography,* 1(4): 248-254.

Hite, J. (1997), 'The Thunen model and the new economic geography as a paradigm for rural development', in *Review of agricultural economics,* 19: 230-40.

IFAD (2011), 'Rural Poverty in Nigeria', Available at: http://www.ruralpoverty portal.org/web/guest/country/home/tags/nigeria, International Fund for Agricultural Development.

Marcellus, I.O. (2009), 'Development planning in Nigeria: reflections on the National Economic Empowerment and Development Strategy (NEEDS), 2003-2007', in *Journal of Social Sciences,* 20(3): 197-210.

Maxwell, S. and Heber-Percy, R. (2001), 'New trends in development thinking and implications for agriculture', in Stamoulis, K. G. (ed.), *Food, Agriculture and Rural Development: current and emerging issues for economic analysis and policy research,* Rome: FAO.

Muoghalu, L.N. (1992), 'Rural development in Nigeria: a review of previous initiatives', in Olisa, M. S. O. and Obiukwu, J.I. (eds.), *Rural development in Nigeria: dynamics and strategies,* Mekslink Publishers, Awka.

Mustapha, A.R. and Meagher K. (2000), 'Agrarian production, public policy and the State in Kano region, 1900-2000', *Working Paper 35,* Drylands Research, Crewkerne, Somerset, United Kingdom.

Olatubosun, D. (1975), *Nigerian neglected rural majority,* Ibadan: Oxford University Press.

Olayiwola, L.M. and Adeleye O.A. (2005), 'Rural Infrastructural Development in Nigeria: Between 1960 and 1990-problems and challenges', in *Journal of Social Science* 11(2): 91-96.

Olorunfemi, A. and Adesina O.C. (1998), 'Politics and Nigerian Agriculture in the first decade of the oil boom, 1970-1980: a preliminary assessment', *The Nigerian Journal of Economic History,* 1(1): 57-69.

Omah, P. (2004), 'Poverty alleviation in Nigeria's post-military era: a case study of Obasanjo's administration (1999-2003)', *An unpublished seminar paper,* Department of Political Science Postgraduate Seminar, University of Nigeria, Nsukka, 15 July.

Onokerhoraye, A.E. (1978), 'Planning for rural development in Nigeria: a spatial approach', in *Community Development Journal,* 13(1): 29-34.

Osagie, E. (2007), 'The New Nigerian Economy: from poverty to prosperity', Benin City: AFBSN Publications.

Philips, A.0. (1987), 'A General Overview of Structural Adjustment Programme', in Philips, A.C. and Ndekwu, E. C. (eds.), *Structural Adjustment Programme in a Developing Economy: The Case of Nigeria,* Ibadan: NISER, 1-12.

Ploeg, J.D. van der, Renting, H., Brunori, G., Knickel, K., Mannion, J., Marsden, T., de Roest, K., Sevilla-Guzman, E. and Ventura, F. (2000), 'Rural development: from practices and policies towards theory', in *Sociologia Ruralis,* 40(4): 391-408.

Presidential Report (1999), 'A report submitted to the President by the committee on streamlining and rationalization of poverty institutions in Nigeria', Abuja: Federal Government of Nigeria.

Blench, Roger (2003), 'Position paper: the rural dimension (Nigeria: drivers of change)', *Paper prepared for DFID,* Cambridge, 22 October. Available at: http://www.rogerblench.info/RBOP.htm

Saheed, A.B. (2010), 'Poverty situation in Nigeria: an overview of rural development institutions, in *Pakistan Journal of Social Sciences,* 7(5): 351-356.

Udeh, C.A. (1989), 'Rural development in Nigeria', in *Habitat Intl,* 13(3): 95-100.

UNDP (2009), 'Nigeria: the human development index: Going beyond income, Human development report', Available at: http://hdrstats.undp.org/en/countries/country_sheets/cty_fs_NGA.html

Vision 2010 Committee (1997), 'Report of the Vision 2010 committee', V11, Book 2, Economic Sectors and Issues, Abuja: Government of Nigeria.

Ward, W.A. and J.C. Hite (1998), 'Theory in rural development: an introduction and overview', in *Growth and Change,* 29: 245-258.

Watts, M. and Bassett, T.J. (1986), 'Politics, the State and Agrarian development: a comparative study of Nigeria and the Ivory Coast', in *Political Geography Quarterly*, 5: 103-125.

Yakubu, O.D. and Aderonmu J.A. (2010), 'Rural poverty alleviation and democracy in Nigeria's fourth republic (1999-2009)', in *Current Research Journal of Social Sciences,* 2(3): 191-195.

African Journal of Science, Technology, Innovation and Development
Vol. 4, No. 2, 2012
pp. 150-172

Sustainable Broadband Connectivity Model for Rural Areas of Tanzania

Fatuma Simba,* Lena Trojer** & Zaipuna O. Yonah***

Abstract

Some of the reasons for lack or limited Information and Communication Technology (ICT) infrastructures in rural areas of developing countries in general and Tanzania in particular, is high cost of establishing such infrastructures, lack of electrical energy and low ICT literacy. Public Private Peoples Partnership (PPPP) is recommended as a suitable model to implement sustainable ICT projects in rural areas. This paper surveys the availability of supporting environments for the provision of broadband rural connectivity: the surveyed environments include initiatives for ICT infrastructure development and institutional frameworks such as policies, strategies, legislations and regulations. The aim of the survey is to investigate the readiness of Tanzania to deploy PPPP model for rural connectivity implementation. Furthermore,

* PhD Scholar, University of Dar es Salaam, Tanzania.
Email: fatmasimba@udsm.ac.tz

** Professor of Information and Communication Technology (ICT) for Development, Blekinge Institute of Technology, Sweden. Email: lena.trojer@bth.se

*** Director of Information and Communication Technology (ICT), Ministry of Communication, Science and Technology, Tanzania.
Email: zaipuna.yonah@mst.go.tz; zaipuna.yonah@gmail.com

the paper proposed implementation strategies in order to adapt the PPPP model for sustainable broadband rural connectivity in Tanzania.

Keywords: Broadband, Connectivity, Rural Area, PPPP, Tanzania.

JEL Classification: O10; O20; O30; O55.

1. Introduction

Rural areas are often characterized by highly sparse population consisting of low income communities, where individuals can rarely afford the costs of ICT services (Siochrú, 2005). Therefore, shared access is the model commonly used to deliver ICT services in rural areas. Implementation of the shared access ICT facilities for rural areas differs widely ranging from donor funded projects, in which the project management remains under the local community at the end of the donor funding time, franchise business model, Public-Private Partnership (PPP) and Public-Private People´s Partnership (PPPP). Brief descriptions of the mentioned models are given in the forthcoming paragraphs.

A donor funded project is a project in which almost all resources required for project implementation are provided by the donor. Most of the donor funded projects are of the form of pilot projects. They often use a "top-down" implementation approach, of which at the end of the donor funding time, the local community may not have enough capacity or knowledge to manage and maintain the project. Therefore, most of the donor funded projects are usually unsustainable after the donor funding time elapsed. A franchise is a business system in which private entrepreneurs purchase the rights to open and run a similar or part of a big business. Nokia Siemens Network (NSN) village connection, n-logue's rural connectivity model and Grameens public payphone are examples of franchising models implementing ICT projects in rural areas. Characteristics of a franchising model are to push delivery and management of services closer to the end users. The NSN village connection is a solution that enables the Global System for Mobile communication (GSM) network operators to extend their network reach to accommodate remote villages, where traditional technology and commercial business models would not be profitable. The NSN village connection is implemented in partnership with local entrepreneurs, who are familiar with potential customers and who can run the local operations. In this model the entire village customer acquisition and care are handled locally, reducing overall sales and marketing expenses to the operator (franchisor). The n-logue´s rural connectivity model employed a three-tier franchise model to implement a village-level kiosk. The locally owned franchises offer a variety of Internet and computer-based services to the rural market. Partners of this model further developed relevant local content and services using the local language aimed at making kiosks useful to the rural society (Paul, 2004 ; Jhunjhunwala *et al.*, 2004). Another example of a franchise model for rural ICT is the Grameen public payphone. The Grameen public payphone aimed at connecting rural areas of Bangladesh through the provision of public shared-access, where the entrepreneurs provide telephone services to local communities for a fee. The project is implemented by a partnership of the GSM network operator and stationary phones in the villages owned and operated by local entrepreneurs (Cohen, 2001). The franchise model is not widely deployed in implementing ICT projects due to the low level of ICT literacy and low income of the rural community. It is rare to find an entrepreneur with both the skills and financial capacity to operate ICT projects in rural areas. It is obvious that providing connectivity to rural areas is not financially viable to commercial operators. Therefore, government intervention is required for rural connectivity viability. This requirement scenario resulted into the Public-Private Partnership (PPP) model gaining popularity, especially in developing countries, in a situation when a government prioritized rural connectivity.

Public-Private Partnership is collaboration between the public sector such as the government and the private sector to implement projects. In this type of partnership, governments have been intervening by providing financial support in terms of subsidies, often from universal access funds initiatives. While PPPs have the potential to run investments in rural areas, it has been experienced that many developing countries do not have enough administrative and regulatory capacities to run PPP projects efficiently. A typical example is vandalization or poor maintenance of equipments especially those intended for ICT projects. This problem is also partly attributed to lack of beneficiary sense of ownership and inclusion (Spio-garbrah, 2010). This shortcoming was taken as an opportunity to involve beneficiaries of the project in the PPP model, which eventually lead to the Public-Private Peoples Partnership (PPPP) model, sometimes abbreviated as 4Ps.

Public-Private Peoples Partnership is defined as a strategic cooperative relationship between the public sector, private sector and the community (people) who agree to share the responsibility for achieving some specific goals (Siochrú & Girard, 2005; Spio-garbrah, 2010). The partnership emphasizes greater involvement of the communities that will eventually benefit from the outcome of the cooperative relationship. The PPPP model is based on the concept that for projects – especially in the rural areas – to be sustainable, the beneficiaries must feel a sense of ownership and inclusion (Spio-garbrah, 2010). In a PPPP, the ownership of the activity under cooperation such as a project is shared. The heart of a PPPP is therefore sharing of risks and benefits. ICT projects that are implemented in collaboration with the community they serve are usually sustainable. This is evident in the winning projects which were selected as the most successful community-based rural ICT projects in the final report of the Commonwealth African Rural Connectivity Initiative (COMARCI). All of the selected projects were developed in partnership with the community they serve (Calindi *et al.*, 2008; Spio-garbrah, 2010). Therefore, such a selection supports the recommendation that a PPPP is a suitable formula for implementation of projects that are unlikely to be profitable in rural areas if owned and managed either by the public sector alone, the private sector alone or a combination of public and private sector partners (Spio-garbrah, 2010). The schematic diagram of the PPPP model is shown in Figure 1.

Figure 1: Schematic Diagram of Public-Private Peoples Partnership (PPPP)

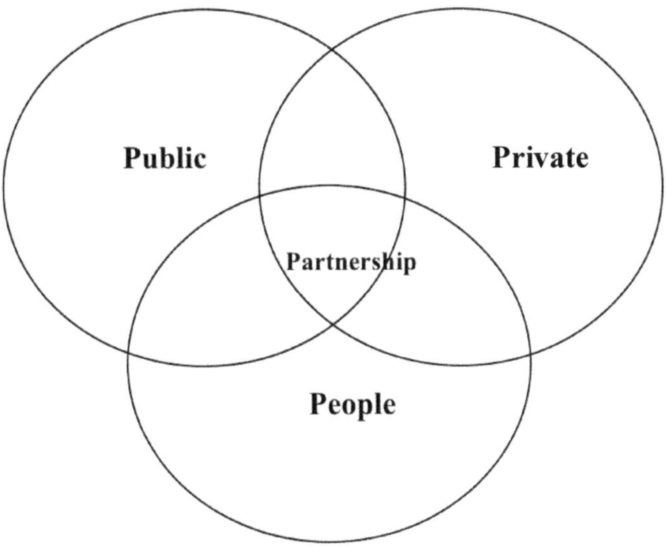

The rest of this paper is organized as follows: Section 2 presents an overview on how to implement sustainable projects. Three case studies of best practices for sustainable project implementation based on PPPP model are presented in order to understand role of different actors and how collaboration/partnership takes place. Section 3 examines the readiness of Tanzania to provide broadband rural connectivity in terms of availability of ICT infrastructure and institutional frameworks (policies, legislations (Acts) and regulations) supporting rural connectivity in the country. With the existing

ICT infrastructures, institutional frameworks and experience from selected best practice projects implementation, a sustainable broadband rural connectivity model adapting the Public Private People's Partnership (PPPP or 4Ps) implementation strategy for Tanzanian context is proposed in section 4. Section 5 carries the conclusion.

2. Sustainable Implementation of ICT Project in Rural Areas

The challenging environments of rural areas result into lack or limited ICT infrastructures, especially the broadband connectivity. In addition, the common models (donor-funded, franchising and PPP) used to implement ICT-based projects in rural areas have shortcomings that lead to unsustainable ICT projects, as explained in section 1. From the literature, the Public Private Peoples Partnership (PPPP) is recommended as a sustainable model for implementation of ICT-based projects in rural areas (Spio-garbrah, 2010; Calindi *et al.*, 2008; Roman, 2009). Also, it has been noted that partnership with the community to be served is essential for the project´s success and sustainability (Calindi *et al.*, 2008; Roman, 2009). However, the PPPP concept and its implementation is still in an infant stage (Spio-garbrah, 2010). Therefore, this paper aims at adapting the PPPP model and proposing its implementation strategy in the Tanzanian context with the main goal of attaining sustainable broadband connectivity in the rural areas of Tanzania. The proposed PPPP model implementation strategy for broadband connectivity in Tanzania can be generalized to other developing countries, because their respective rural areas usually pose similar characteristics with regard to ICT infrastructure development. The following three projects: rural wireless broadband networks in Peru, rural broadband connectivity project in Dominican Republic and sanitary intervention project in Nigeria, were selected as examples of best practices in implementation of the PPPP model, in order to understand the role of different actors and how collaboration/partnership takes place.

The Rural Wireless Broadband Network in Chancay-Huaral Valley District in Peru

The Chancay-Huaral Valley is a coastal district of Peru with many small farms. Farmers of Huaral were unable to capitalize on the great economic potential of their fertile land, abundant water and proximity to the nearby markets within Peru. A major challenge has been farmers' inability to adjust agricultural production to market fluctuations due to poor communications. Poor communications has also resulted into inefficient management of the river waters for irrigation (Saravia, 2005).

A rural wireless broadband network was established to make agricultural information available to farmers. The specific objectives were: (1) To train farmers in the effective use of agricultural information, (2) To develop an agricultural information system that efficiently provides information via the internet to the farmers, (3) To strengthen local capacity for obtaining, distributing and using agricultural information (Saravia, 2005). The project deployed a wireless network that connects 13 telecenters. The project has been deployed with active participation of the local farmers' association, responsible for management of water and irrigation. Technical assistance has been provided by a Non-Governmental Organization (NGO) called CEPES (the Peruvian Center of Social Studies / the Centro Peruano de Estudios Sociales). The NGO provided ICT training to young people who later took ICT jobs in the project (Saravia, 2005). A remarkable strength that provides sustainability in this project is the collaboration climate that has been created. Existing institutions in the valley pull together their forces and resources to plan and execute this project. Services offered in this project were the agricultural information via internet and Voice over Internet Protocol (VoIP). The VoIP service was not a target in the initial project planning; however, it later came up as a specific demand from project beneficiaries. This shows that the local community was pro-active in maximizing the project capabilities.

Management of the project was divided into two parts: management of the services that the project is providing and management of the equipment and the physical aspects of the network. Service management was taken care of by administrators of the thirteen communication centres, who have been trained for that. On the other hand, the CEPES technical team handled management of the equipment, configuration, maintenance and technical support. Twelve local people were trained to use the network, to identify connection errors, routine maintenance, to manage, configure and administer the network. Upon completion of their training, they were expected to take charge of network administration tasks from CEPES. There was also a plan for the project's economic sustainability. It was planned that revenue from the internet and telephone services will be used to cover costs of interconnection with the public network and for paying technicians responsible for network maintenance and technical supports in each location.

Rural Broadband Connectivity Project in Dominican Republic

INDOTEL, the Dominican Republic communications regulatory authority launched the rural broadband connectivity project as part of the government's e-Dominicana strategy in 2007. The project objectives were to provide telephone services through public call centers and broadband internet service through internet cafes to 508 localities throughout the country (Roman, 2009). This project also aimed at providing training to both end users and entrepreneurs in the use of the telephones and computers as well as in managing public call centres and cyber cafés. The project included a program to develop web pages with important information about each community, such as location, how to reach it, tourist attractions and products made by the local community. In order to promote entrepreneurship, the Internet access and public call centres were encouraged to be owned and managed by local entrepreneurs.

The project implementation started by establishing the status of telecommunications infrastructure in the area and consultations were made to all stakeholders in order to secure their support and involvement in the project. It was established that there were existing small entrepreneurs who use satellite and wireless technologies to install local telecenters, cyber cafes and public call centres, where the local population pay to use the services. The consultation exercise involved stakeholders such as public institutions and local entities, telecommunication operators, service providers and NGOs.

Establishing contacts with civil society agencies and NGOs was a strategic move, since most of them consider internet access as a working tool and would use it to communicate with their distant offices or staff located in rural areas. For this reason, rural broadband connectivity projects are attractive to civil society agencies and NGOs. Before launching the full scale project, the regulator did a pilot implementation in a small community to confirm whether the rural broadband connectivity project was economically and technically viable (Roman, 2009).

In the Dominican Republic, the rural broadband project was financed by using the Universal Access Funds (UAF) through tender processes supervised by the regulator. In this process, potential investors (telecommunication operator companies) are given a certain time to prepare their bids which are evaluated according to tender procedures. The company with a bid that meets all the technical specifications and asks for the least amount of subsidy from the fund is awarded the project to carry out commercial network roll out (Roman, 2009). In this case study, the regulator played a vital role in ensuring provision of rural connectivity.

Sanitary Intervention Project in Nigeria

This was a project aimed at finding a long-term solution to finance a sanitary intervention project. The mission was to promote safe sanitary and hygiene practices through hygiene education and provision of public convenience facilities that are modern, functional and well maintained (Asabia, 2009).

The target areas for provision of sanitary convenience facilities were motor parks, markets, open spaces, central business areas, commuter points and high-density areas. The model adopted to finance sanitary intervention was called public-social private partnership (Asabia, 2009). This is basically a 4Ps model where the unmentioned people's P is represented by the social component of the model. Roles and responsibilities of partnership in the sanitary intervention project were mentioned as follows (Asabia, 2009): State and local government were responsible to provide sites to locate the public convenience facilities and to provide an enabling environment for project implementation. The facilities construction costs were financed by the private sector; an NGO. The NGO took lead in engaging local community and other stakeholders located in the sites earmarked for construction of public conveniences to ensure support and ownership of the project. Community and other stakeholders were educated about basic health and hygiene requirements and the link between diseases and unsafe sanitary practices with the ultimate aim of bringing about behavioural change. To ensure project sustainability, the NGO runs and maintains the facility for an interim period of two years, after which a memorandum of understanding is signed, to enable the community or stakeholders in the target area to take over the management and ownership of the facility through a governing council comprising of key stakeholder representatives. The facilities are operated on a pay per use system. Revenue generated from usage is used to pay cleaning staff wages and to cover maintenance costs.

There are four (4) lessons that can be drawn from the projects presented as case studies of the PPPP model for project implementation. The first lesson learned is that: the presence of a governmental can make a project move fast as in the case of the Dominican Republic, where the regulator took a lead in all the steps required for a rural broadband project to take off viably. However, it is not a rule of thumb that the government/regulators are the ones to lead the PPPP initiatives, any of the partnership stakeholders can lead, especially the people (local community or local entrepreneurs), because, they are the ones who properly know their needs. This was very evident in Peru's and Nigeria's projects. Another lesson learned is the importance of local community participation in all project phases in order to deliver relevant and useful services. This aspect is more evident in the case study from Peru, where the local community was able to demand relevant services. On the other hand, all case study projects demonstrated the usefulness of nurturing project ownership by the local communities/local entrepreneurs for sustainability.

3. Readiness of Tanzania to Deploy PPPP Model for Broadband Rural Connectivity

The following section investigates the availability of supporting environments for rural connectivity, such as the availability of telecommunication infrastructures, institutional framework (policies, regulations, strategies and legislations) and initiatives for infrastructure development, which can be used to gauge readiness of Tanzania to deploy PPPP model for broadband rural connectivity.

Telecommunication Infrastructures

The Tanzania Communication Regulatory Authority (TCRA) is responsible for licensing and enforcing license conditions of broadcasting, postal, and telecommunication operators, manage radio frequency spectrum and establish standards for regulated goods and services. In addition to the mentioned responsibilities, TCRA requires all operators to expand their services up to rural areas in their license obligations. By the year 2011, TCRA had licensed two wired operators, Tanzania Telecommunication Company Limited (TTCL) and Zanzibar Telecommunication Company Limited (Zantel) to provide fixed-line telecommunication services, network services and facilities throughout the country (Tanzania mainland and Zanzibar). The wireless mobile communication technology entered the Tanzanian market in 1994, when the then Mobitel Company, currently branded as Tigo, was first registered as the only privately owned wireless mobile network operator. Currently there are seven wireless mobile operators, namely Tigo, Vodacom, Zain, TTCL, Zantel, Benson and Sasatel. Their respective quarterly (Jan - March, 2011) subscription market share is shown in Figure 2.

Network coverage of fixed-line network operators is mainly up to levels of regional or district headquarters. Apart from the wired network, the wireless infrastructures are also in place from the mobile wireless cellular networks operators, which provide voice as well as broadband data and internet (multimedia) services. With wireless operators, coverage for voice services is almost countrywide while for broadband multimedia services, the coverage is in the urban areas, basically in cities. Furthermore, the TCRA which is responsible for allocating radio frequency to telecommunication networks and ICT services operators, has strategically reserved the extended GSM spectrum for operators aiming to deploy broadband network coverage in suburban and rural areas of Tanzania. So far there is an operator, called Rural NetCO, which has been allocated the extended GSM spectrum and is dedicated to extending coverage of broadband mobile wireless networks to rural areas in the country. This network is based on the third generation

(3G) Universal Mobile Telecommunication Systems (UMTS) at 900MHz frequency band. It is a shared network, in which its design strategy is to re-use existing infrastructures such as sharing network base station sites with other telecommunication operators. During the time of writing this paper, the network was still under development. Therefore, with the current status of both wired and wireless technologies, rural areas of Tanzania are still unconnected with regards to broadband network capacity.

Figure 2: Quarterly Operator's Subscriptions Market Shares (January-March, 2011)

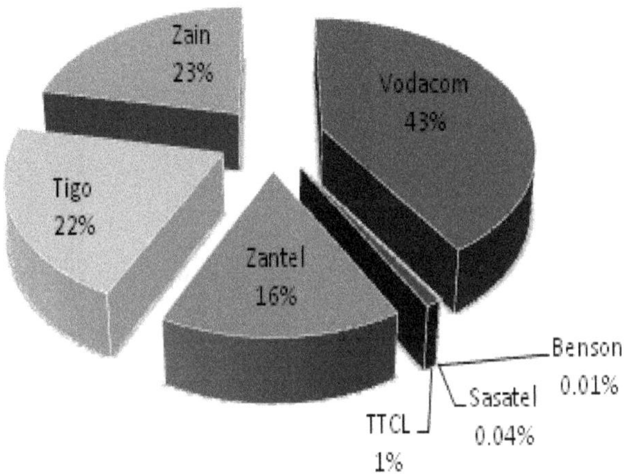

Initiatives for Broadband Infrastructure Development in Tanzania

There are efforts in Tanzania that aim to develop broadband ICT infrastructures. A typical example of such efforts is the National ICT Broadband backbone (NICTBB) infrastructure project. This is a construction of a terrestrial national-wide ICT backbone by using optic fibre cable technology to cover all regions and district headquarters in Tanzania mainland and Zanzibar. The implementation strategy of the national ICT backbone project is to use the existing networks segments from multiple utility companies such as Tanzania Electric Supply Company (TANESCO), Tanzania Railways Corporation (TRC), Songo Songo Gas Company (SONGAS), Tanzania Zambia Railways Authority (TAZARA) and Tanzania Telecommunication Company Limited (TTCL) as shown in Figure 3. The national ICT backbone aims to establish a carrier of carriers' network, which can be leased to network services or content providers. In addition, the backbone is aimed to provide cross border connectivity to the neighbouring countries: Kenya, Uganda,

Rwanda, Burundi, Democratic republic of Congo (DRC), Zambia, Malawi and Mozambique. Phase 1 of the NICTBB project which includes utilization of the existing optic fibre cable over pylons owned by TANESCO and construction of new direct buried fibre system along routes of missing links, was completed in April, 2010.

Figure 3: The National ICT Backbone in Tanzania

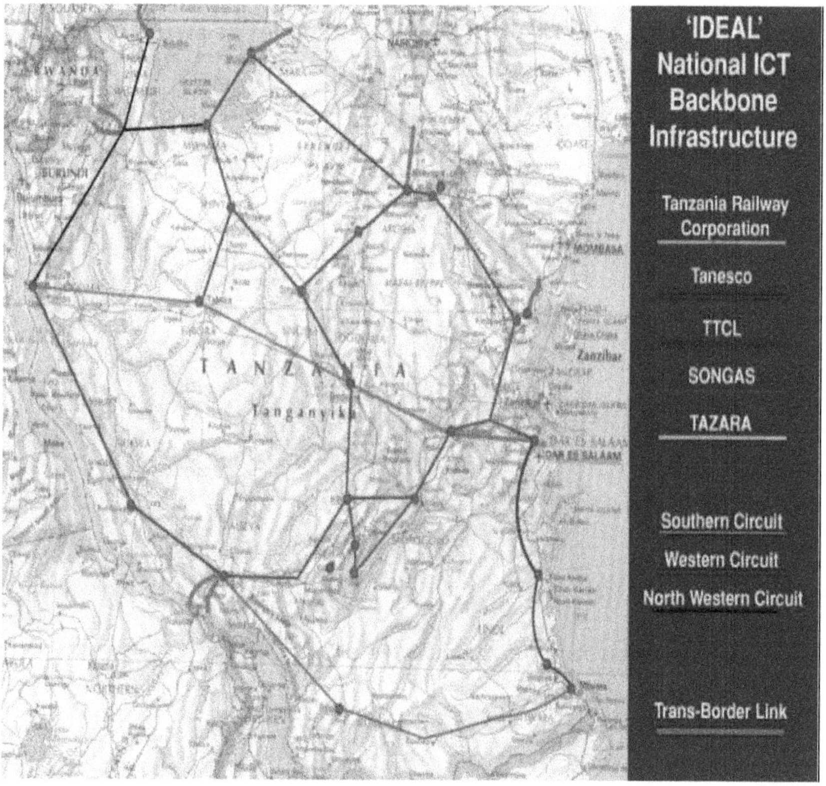

Source: Pehrson & Ngwira (2006)

Tanzania is also connected to the rest of the world by using submarine cables, in addition to satellite systems. Examples of such submarine cables are the SEACOM and the Eastern Africa Submarine Cable System (EASSY) along the east African coast. The SEACOM cable was launched on 23rd July 2009 and has a capacity of 1.28Tb/s (terabits per second). EASSY has a capacity of 1.4 Tbps and was launched on 7th April, 2010. The current status (2012) of broadband infrastructure, both terrestrial (NICTBB) and submarine cables in Tanzania is shown in Figure 4.

Figure 4: Tanzania national ICT backbone and Submarine Cables

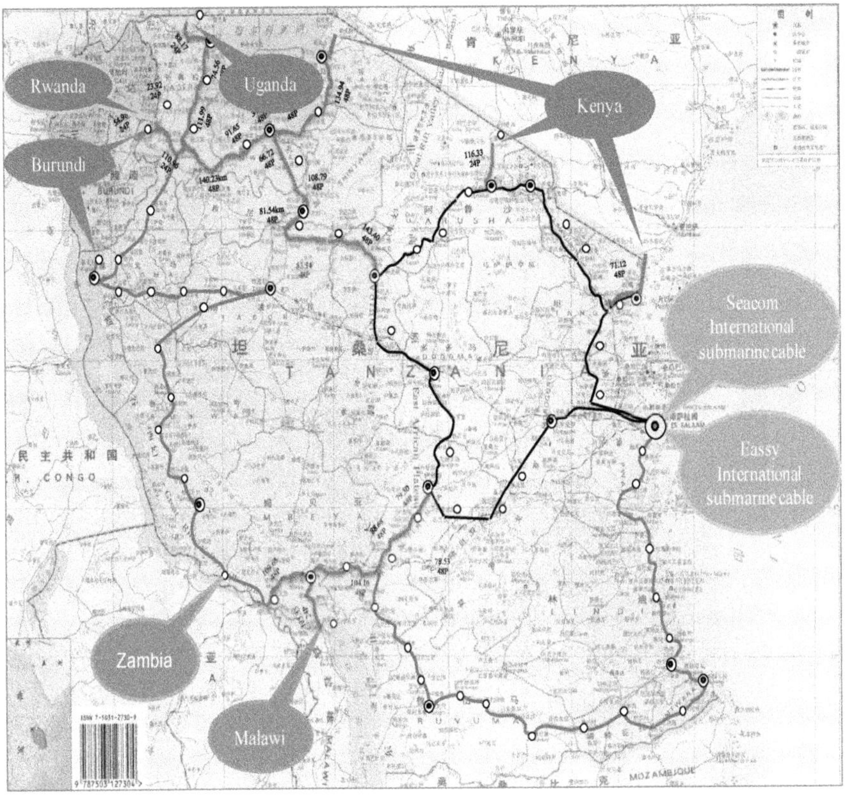

Source: Ministry of Communications, Science and Technology (MCST), Tanzania.

Institutional Frameworks

This section explores institutional frameworks such as policies, regulations, legislations and strategies which support rural connectivity in Tanzania. Existence of such frameworks is a useful tool to enforce and foster implementation of rural connectivity projects.

a. Tanzania National Development Vision 2025

The national development vision aims at a Tanzania of 2025 to be a nation imbued with five main attributes: (1) High quality livelihood (2) Peace, stability and unity (3) Good governance (4) A well educated and learning society (5) A competitive economy capable of producing sustainable growth and shared benefits. The objective of this development vision is to awaken, co-ordinate and direct people's efforts, minds and national resources towards the five main attributes. Upon achievement of the five attributes, Tanzania is envisioned to be an active participant in the global competitive economy of the 21st century, which is characterized by advanced technology, high productivity, modern and efficient transport and communication infrastructure with highly skilled and innovative manpower (United Republic of Tanzania, 2000).

b. National ICT Policy

In 2002, Tanzania set off a multi-stakeholder ICT policy development initiative that led to the development of a national ICT policy and its adoption by the Government in 2003. The policy is currently (2011) under review for improvement. The policy articulates ten focus areas drawn from the aspirations of Tanzania's Vision 2025. One of the focus areas is the ICT infrastructure, with an objective of establishing mechanisms that will result in least cost access to bandwidth for institutions or individuals in Tanzania. The National ICT Policy stipulates that, "Tanzania should have a universally accessible broadband infrastructure and ICT solutions that enhance sustainable socio-economic development and accelerate poverty reduction national-wide" (Ministry of Communications and Transport, 2003). To achieve this objective, the Government is committed to support, through incentives and directives, bona fide institutions actively involved in the development and application of ICT infrastructure and services (Ministry of Communication and Transport, 2003). Another focus area of ICT policy is the universal access, where the Government is committed to reduce the ICT access gap between the rural and the urban areas by activating the universal communications access fund, offering special incentives to investors in rural ICT provisions, supporting the construction of rural telecentres and involving local government authorities in ICT utilization and promotion (Ministry of Communications and Transport, 2003). As part of the implementation of the national ICT policy, Tanzania embarked on an initiative for development of an open national ICT backbone network in 2005.

c. The National Strategy for Growth and Reduction of Poverty (NSGRP)

Introduced in 2005, this strategy which is popularly known as MKUKUTA in Swahili, was revised in 2010 into MKUKUTA II. Among other objectives, the strategy aims to promote the use of PPP model for developing and operating ICT infrastructures. It also looks for efforts to support increased access and application of ICT which will eventually increase productivity in government, business, education and Small To Medium Enterprises (SMEs) development (NSGRP, 2005; NSGRP II, 2010).

d. National Rural Development Strategy (RDS)

The strategy came into existence in the year 2001 with the aim to promote introduction of ICT in rural areas through developing telecentres. The telecentres are responsible for providing ICT services such as voice, fax, e-mail, internet access, distance education, telemedicine, news distribution, access to information on market and weather conditions (RDS, 2001).

e. Universal Communications Service Act 2006

The Act established a fund responsible for promoting ICTs in rural and underserved urban areas by subsidizing operators investing in rural areas (UCS-Act Tz, 2006; Pehrson & Ngwira, 2006). The fund receives contributions from TCRA, development partners and telecommunication operators who contribute 0.3% from their annual growth turn over.

f. Converged Regulatory and Licensing Regime

In 2005, TCRA introduced a converged licensing framework, which is a technology- and service - neutral framework. The converged framework ensures efficient utilization of network resources, in such a way that an individual network can be used to provide a broad range of ICT services, which will eventually lead to address market and technological developments. The converged licensing regime allows leasing of excess capacity of communications infrastructures owned by utility companies in order to provide communication services to customers. Moreover, it provides a framework for all communication service providers to build a nationwide backhaul and interconnect with each other.

In 2005, Tanzania prepared different communication regulations which in one way or another support provision of broadband connectivity. Regulations relevant to broadband connectivity are the Tanzania communication regulations for: broadband services, quality of service, access and facilities, radio communication and frequency spectrum, and interconnection.

Table 1: ICT Initiatives for Education

Initiative (projects)	Description
Tanzania beyond Tomorrow	An e-learning initiative launched by MoEVT in partnership with technology companies (Accenture, Intel, Microsoft and Cisco) and NGOs (NetHope, AMREF, World Vision) aims at integrating ICT in the teaching and learning processes.
TanSSe-L (CoICT-UDSM)	The project is under the College of Information and Communication Technology (CoICT), University of Dar es Salaam. It aims at providing e-learning services to rural secondary schools. It has three pillars: interactive learning management system, e-learning contents for self learning and connectivity solution.
The e-School Forum	Nine task forces were formed, focusing on key areas for ICT in secondary education (1) ICT infrastructure development (2) technical resources, (3) student management (4) content and curriculum development (5) e-learning (6) sensitization (7) human resources (8) programme co-ordination and (9) funding. At the time of writing this paper, the e-School programme proposal was still under review by the MoEVT.
Science, Technology and Higher Education Program (STHEP).	It is a programme under the MoEVT and the Ministry of Communication Science and Technology (MCST) that aims at improving development of human capital in the areas of science and technology and to create a knowledge based economy. This program focuses on National Research and Education Network (NREN), Education Management Information system (EMIS), e-Library and e-Learning.
Zain, Build a Nation project	670 schools in Tanzania have benefited with textbooks or educational tools such as computers provided by the then Zain, now Airtel mobile network operator.
Bridge IT project	The project is implemented under the management of International Youth Foundation. It is about the use of mobile phones to teach Maths and Science in class 5 and 6. It is operational in 150 primary schools. Development of course materials is done by Pearson Foundation, hosting of the course materials is by Vodacom. Delivery of the course materials is through Nokia phones to television sets in the classrooms. Contents assist teachers in the classrooms.

continued on next page

Table 1 continued

Initiative (projects)	Description
Computer for Schools Project	Barclays bank and Digital Links International company formed a partnership to spur the growth of ICT in schools across three countries in East Africa (Tanzania, Uganda, and Kenya). The project sets a target to place 10,000 computers in approximately 500 schools. The implementation strategy is through collaborative partnerships with organizations in each country. For Tanzania, the project is implemented by Tanzania Education Authority (TEA), Tanzania Commission of Science and Technology (COSTECH), and Mkombozi centre for street children.
Distance Learning Education Services (DILES) (IICD Supported)	The project develops teaching and learning materials for secondary schools. These resources are available online (http://www.diles.or.tz).

g. ICT for Education Projects

In Tanzania, there are number of pilot projects aimed at integrating ICT in the education system. The projects are currently challenged by lack of connectivity to make them more beneficial. Therefore, most of the existing ICT for education initiatives aim at providing computers to schools, and sometimes training to teachers and students. The existing projects on ICT for education are formed under different collaboration models; the most common model being a Public-Private Partnership (PPP), which is a collaboration between the Ministry of Education and Vocational Training (MoEVT) with technology companies. Another model is the donor funded model, where the efforts are from either the private or public sector to support schools by providing computers or capacity building through training. Table 1 provides a brief description of indicative sample projects. The list is not exhaustive.

The ICT for education initiatives summarized in Table 1, illustrates that Tanzania has a number of ICT for education initiatives running concurrently. Many of these initiatives are pilot projects that are not well documented with no clear strategic plan for their implementation and there is no centralized coordination. The missing coordination and strategy for implementation to the many ICT for education initiatives implies that opportunities to combine, or associate related projects are missed, hence duplication, lack of experience sharing, and a potential for ineffective use of resources and opportunities is inevitable. Tanzania is currently (2011-2012) preparing a

National School Connectivity Plan (NSCP) under the Ministry of communication, science and technology in collaboration with International Telecommunication Union (ITU). The NSCP aims at providing an ICT broadband infrastructure master plan to facilitate implementation of broadband connectivity solution for primary and secondary schools as well as to tertiary education. Among other targets, the NSCP intends to address the lack of coordination and absence of a single ICT for education implementation strategy.

This section presented the existence of telecommunication infrastructures, institutional frameworks and initiatives for broadband connectivity in the country and ICT for education projects. Collectively, all these efforts demonstrate readiness of Tanzania to provide rural connectivity. The following section proposes implementation strategies in order to build sustainable broadband rural connectivity in Tanzania.

4. The Proposed Model for Provision of Sustainable Broadband Rural Connectivity

Availability of broadband infrastructures, institutional frameworks, ICT for education projects and the governmental will are the potential enabling tools for PPPP implementation in Tanzania. Having the tools and knowledge from the best practice projects implemented based on PPPP model, a sustainable model for broadband rural connectivity suitable for the Tanzanian context is proposed as shown in Figure 5. Roles of the different actors in the model are explained in the forthcoming sections.

Public Sector

The public sector can be made up of the communication regulatory authority and/or the Ministry responsible for communications, science and technology. The main roles of the public sector are:

- To create and enforce enabling policy and regulatory frameworks for PPPP.
- To train the local community in basic computer literacy, Internet use as well as services and applications delivered by broadband networks.
- To enforce as well as contribute the subsidy funding for universal communications access fund to private sectors in order to facilitate ICT infrastructure and service deployment to rural areas.
- To encourage the private sector to rollout commercial networks in rural areas.
- To coordinate formation of the PPPP.

Figure 5: The PPPP Model of Rural Broadband Connectivity in Tanzania

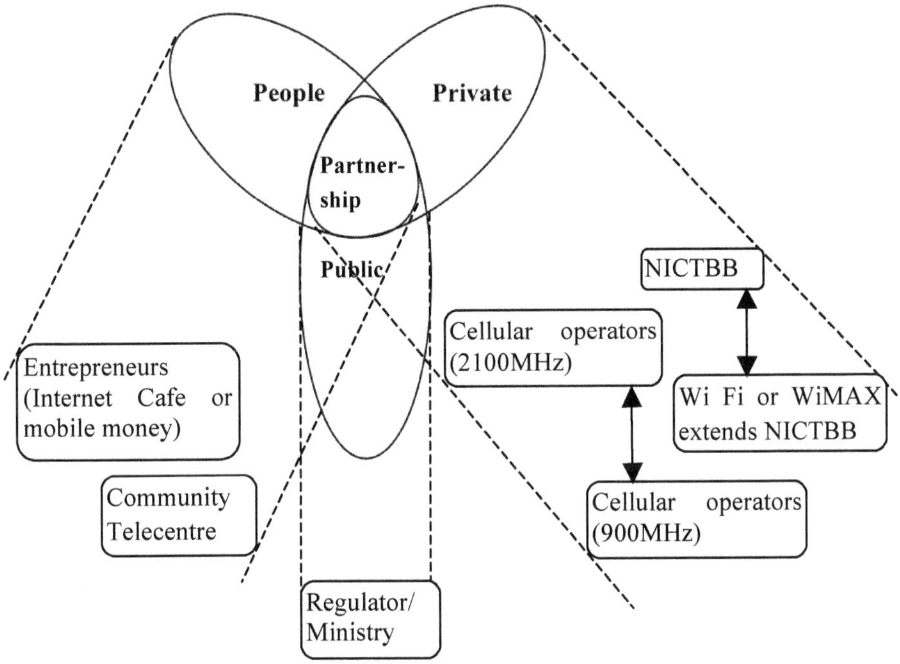

Private Sector

The private sector in this context is proposed to have two (2) tiers; the upper tier also known as the backbone tier and the lower tier known as the access network tier. The architecture of the private sector in the Tanzanian PPPP model is shown in Figure 6. The upper tier (backbone tier) is composed of cellular mobile operators. These are the operators that have wide coverage in the urban areas, but their networks are not extended to reach rural areas, due to the high cost associated with network roll out and maintenance in rural areas. Another candidate for the backbone tier is an operator managing the NICTBB infrastructure. The objective of the backbone tier is to provide local and international connections to the access network tier, which is made up of operators who have infrastructures in rural areas. The access network tier is responsible to provide broadband network capacity in the rural areas. In this context, the access network tier can be made up of Wireless Fidelity (WiFi) or Worldwide Interoperability for Microwave Access (WiMAX) wireless operators extending the coverage of the NICTBB. The access network tier can as well be made up of a wireless cellular mobile operator of 3G broadband access network at 900MHz frequency band to extend coverage of the existing 3G at 2100MHz broadband mobile wireless network.

Figure 6: Two Tiers of Private Sector in the PPPP Model for rural connectivity in Tanzania

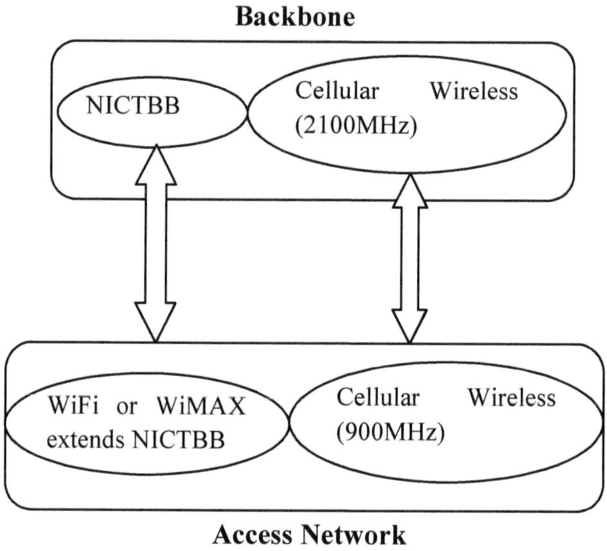

Different roles of the two tiers are as follows:

Backbone Tier

- Provide local and international connections to the access network tier
- Develop and offer value added services
- Create environment for franchise business model with access network tier
- Train the access network operators for potential business opportunities
- Train the local community in basic computer literacy, Internet use as well as services and applications delivered by broadband networks.

Access Network Tier

- Roll out the commercial broadband access network infrastructure
- Develop and offer value added services
- Create environment for franchise business model with local entrepreneurs

- Train local entrepreneurs for potential business opportunities
- Train the local community in basic computer literacy, Internet use as well as services and applications delivered by broadband networks.

People´s Sector

The people or local community can be the local government or management responsible for a shared local ICT facility such as telecentres. Another potential local partners to represent the people's part are the existing entrepreneurs in rural communities who are already providing some forms of telecommunication services such as internet cafes or mobile money transfer to others within the community. The PPPP model can benefit from the ICT-based local entrepreneurs from their ICT literacy and experiences. Roles of the people's part in the partnership can be:

- Make in-kind contribution to set - up network, for example provide land, labour and site security.
- Train the local community in computers and Internet use.
- Strive for participation and local ownership of the rural broadband connectivity, which will lead to sustainability and service relevance.
- Demand and maximize use of the value added services.

Sustainability aspects of the proposed PPPP model for broadband rural connectivity in Tanzania are considered into two aspects: financial and the partnership (stakeholders working together) sustainability. In addition to the subsidies offered by the public sector and revenue collected from the main intended service to be offered, other value added services relevant to the local community can contribute to the rural connectivity project´s financial sustainability. Providing need-driven services that are affordable to the local community, which also inspire social-economic development at the community level will generate revenue that in turn contribute to the financial sustainability of the project.

The training component appears to be a role for all actors in the proposed PPPP model due to the fact that capacity building to the local community is essential to ensure sustainability of the project. People in the community have to understand the usefulness and potential of broadband Internet as well as of the services and applications that it can deliver. If the local community feels empowered by the broadband rural connectivity projects, they will participate more actively in seeking ways to keep it running. Capacity building by formal training is not the only ingredient for sustainability. Awareness creation to the community about services to be provided by the broadband network and how to access and use them can also add to the sustainability of the rural broadband connectivity. Therefore, it is necessary for the people to be trained to become customers of the service and thereby ensure the project's sustainability. Training for potential business opportunities between backbone tier, access network tier and local entrepreneurs is essential in order to foster business partnership climate. In order to enhance sustainability, the partnership should strive to nurture local community inclusion, involvement and ownership throughout all the implementation phases of rural broadband connectivity projects.

Participatory action research is a practical approach which involves all participants affected by the issue under study (Rydhagen, 2002). Active participation of actors, which can be brought about by the participatory approach, strengthens partnership and trust among the stakeholders. Due to the requirement of PPPP model to maintain the strategic partnership in all phases and throughout the project, the participatory approach is recommended in the process of nurturing partnerships, because it can build a climate where rural communities feel a sense of inclusion and ownership. Furthermore, having the existing policies, legislations, strategies and regulatory framework supporting rural connectivity will protect, promote and support its development and existence, hence its sustainability.

5. Conclusion

This paper has identified the availability of supporting and enabling tools such as broadband connectivity, Integration of ICT in the educational system, governmental will and institutional frameworks, favourable for adopting PPPP model for rural broadband connectivity in Tanzania. By having such tools and the supporting environments, a PPPP model for sustainable rural broadband connectivity implementation in Tanzania has been proposed. The Government of Tanzania through its Ministry of Communication, Science and Technology in collaboration with International Telecommunication Union (ITU) are formulating the national school connectivity plan (NSCP). The objective of the NSCP is to develop a nation-wide master plan for providing broadband connectivity to all schools in Tanzania. The PPPP model for rural broadband connectivity proposed in this paper can be a very useful input to the NSCP.

References

Asabia, A. (2009), 'Presentation on public, private and people partnership model for sanitation at the 6th earth watch conference on water and sanitation 2008', in *International NGO Journal*, 4(8): 362-367.

Calindi, V., Tongia, R., Ross, P., Pulkkinen, J., Akwetey, L. and Field, D. (2008), 'The Commonwealth African Rural Connectivity Report', in *Commonwealth African Rural Connectivity Initiative (COMARCI).*

Cohen, N. (2001), 'What Works: Grameen Telecom's Village Phones', in *A Digital Dividend Study by the World Resources Institute.*

Jhunjhunwala, A., Ramachandran, A. and Bandyopadhyay, A. (2004), 'n-logue: the story of a rural service provider in India', in *The Journal of Community Informatics,* 1(1): 30-38.

NSGRP (2005), 'The United Republic of Tanzania National Strategy for Growth and Reduction of Poverty (NSGRP)', United Republic of Tanzania, Vice President´s Office, Dar es Salaam.

NSGRP II (2010), 'National Strategy for Growth and Reduction of Poverty II', United Republic of Tanzania, Ministry of Finance and Economic Affairs, Dar es Salaam .

Paul, J. (2004), 'What works: n-Logue´s rural connectivity model: deploying wirelessly-connected internet kiosks in villages throughout India', Washington, DC: World Resources Institute. Available at: http://www.digitaldividend.org/pdf/nlogue.pdf

Pehrson, B. and Ngwira, M. (2006), *Optical Fibre for Education and Research Networks in Eastern and Southern Africa,* University of Malawi. Available: http://www.idrc.ca/uploads/user-S/11083295861PAREN_Reportv15.doc

RDS (2001), 'Rural Development Strategy (RDS)', Prime Minister`s Office, United Republic of Tanzania, Dar es Salaam.

Roman, E. S. (2009), 'Bringing broadband access to rural areas: a step-by-step approach for regulators, policy makers and universal access program administrators: the experience of the Dominican Republic', in *9th Global Symposium for Regulators (GSR),* 10 - 12 November, Beirut, Lebanon.

Rydhagen, B. (2002), 'Feminist Sanitary engineering as a participatory alternative in South Africa and Sweden', Doctoral Dissertation Series Number: 2002:06, Blekinge Institute of Technology.

Saravia, M. (2005), 'Rural telecommunication networks in Peru, case studies 3 and 4 of innovative technologies and community ownership: a new model of ICT access for the rural poor', in *A report for the United Nations Development Programme (UNDP), Series: Making ICT Work for the Poor,* 99-141.

Siochrú, S. Ó. (2005), 'Community ownership of ICTs: new possibilities for poor communities', *WSIS Briefing Paper*, 1-6.

Siochrú, S. Ó. and Girard, B. (2005), 'Community-based networks and innovative technologies: new models to serve and empower the poor', *A report for the United Nations Development Programme (UNDP), Series: Making ICT Work for the Poor*, 185.

Spio-garbrah, E. (2010), 'Driving rural connections: leveraging public-private-people's partnerships to improve rural connectivity and adopting the 4P approach to develop, promote and accelerate ICT connectivity in the developing world', in *Mobile World Congress 2010, Special Report From Barcelona*, (4): 30 - 38.

Ministry of Communications and Transport, The United Republic of Tanzania (2003), 'National Information and Communications Technologies Policy', Available at: http://www.tanzania.go.tz/pdf/ictpolicy.pdf

UCS-ActTz (2006), 'Universal Communication Service Act', United Republic of Tanzania, Vice President's Office, Dar es Salaam.

United Republic of Tanzania (2000), 'Tanzania National Development Vision 2025'. Available at: http://www.tanzania.go.tz/vission_2025f.html

Acknowledgement

Authors are grateful to the Swedish International Development Agency (Sida) for sponsoring this study.

African Journal of Science, Technology,
Innovation and Development
Vol. 4, No. 2, 2012
pp. 173-187

Lithogeochemistry and Industrial Appraisal of Igbetti Marble, South Western Nigeria

Oluwatoyin O. Akinola[*] & Olusola A. Olaolorun[**]

Abstract

Mineralogical determinations from optical and X-ray diffraction studies show that the Igbetti marble body in southwestern Nigeria is composed of white and grey varieties, dolomite and calcite as the principal components of the two rocks. The white marble variety contains essentially dolomite (60%) and calcite (35%) while the grey variety contains dolomite (43%), calcite (35%), quartz (8%), tremolite (7%) and chlorite (4%). Major and trace elements composition using Atomic Absorption Spectrophotometry (AAS) and X-ray Fluorescence (XRF) respectively indicates that the white marble variety contains SiO_2 (ca. 0.11%), MgO (ca. 21.5%), CaO (ca. 40.7%) while Al_2O_3, Fe_2O_3 and MnO account for 0.02%, 0.02% and 0.01% respectively. The grey variety contains SiO_2 (ca. 0.33%), MgO (ca. 20.4%), CaO (ca. 42.4%). Other oxides: Al_2O_3, Fe_2O_3, Na_2O, K_2O and TiO_2 altogether account for less than 0.5%. Physical tests on both marble varieties show much similarities as their values are comparable. Values of apparent porosities (0.50% - 0.80%), bulk density (2.72-2.80 g/cc), compressive strength (89.56-91.50 Mpa), shear strength (13.28-13.50 Mpa),

[*] Department of Geology, Ekiti State University, Ado-Ekiti, Nigeria.
Email: oluwatoyinakinola@yahoo.com

[**] Department of Geology, Ekiti State University, Ado-Ekiti, Nigeria.
Email: solaolaolorun@gmail.com

tensile strength (3.79-3.94 Mpa), whiteness (75-86), specific gravity (2.68-2.79), pH (8.1-8.6) are within the limits for other known marble deposits within the country. An overview of economic evaluation shows that the dolomitic Igbetti marble is a very viable refractory raw materials for the steel plant, flux stone in iron smelting, manufacture of sheet glass, furnace lining and production of magnesia lime.

Keywords: Lithogeochemistry, Igbetti Marble, Dolomite, Refractory, Fluxstone, Nigeria.

JEL Classification: O10; O20; O30; O55.

1. Introduction

Marble is a major industrial raw material for the cement and construction companies in Nigeria where such industries are the primary consumers of most sedimentary carbonates like limestone and their metamorphosed products including dolomite. Others include the glass, ceramics and steel industries. Applications also exist in the chemical, environmental, and agricultural industries. Marble and dolomite are useful aggregates in civil engineering construction, particularly in structures requiring considerable strength and reinforcement. Scott and Durham (1984) and Dada (1993) identified about two hundred end uses of raw marble and their calcined products. Most of the economic marble deposits in Nigeria are associated with the schist belts of the basement complex, where they occur as lensoid bodies within the miogeosynclinal deposits. Notable among these deposits are the Igbetti, Igarra, Ubo, Ososo, Kwakuti, Jakura, Burum, Elebu, and Ukpilla Marbles. Probably the most well known of these bodies within the southwestern Nigeria is the Igbetti marble whose economic potentials have been highlighted in the work of Emofurieta and Ekuajemi (1995). However, the current investigation presents a combined systematic geological appraisal, petrographic features, geochemical properties, and assessment of physical and industrial properties to provide a comprehensive evaluation of the marble body.

2. Regional Geological setting

The Precambrian rocks of Nigeria lie within the Pan-African mobile belt, specifically between the West African and Congo Cratons (Figure 1). Rocks within this domain have been categorized into three broad groups viz., the migmatite-gneiss complex, the schist belts and the Pan African granitoids. (Figure 2). The migmatite gneiss complex has a long evolutionary history (Emofurieta and Ekuajemi, 1995) and displays chemical variations indicative of having been derived from heterogeneous progenitors (Elueze, 1982).The age of this suite is mainly between 2.8 and 2.0 Ga. However, older dates (3.0 Ga) have been recorded in some places (Dada *et al.*, 1996). The schist belts consists of essentially low-grade metasediments and metabasic rocks that outcrop in a series of distinctly N-S trending synformal troughs infolded into the crystalline migmatite-gneiss complex. The belts show distinctive petrological, structural and metallogenic characteristics, and are more prominent in the western half of the country. The schist belts have attracted a lot of interest and study because of gold, Banded Iron Formation (BIF), marble and other mineralization associated with them. The works of (Rahaman *et al.*, 1983) indicate a lower Proterozoic age for this deposit. Among the schist belts in southwestern Nigeria are the Iseyin, Ife-Ilesha, Egbe-Isanlu, Igarra and Lokoja (Rahaman, 1976; Odeyemi, 1988; Elueze, 1993; Annor *et al.*, 1996). The Igbetti marble occurs within the Iseyin-Oyan schist belt.

Figure 1: Map showing Nigeria within the Pan African province located between the West African and Congo Cratons

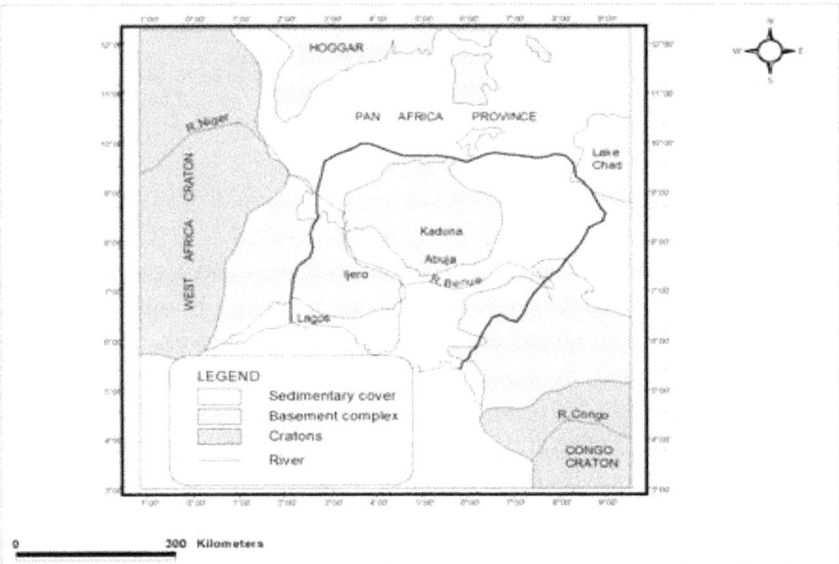

Figure 2: Generalized Geological Map of Nigeria showing the Basement Complex Rocks, Schist Belts, the Younger Granites and the Sedimentary Basins

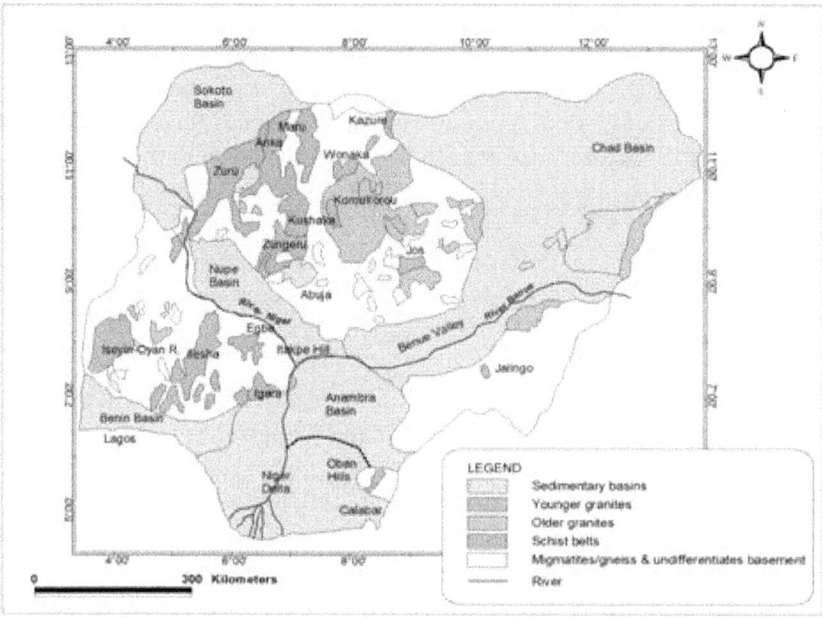

3. Field Relationships

Igbetti town is located at about 180 km NNE of Ibadan and about 60 km NW of Ilorin. The area lies between latitudes $8^{o}\ 34^{1}$ N to $8^{o}\ 53^{1}$ N and Longitudes $3^{o}\ 55^{1}$E to $4^{o}\ 15^{1}$E. The Igbetti area is dominated by gneisses, granite, amphibolite and metasediments including quartzite, quartz schist and marble (Figure 3). The marble occurs as N-S trending lenses delimited in the east by the porphyroblastic gneiss and in the west by the migmatite-gneiss complex. It also makes contact with the NE-SW trending quartz schist and outcrops distinctly in two areas characterized by low-lying physiographical features in the northern and southern parts of the study area. The main mining activity is located in the northern segment along Igbetti-Igboho road. The geologic contacts between the marble deposit and other lithologies are poorly exposed in most of the area. In the southern segment however, substantial part of the deposit is also exposed where River Yegun flows across the marble deposit. The carbonate rock occurs at a relatively shallow depth and is overlain by poorly consolidated gritty sands (Figure 4). The

Igbetti marble is mainly white in colour, but minor grey varieties also occur. It is essentially a fine-medium grained equigranular rock.

Figure 3: Geological map of Igbetti area

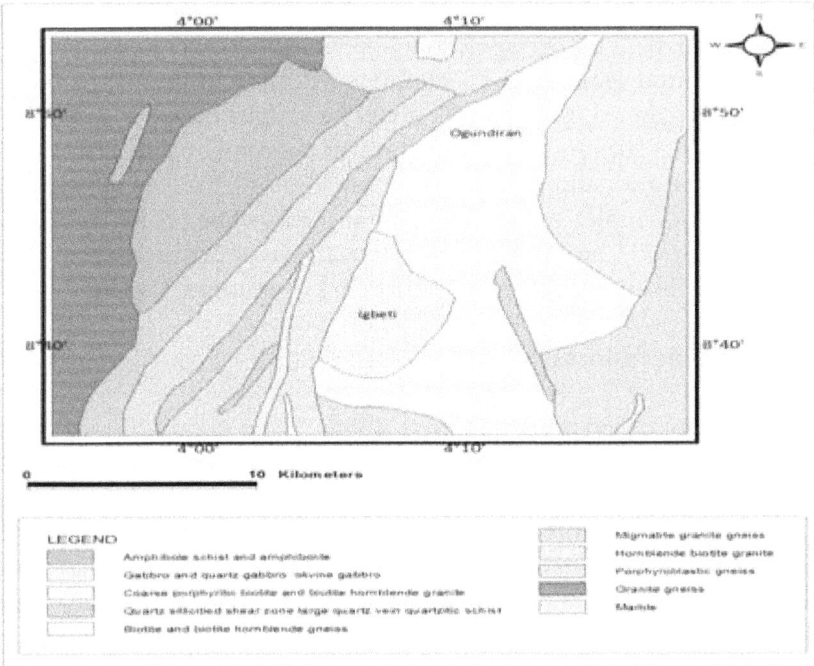

Source: Olayinka, *et al*. (2004)

Figure 4: Photograph showing exposure of the fine grained white Igbetti Marble at the mines with conspicuous block jointing

4. Sampling and methods

Ten representative samples each were collected along a vertical profile at ten (10)-meter interval from the surface exposed by mine excavations in the northern and southern quarries. Some isolated outcrops are also sampled to ensure consideration for all the textural varieties. Each sample was prepared into thin section for petrographic examination and another portion pulverized for chemical analysis. The resulting powder was loaded into a diffractometer and scanned from 0° to 60° under Fe-k alpha radiation 28kv, 8mA scanning rate 2° 20cm/min and time constant 4 seconds, (raise $4x10^{2}$ C.P.S). Mineralogical evaluations were based on X-ray diffraction through the powdery rock samples and petrographic analysis, while a combined X-Ray Fluorescence (XRF) and Atomic Absorption Spectrophotometry (AAS) were used for the chemical analysis at Activation Laboratories, Canada.

5. Petrographic features

Combined optical analysis (Figure 5, Table 1) and X-ray diffractograms (Figure 6a, Figure 6b) reveal that the carbonate bodies are composed of predominantly calcite and dolomite. However, the gray variety shows some traces of quartz, chlorite and tremolite. Petrographic analysis (Figure 5) indicates that the Igbetti marble is characteristically granoblastic in texture with fine to medium grained equidimensional crystals of calcite that exhibit rhombohedral cleavage and undulose extinction. The dolomite crystals are generally sub-angular, grayish in colour, with low birefringence. These two minerals alone constitutes about 95% of the mineralogical composition in Igbetti white marble and about 78% of the gray variety making them to be dolomitic marbles. Euhedral crystals of quartz accounts for 8% of the total composition in Igbetti gray marble. The angular quartz crystals remain largely unaltered. Tremolite crystals occur as acicular minerals with fibrous habit and crystal laths set in a matrix of calcite and dolomite. Optical examination of the samples further reveals that the marble bodies show marked variation in terms of mineralogical composition. The dolomite content of Igbetti white and gray marbles are coincidentally equal (Table 1). However, the values are much greater than the Ososo and Jakura marbles (Emofurieta and Ekuajemi, 1995).

Figure 5: Photomicrograph of Igbetti gray marble in transmitted light showing euhedral calcite (C) and quartz (Q) crystals, subhedral dolomite (D) and acicular tremolite (T) crystals

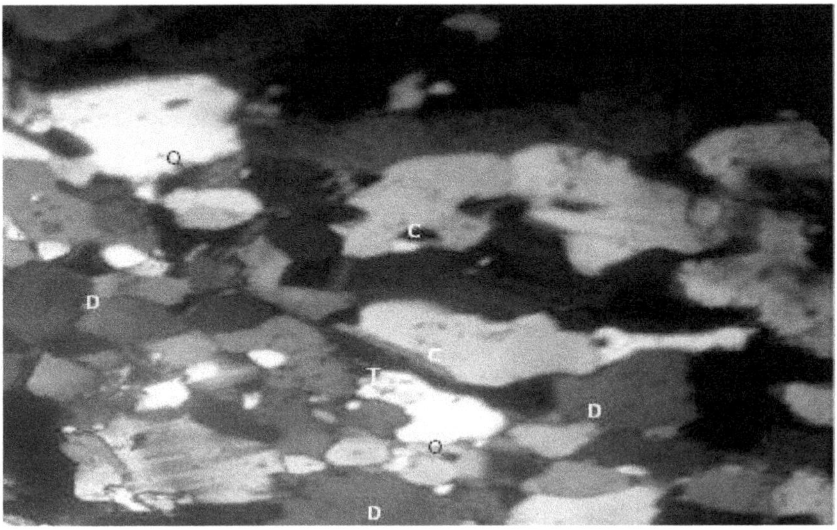

Table 1: Average relative mineralogical composition of Igbetti marble compared to others

Minerals	*This Study*		*Reference Samples*		*Industrial Specifications*			
	Igbetti(10) (A)White	Igbetti(10) (B) Grey	*Ososo (21)	*Jakura (33)	(W)	(X)	(Y)	(Z)
	Mean(%)	Mean(%)	Mean(%)	Mean(%)				
Dolomite	35	35	2.00	0.33				
Calcite	60	43	95.62	96.73	95.0	95.0	95.00	98.00
Quartz	-	8	0.37	0.52	1.00	1.00	1.00	1.00
Tremolite	-	7	0.17	0.12				
Chlorite	-	4	-	-				
Muscovite	-	-	0.85	0.75				
Feldspar	-	-	0.20	0.19				
Others	5	3	0.79	1.36	4.00	4.00	4.00	1.00
Reserve**	60 MT	-	20 MT	75MT				

(W) = NIDB, Lagos mineralogical specification; (X) = West African Portland Cement, Lagos; (Y) = Ceramic Manufacturers Limited, Kano; (Z) = Metal Box Toyo Glass Limited, Lagos. *After Emofurieta and Ekuajemi, (1995); **after Erhuero, (1986). MT = Million Tonnes

Figure 6a: X-ray diffraction trace of Igbetti white marbe.

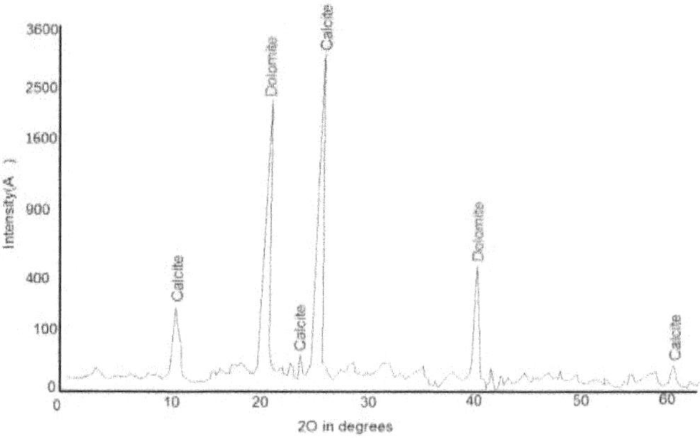

Figure 6b: X-ray diffraction trace of Igbetti gray marble.

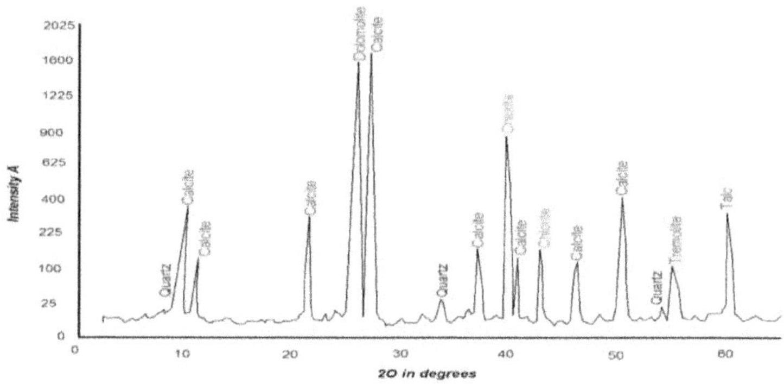

6. Chemical features

In Table 2 and 3, the average concentrations of the oxides of the two investigated marble deposits are presented along with published references. The analytical results reveal that the average SiO_2 concentration in Igbetti white marble (0.33%) coincidentally triples that of Igbetti grey variety (0.11%) and lower than the average value for most Nigeria marbles. Mean Al_2O_3 content of the white and grey marble varieties are both 0.02%. This mean value is comparable to the Sharpfell marble (Dowrie *et al.*, 1982), marginally differs from the Jakura (Okunlola *et al.*, 2003) marbles. The average CaO concentration of the two Igbetti marble varieties is comparable, and they are consistent with those of Kwakuti and Sharpfell but higher than those of Burum and Elebu marbles, while they are markedly lower than those of Jakura, Ososo, Ukpilla and Igwe marble varieties. The average Fe_2O_3 content of Igbetti white (0.02%) and grey (0.03%) marble compare with Jakura (0.02%) marble, marginally lower than that of Ososo and Sharpfell marbles but lower than those of Burum, Kwakuti, Ukpilla and Igwe varieties (Table 2). The average MnO and K_2O concentrations for the investigated marbles are either beyond detection limit (i.e. grey marble) or generally less than 0.03 and this is consistent with their concentrations in the references (Table 2). The average MgO values of the two Igbetti marble varieties are comparable with those of Burum and Elebu, lower when compared with Sharpfell marble, but significantly higher than those of Jakura, Ososo, Kuwakuti, Ukpilla and Igwe marbles. The loss on ignition (LOI) is high with the white and grey marbles having values of 37.6% and 36.5% respectively that compare with those reported for Kwakuti marble (ca. 35.63%).

Table 2: Chemical composition of Igbetti white marble

Oxides	1	2	3	4	5	6	7	8	9	10	Average
SiO_2	0.14	0.09	0.13	0.18	0.14	0.09	0.08	0.08	0.08	0.09	0.11
Al_2O_3	0.02	0.02	0.01	0.03	0.03	0.01	0.04	0.01	0.01	0.02	0.02
Fe_2O_3	0.01	0.01	0.01	0.02	0.02	0.05	0.03	0.03	0.03	0.04	0.02
MnO	-	0.02	0.02	0.02	0.02	0.01	-	0.01	0.01	-	0.01
MgO	20.9	21.0	20.3	20.0	22.4	19.6	19.8	24.6	22.0	20.7	21.5
CaO	38.7	39.9	42.4	41.1	40.9	40.3	40.5	41.0	40.8	40.9	40.7
Na_2O	0.02	0.02	0.02	0.01	0.03	0.05	-	-	0.01	0.03	0.02
K_2O	0.01	0.01	0.01	0.01	-	0.02	0.03	0.01	-	0.01	0.01
TiO_2	-	0.02	-	-	-	-	0.01	-	-	-	-
LOI	40.8	35.7	37.4	38.3	36.5	37.6	37.1	37.9	36.7	35.9	37.6
Total	100.6	96.79	100.3	100.2	100.0	97.7	97.6	103.6	99.6	97.7	99.9

Table 3: Chemical composition of Igbetti Grey Marble

Oxides	1	2	3	4	5	6	7	8	9	10	Average
SiO_2	0.29	0.40	0.36	0.33	0.31	0.40	0.43	0.45	0.28	0.33	0.33
Al_2O_3	0.02	0.03	0.02	0.01	0.01	-	0.03	0.04	0.02	0.05	0.02
Fe_2O_3	0.02	0.02	0.04	0.01	0.03	0.04	0.05	0.05	0.04	0.03	0.03
MnO	0.01	0.01	-	-	-	-	-	-	-	-	-
MgO	20.3	21.4	20.8	19.6	19.45	20.5	20.8	20.3	20.4	20.4	20.4
CaO	42.4	38.1	44.2	43.6	42.3	42.7	45.0	43.0	44.6	42.4	42.4
Na_2O	0.03	0.04	0.04	0.04	0.01	0.01	0.03	0.03	0.02	0.05	0.03
K_2O	0.03	0.02	0.02	0.02	0.01	-	0.02	0.03	0.02	0.02	0.02
TiO_2	-	-	-	-	-	-	-	-	-	-	-
LOI	36.7	38.11	35.4	35.8	37.0	37.2	34.5	36.5	35.2	35.4	36.5
Total	99.8	98.1	100.9	99.4	99.1	100.8	100.9	100.4	100.6	98.7	99.7

7. Physical and Industrial assessment

The industrial suitability of marble depends largely on physical properties such as porosity, hardness, bulk density, specific gravity, pH, tensile, compressive and shear strength; and chemical characteristics such as major and trace element concentration. Apparent porosity was determined by immersing an oven-dried sample weighing 2g in water for 24 hours. The sample was removed and re-dried. The percentage increase in weight relative to the original weight of the sample was calculated. The dried samples were weighed and immersed in water of known volume. The ratio of the original sample weight and water volume change was measured as the bulk density. For the determination of pH, 5g of the powder of each of the selected samples was thoroughly stirred in distilled water and a digital pH meter was inserted and the pH recorded. Loss on Ignition was determined by heating 10g of powdered samples in a muffle furnace at 950°C for 3 hours. The mechanical tests were carried out by compressing cube-shaped samples between two points in load testing device. The point load index was calculated as ratio of applied load to the square of distance between loading points. The compressive and shear strengths were determined by converting the point load index.

The mechanical tests were carried out at Trevi Foundations, Lagos and the result presented in Table 4.

Compressive strength values (90.23 Mpa) and (91.36 Mpa) respectively are also within close limits. The tensile strength values vary marginally, with the white and gray marble samples recording 3.89 and 3.81 respectively. Shear strength values are also comparable with the two marble varieties recording 13.39 and 13.46 respectively. These values are marginally lower than those recorded for Cheetor marble (Scott and Durham, 1984) and Mfamosing Limestone (Table 5). The specific gravity values are within the range for most Precambrian marbles (Boynton, 1980; O'Driscoll, 1988). Whiteness is 85% for the white marble variety and 71% for the gray type. These values are generally lower than the British whiting (Ofulume, 1991) and Indiana Marble (Boynton, 1980; Power, 1985).

The use of marble as raw material is dependent on the extent to which its properties meet the industrial specifications. Physical property determination (Table 4) shows that there is significant difference in apparent porosity values for the white (0.59%) and the gray (0.77%) marbles. The hardness (3.1) values of the two marbles remained largely the same. However, the mean bulk density values (2.77g/cc and 2.81g/cc) for both white and grey marbles respectively are comparable.

Table 4: Chemical composition of Igbetti marble compared with similar bodies from other locations.

Oxides	A*	B*	(C)	(D)	(E)	(F)	(G)	(H)	(I)	(J)
SiO_2	0.11	0.33	0.43	3.81	1.18	-	12.52	3.47	4.81	-
Al_2O_3	0.02	0.02	0.06	0.16	0.08		0.51	1.00	0.58	0.02
Fe_2O_3	0.02	0.03	0.02	0.15	0.07		0.27	0.21	0.18	0.06
MnO	0.01		0.03	0.01	0.03					0.03
MgO	21.5	20.4	0.58	20.75	1.75	19.9	11.43	2.23	0.88	26.85
CaO	40.7	42.4	54.17	31.0	53.64	29.5	39.50	51.29	49.00	38.28
Na_2O	0.02	0.03	0.03	0.05	0.01				0.45	0.03
K_2O	0.01	0.02	0.06	0.12	0.02					0.01
TiO_2			0.01	0.17						
P_2O_5				0.03			0.03	0.03		
LOI	37.6	36.5	43.81	43.56		44.5	35.63	41.53	39.1	
Total			99.87	99.88		93.9	99.89	99.76	95.04	
$CaCO_3$					95.72	52.60	70.50	91.6	89.49	97.0
$MgCO_3$					3.67	41.6	23.0	4.60	1.85	

* This Study. A* =Igbetti white marble, B*= Igbetti grey marble, (C) =Jakura marble (Okunlola, et al.,2003); (D)= Burum marble (Okunlola, et al., 2003); (E)= Ososo marble (Emofurieta and Ekuajemi 1995); (F)= Elebu marble (GSN Report No. 1192); (G)= Kwakuti marble (GSN Report No 1192); (H)= Ukpilla marble (GSN Report No 1192); (I)= Igwe marble; (J)= Sharpfell marble

Table 5: Physical properties of Igbetti Raw marbles

Physical properties	1	2	3	4	Mean	5	6	7	8	Mean
Apparent porosity (%)	0.50	0.58	0.61	0.67	0.59	0.8	0.77	0.73	0.78	0.77
Hardness	3.0	3.0	3.2	3.1	3.1	3.1	3.1	3.1	3.2	3.1
Bulk Density	2.72	2.75	2.81	2.78	2.77	2.76	2.73	2.9	2.84	2.81
Compressive Strength (Mpa)	90.65	90.4	89.56	90.30	90.23	91.50	91.19	91.43	91.33	91.36
Tensile Strength	3.94	3.90	3.86	3.86	3.89	3.79	3.80	3.82	3.81	3.81
Shear Strength	13.46	13.36	13.28	13.47	13.39	13.51	13.49	13.44	13.41	13.46
Whiteness	86	84	85	85	85	72	70	69	73	71
Specific Gravity	2.73	2.71	2.71	2.75	2.73	2.78	2.78	2.78	2.80	2.79
pH	8.1	8.1	8.1	8.2	8.1	8.5	8.6	8.61	8.6	8.6

1-4 = Igbetti White marble variety; 5-8 = Igbetti Gray marble variety

8. Conclusion

The Nigeria schist belt hosts various sizes of lensoid marble bodies of variable chemical and physical properties. Although, marble and dolomite are commonly used aggregates in civil engineering construction in structures requiring considerable strength and reinforcement, the use of marble as industrial material depends on a series of specifications. The Igbetti marble has physical properties that are comparable to other Nigerian marbles and will be a useful refractory raw materials for steel plant, flux stone in iron smelting, sheet glass manufacture, furnace lining and production of magnesia lime.

References

Annor, A. E., Olabaniyi, S. B. and Mucke, A. (1996), 'A note on the Geology of Isanlu area in the Egbe-Isanlu Schist belt, S.W. Nigeria', in *Journal of Mining and Geology*, 32 (2): 47-51.

Boynton, S. (1980), *Chemistry and technology of limestone*, New York: John Wiley and Sons Inc.

Dada, S. S., Briqueu, L., and Birck, J. L. (1996), 'Pb-Pb and Sm-Nd isotopic study of meta-igneous rocks of Kaduna: implication for the Archean mantle in Northern Nigeria', in *32nd Proceedings of the Annual Conference of Nigeria Mining and Geoscience Society*.

Dada, O. (1993), 'Environmental impact assessment of mining projects in Nigeria: the statutory requirement', in *Proceedings National Workshop on Review of Minerals Acts*.

Dowrie, D. G., Walden, I. and John, F. (1982), 'Modern lime burning plant at Shapfell quarry', in *Management and Products Report*, 63-171.

Ekwueme, B. N. (1987), 'Structural orientations and Precambrian deformational episode of Uwet area, Oban massif, Nigeria', in *Precambrian Research*, 34: 269-289.

Elueze, A.A. (1982), 'Geochemistry of the Ilesha granite gneiss in the basement complex of southwestern Nigeria', in *Precambrian Research*, 19:167-177.

Elueze, A.A. (1993), 'Geochemical variations and geotectonic implications of mafic assemblages in the proterozoic domain', Odo Ese area, Nigeria, in *Occasional CFEG*, 23: 90-93

Emofurieta, W.O. (1985), 'The geochemistry and petrography of two prominent gneiss in the basement complex around Igbetti, S.W Nigeria,' in *Journal of Mining and Geology*, 22 (1& 2): 125-135.

Emofurieta, W. O. and Ekuajemi, V. O. (1995), 'Lime products and Economic Aspects of Igbetti Ososo and Jakura Marble deposits in S. W Nigeria', in *Journal of Mining and Geology*, 31(1): 89-97.

Erhuero, J.B. (1986), 'Installed Capacity Utilization Problems in the Nigerian Cement Industry: the case of Bendel Cement Company Limited', *Unpublished M.Sc. Dissertation*, University of Benin, Nigeria.

Odeyemi, I.B. (1988), *Lithostratigraphy and structural relationships of the upper precambrian metasediments in Igarra Area, Southwestern Nigeria*, In: Geological Survey of Nigeria Publication, *The Precambrian geology of Nigeria*, Kaduna, Nigeria: Esho Publishers.

O'Driscoll, M. (1988), 'Burnt lime/dolomite', Seeking markets green, in *Industrial Minerals*, 22: 1-10.

Ofulume, A. B. (1991), 'The Jakura Marble as fillers and Extenders in paints and plastics industries', in *Journal of Mining and Geology*, 27(2): 187-193.

Okunlola, O.A., Ogedengbe, O. and Ojutalayo, A. (2003), 'Compositional features and industrial appraisal of the Baba Ode talc occurrence, South Western Nigeria', in *Global Journal of Geological sciences*, 1: 63-72.

Olayinka, A.I., Amidu, S.A. and Oladunjoye, M.A. (2004), 'Use of electromagnetic profiling and resistivity sounding for groundwater exploration in the crystalline basement of Igbetti, southwestern Nigeria', in *Global Journal of Geological Sciences*, 2(2): 243-253.

Power, T. (1985), 'Limestone specification, limiting constraints on the market. Industrial minerals and Rocks', in *Proceedings of the American Institute of Mining, Metallurgical and Petroleum Engineers*, 5thedition, 709-722.

Rahaman, M.A. (1976), *Review of the Basement geology of Nigeria*, In Kogbe, C. A. (ed.), *Geology of Nigeria*, Surulere, Lagos: Elizabethian Publishing Co.

Rahaman, M.A., Emofurieta, W. O. and Caen-Vachette, M. (1983), 'The potassic grantes of the Igbeti area: further evidence of the polycyclic evolution of the Pan-African belt in southwestern Nigeria', in *Precambrian Research*, 22: 75-92.

Scott, T.W. and Dunham, A.C. (1984), 'Problems in the evaluation of Limestone for diverse Markets', in *Proceedings of the 6th Industrial Minerals International Congress*, Toronto.

African Journal of Science, Technology, Innovation and Development
Vol. 4, No. 2, 2012
pp. 188-209

Environmental Impact of Underground Natural Gas Storage

Charley I. Anyadiegwu* & Emmanuel E. Anyanwu**

Abstract

The environmental impact of injecting natural gas in underground reservoirs for storage is presented taking depleted oil/gas reservoirs for consideration. Several information on underground gas storage facilities were gathered, which were the bedrock of the environmental impact analysis. The impact of natural gas in underground reservoirs on the environment include: contamination of atmospheric air with pollutant gases (greenhouse gases emissions), ozone layer depletion by produced gas flaring, pollution of environment by produced water, soil contamination by oil and gas leakages, effect of dumping drilling and production wastes on sites and air/soil/water contamination by the hazardous chemicals used for gas treatment and pipeline transportation. Several control measures were outlined and discussed in this work for the regulation of the impact of underground storage of natural gas. The use of advanced technology and trained manpower play a vital role in improving the environmental safety during the operation of natural gas transportation and storage systems.

* Department of Petroleum Engineering, Federal University of Technology, Owerri. Email: cicanyadiegwu@yahoo.com

** Department of Mechanical Engineering, Federal University of Technology, Owerri. Email: dreeanya@yahoo.com

Keywords: Environment, Natural gas, Gas storage, Greenhouse gases, Waste treatment.

JEL Classification: O10; O20; O30; O55.

1. Introduction

Normative acts related to environmental quality, natural gas purity, and control of emissions of pollutants contained in natural gas-driven equipment exhausts demonstrate that the world is concerned with the problems of environmental protection and people safety and health (Vlasenko *et al.*, 2008). Depleted oil and gas reservoirs are prime candidates for conversion to storage. The size of the reservoir is determined by calculations from geological data or from the oil production reservoir pressures. In considering a depleted oil fields, it should be recognized that the gas withdrawal take about 120days in a given year (Katz and Tek, 1981). This requires more wells than used during oil production, and enlarged gathering and injection pipeline system from the well to the central station. A delivery system can be installed to cover the market demand for the year. Some flexibility is needed, since variation in weather causes varying demands. Storage field pipelines may require some period of reduced load in summer for testing. Natural gas is injected into the porous sandstone through the surface facilities during the period when the demand is low and withdrawn for use during the period when the demand for gas is high. For temperate countries the periods correspond to summer and winter periods respectively.

The two basic questions that come into one's mind are: (1) Is it possible to operate underground gas storage in Nigeria; and (2) How environmental friendly is it. This research work is aimed at presenting the safe and environmental friendly way of operating underground gas storage facilities without having adverse effects on the environment (human, air, soil, water, flora and fauna).

Underground Natural Gas Storage

Natural gas, like most other commodities, can be stored for an indefinite period of time. The exploration, production, and transportation of natural gas take time, and the natural gas that reaches its destination is not always needed right away, so it is injected into underground storage facilities. These storage facilities can be located near market centers that do not have a ready supply of locally produced natural gas. There are typically three (3) major types of underground natural gas storage. They are: 1. Depleted reservoirs in oil or gas fields, 2. Aquifers; and 3. Salt cavern formations.

- Depleted oil/gas reservoirs: Depleted reservoirs are those formations that have already been tapped of all their recoverable natural gas. This leaves an underground formation, geologically capable of holding natural gas. These are the most prominent and common form of underground storage.
- Aquifers: Aquifers are underground, porous and permeable rock formations that act as natural water reservoirs. In some cases they can be used for natural gas storage. Usually these facilities are operated on a single formation and are not known ahead of time.
- Salt Caverns: These are formations formed out of existing salt deposits. These underground salt deposits may exist in two possible forms: salt domes and salt beds. Salt domes are thick formations created out from natural salt deposits, while salt beds are shallower, thinner and wider formations.

The typical injection and withdrawal trend in an oil-depleted underground gas storage reservoir which is a detailed step-by-step involved in an underground natural gas storage is shown in the Figure 1.

Environmental Impact Assessment (EIA) refers to assessment of impacts of a project on the natural, health, social and economic well being of the communities in the project area. EIA process ensures that measures are put in places that assist in the reduction of negative effects and enhancement of positive effects. EIA is a statutory requirement for all categories of Petroleum Exploration and Production (E&P) as well as gas projects. It was made mandatory by various legislation, which includes the (Petroleum Act, 1969) and EIA Act No 86, (1992) (Echefu and Akpofure, 2003).

Department of Petroleum Resources (DPR) is empowered to supervise the entire operations of the oil and gas industries by virtue of section 191 of (NNPC Act, 1979). This act empowers DPR to ensure that operators in the petroleum industry in Nigeria do not degrade the environment in the course of their operations. DPR also enforces the clean up and restoration of oil spills/gas leaks and impacted environment to acceptable levels, and controlling new projects that may adversely impact the environment (Shell Petroleum Development Company of Nigeria Limited, 2003).

Figure 1: Schematic of Natural Gas Storage

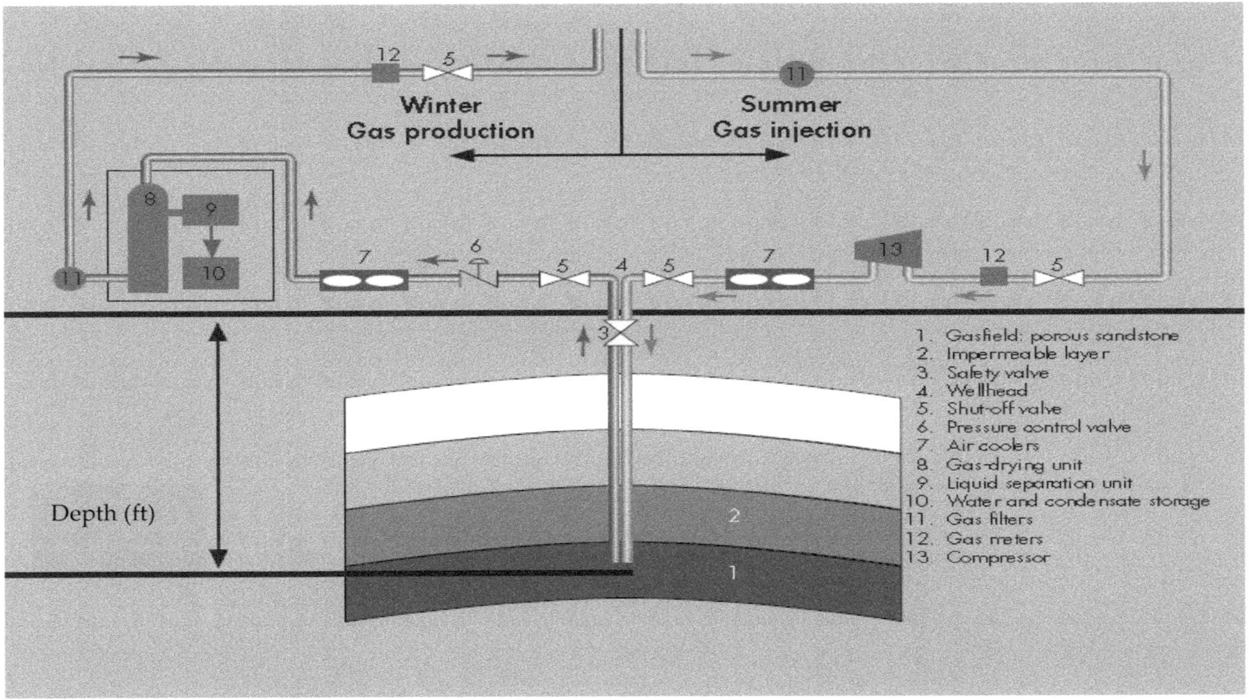

Schematic representation of natural gas storage.

Source: Dietert, J. and Pursell, D. (2008).

Environmental Impact Assessment (EIA)

The EIA process provides the following:

- Describes the project or operation
- Describes the environment that will be affected.
- Predicts the impacts on the environment
- Adopts options, techniques and controls to reduce negative impacts of oil spills/gas leaks
- Monitors the projects or operation to ensure that the identified key impacts in the environment are minimized
- Ensure compliance with regulatory requirements of DPR/Federal Environmental Protection Agency (FEPA)
- Comply with the Health, Safety and Environment (HSE) policy
- Minimize the impacts of our activities on the environments
- Ensure continuous improvement in the environmental performance
- Enhance public image and guard against unnecessary litigation.

2. Environmental Protection, Safety and Quality

Environmental Concerns

One major environmental problem of Underground Gas Storage (UGS) is gas leakage. UGS wells are subject to cyclic stresses of injection and production as gas is stored during times of peak supply for use during times of peak demand. Repeated stress on the cement sheath and the formation in which the gas is stored can result in cement sheath damage or debonding and a loss of stored gas reserves. This loss of stored gas as a result of the presence of surface gas leaks poses a danger. UGS wells are placed near populated areas, where their stored energy-on-demand is most needed; as a result, any unwanted annular flows that might occur would present an unacceptable safety risk (Moroni *et al.*, 2008). The causes and prevention of gas leakages are presented in Table 1.

Environmental and safety concerns often require that storage operations be suspended on wells with gas leaks to surface. There could be incorporation of a self-repairing sealant material as part of a large-scale UGS development. To minimize the possibility of unwanted annular gas flows and the resultant loss of UGS capacity, self-healing cement (SHC) could be pumped and placed as part of primary cementing operations (Reis, 1996).SHC is a unique isolation material with the built-in ability to self-repair.

Table 1: Causes and Prevention of Oil and Gas Leakages

Causes of spill/leakages	Prevention measures
Production Ops (equipment failure/Human error etc	Preventive maintenance Good design and operating procedure Safety devices Good drainage system eg water Continuous staff/contract personnel training Constant vigilance Adherence to operating procedures Improvement/updating of procedure
Corrosion (pipelines)	Wrapping of pipelines Cathodic protection Replacement of ageing flowlines (max of 15 years swamp , 20yrs for land)
Sabotage	Fencing Surveillances Improved community relationship Community education via open forum

Source: Reis (1996).

Whenever the cement sheath integrity is compromised by the formation of cracks or a debonding of the cement from the formation or casing (also known as microannulus), and gaseous hydrocarbon begins to flow through or around the cement sheath, SHC activates automatically, efficiently sealing leak paths and re-establishing well integrity. It was shown that foam, because of its unique structure, reduces gas flow in porous media. This blocking action of foam appears to be especially suitable for sealing leaks in underground gas storage reservoirs. Such reservoirs often have permeable areas in the overlying caprock that allow vertical migration of gas from the storage zone to the upper formations. The escaped gas represents both a safety hazard and an economic loss. The amount of foaming agent required to seal a leak depends on the adsorption-desorption properties of the agent. Foam generation should be an effective and economical method for reducing or stopping gas leakage from an underground storage reservoir.

Safety Hazards

The safety risk is always fire or explosions; hence the management of toxic, flammable and explosive substances is very essential. First, it is worthy of note that UGS are the safest and most secure ways of storing large quantities of natural gas. The stored gas is not in contact with oxygen and cannot ignite within the reservoir. In addition to flammable and explosive risks due to gas nature, operation of the UGS manages toxic risks. Gas extracted during the withdrawal phase is estimated to contain up to 4.5% hydrogen sulphide which is acidic and dangerous when inhaled (Coffin and Lebas, 2007). Therefore, safety issues have to be considered in the very early stages of the design studies in order to have safe installations and processes with the lowest possible impact on surrounding populations and company employees. The potential risk in the case of an accident relates to the dispersion of hydrogen sulphide cloud.

Analysis of the Impact of UGS on the Environment

The minimization of environmental impacts on the surface and protection of ecological interests is very vital. Potential environmental impacts at ground surface mainly consist of:

i) Emission of greenhouse gases in the atmosphere (Methane, carbon dioxide, etc.). Emissions of greenhouse gases in the atmosphere and their reduction at the source are typical concerns of gas storage. Installations and processes are designed to minimize these emissions. For instance, electrically driven compressors are generally preferred to gas-fuelled compressors (Coffin and Lebas, 2007).

ii) Production of waste: Waste originating from storage activities (domestic wastewater, storm water and used oil) is similar to that generated by oil production and represents a small volume. They will be eliminated and treated through authorized channels to eliminate or minimize their impact on the environment.

iii) Crossing of protected areas of ecological interest (woods, wildlife sanctuaries). Potential impacts to areas of ecological interest may be generated only temporarily during pipe laying. A new gas pipeline associated with gas storage activities would cross two areas of ecological interest (land and water). Regarding crossing of rivers, specific methods minimizing water and bank disturbance will be used. Finally, works will be conducted at the most appropriate period of the year in order to preserve animal habitats and nesting places.

Impact on atmospheric air

Experimental analysis targeting various aspects of environment-related activities on UGS facilities and mitigation of environmental impacts tentatively comprises two major parts:

i) Analysis of normative and experimental data on the state of natural-anthropogenic systems during underground gas storage; and
ii) Nature-conservative measures and solutions ensuring environmental safety and UGS stability.

Table 2: Sources of pollutant emissions into the environment

UGS surface equipment	Exhaust gas	Natural gas	Glycol	Methanol	Luboil	HC condensate	Formation water
Gas compressor plant	X	X			X		
Gas drying units	X	X	X	X	X	X	X
Separation station		X		X		X	X
Fire heater / heating boiler	X		X				
Commercial tank		X	X	X	X	X	X
Flare	X	X					
Vent stack		X					
Safety valves		X	X	X	X		
Motor transport	X				X		

Source: Vlasenko et al. (2008).

Sources of pollutant emissions into the environment

A general review of the main sources of pollutant emissions formed in the process of UGS construction, normal operation or temporary failures in the work of UGS surface equipment is given in Table 2.

Fuel gas composition

The advanced technologies intended for mitigating emissions of pollutants from gas turbine units (GTU) are greatly sensitive to fuel gas parameters and any deviation from them may result in increasing pollutant emissions. Therefore, according to normative documents developed for GTU, fuel gas is conditioned, i.e. it has stable composition, is dried and meets salable gas requirements. There are requirements for quality of combustible natural gases used as feed and fuel for industrial and public services for various countries. They extended to salable natural gases fed from fields, gas-compressor plants and underground gas storages into trunk gas pipelines and to gases transported by gas supplying and trading companies. For various countries, there are parameters of fuel gas, which are important for GTU operation, including component composition, admixtures presence and temperature and pressure fluctuation. Thus the quality of natural gas fuels considered as feed and fuel for industrial and public utilization is regulated in different countries at a level national standards or technical codes of companies. The norms regulating the presence of pollutants in natural gas and their permissible concentrations correspond to treatment possibility provided in normative acts. In reality, all marketable products are controlled.

Emissions from surface and underground equipment

Emissions from UGS power-generating equipment have the greatest effect on the atmospheric air. Summary results of experimental determination of ecotoxicant content (nitric oxides, carbon oxide, benzapyrene (BP)) in exhaust gases of fuel-powered equipment (gas turbine units, gas compressors and boilers) used at Gazprom's facilities are given in Table 3. The results are given for the periods between 1998 and 2007.

Table 3: Ecotoxicant emissions from fuel-powered equipment during natural gas burning at Gazprom

Source of pollutant emission	Matter concentration			Emission intensity			Specific emission per unit of work		
	mg/m^3		mcg/m^3	g/s		mcg/s	g/KWh		mcg/KWh
	NO_X	CO	BP	NO_X	CO	BP	NO_X	CO	BP
Gas turbine unit	50-800	50-650	0,2-2,2	1,6-23,0	0,6-40,0	10,4-99,5	1,4-5,8	0,3-7,0	3,6-59,5
Gas engine compressor	1000-2000	500-2000	0,2-2,6	2,6-11,0	2,1-6,3	0,2-2,8	10,5-20,9	4,2-19,6	0,6-9,2
Boiler	125-400	740-810	0,01-0,1	0,02-13,3	0,04-6,0	0,003-0,02	0,05-0,2 kg/GJ		
Fire evaporator	2,48-2, 65	-[X]	Not detected[XX]						

[X]- not found; [XX]- not analyzed

Source: Vniigaz (2008)

Greenhouse gas emissions

Methane emissions are discharged into the atmosphere during burn-free technological operations as a part of natural gas losses. When natural gas is burned during fuel-powered equipment operation, emission into the atmosphere takes place. Usually these emissions consist of carbon dioxide with a slight content of methane as a product of incomplete burning of HC fuel. Analysis of data on natural gas accounting shows that an average world level of gas losses during its production between 1970 and 2000 was decreasing from 24 to 15% of its gross production generally due to reinjection into pay beds used in practice in OPEC countries (VNIIGAZ Ltd, 2008).

According to examination of the USA gas industry facilities in 1991-1996, a total annual methane emission amounted to 1.4±0.5% (over 8.8 bcmy) of the gross production in the country. According to measuring companies' data obtained for the period between 1996 and 1997 and since 2002 to the present day, the volumes of natural gas leakage from the Russian export gas transmission system account for less than 1% of transported gas volume. At that actually 2/3 of the total emission into the atmosphere (in CO_2 equivalent) falls at carbon dioxide. Emission occurs during natural gas burning when gas-compressor units are under operation. Carbon dioxide from gas flaring forms the bulk of the emissions from oil and gas operations. Other gases emitted during oil and gas operations are hydrocarbons, nitrogen oxides and sulphur oxides. Figures 2 and 3 show the total gas emissions during the operations of Shell Petroleum Development Company in 2006.

Figure 2: Total Hydrocarbon Emissions during SPDC 2006 operations

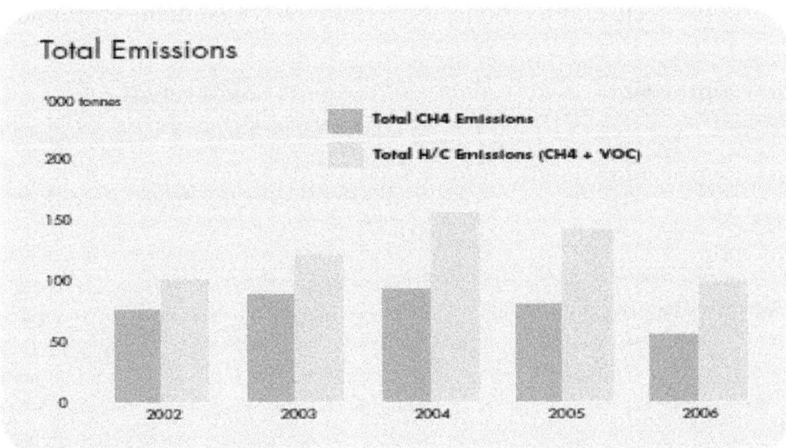

Source: Shell Petroleum Development Company of Nigeria Limited (2007).

Figure 3: Nitrogen Oxides Emissions during SPDC 2006 operations

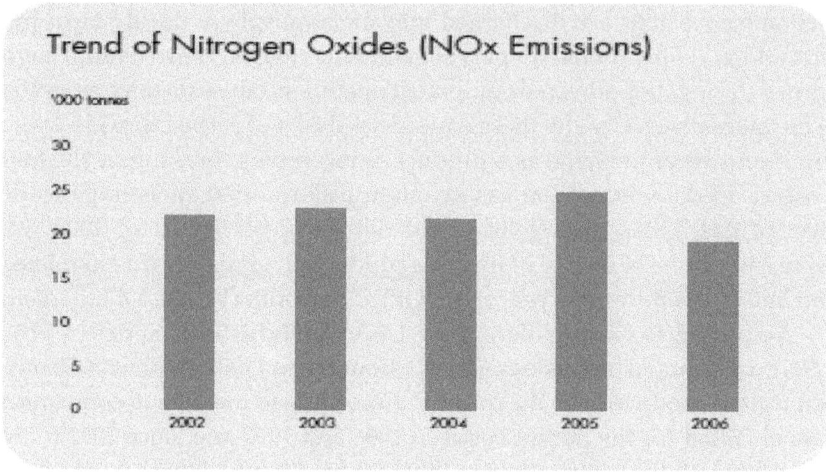

Source: Shell Petroleum Development Company of Nigeria Limited (2007).

Methane and CO_2 emissions take place through the whole activity of underground gas storage facility. A distinctive feature of gas-compressor units at compressor station lies in the fact that gas transmission technology does not consider permanent natural gas emissions into the atmosphere. Natural gas emission occurs occasionally during technological operations carried out on maintenance basis.

The equipment, which is monitored for methane leakage at UGS, is given in Table 4.

Table 4: Objects and methods of control of UGS methane emissions

Objects under control	Control methods
UGS cap	Contact with the use of gas analyzers
Well	Bioindication
Shutoff valves	Remote sensing on the basis of thermal insulation,
Flange joints	laser and spectrozonal equipment
Stack valves	

Source: Vlasenko *et al.* (2008).

Impact of waste and its treatment

Waste waters

In the process of UGS operation there are production and consumption wastes of hazard. For ecological characteristic of an enterprise the wastes fortune is of the most importance. Waste treatment in most countries is regulated at a level of national state, regional and corporate standards. Production and consumption waste treatment at UGS facilities includes:

- utilization;
- neutralization;
- burial of waste within own territory;
- storage within own territory;
- transfer of wastes to other enterprises for storing and/or burial

Five classes of hazards exist for wastes from an underground storage facility. Distribution of wastes by classes of hazards is represented in Table 5.

Table 5: Distribution of wastes by classes of hazards

Class of Hazard	Type of waste
Class I	Mercury lamps
Class II	Exhaust accumulators
Class III	Oil sludge, filters, oil sand
Class IV	Garbage, solid domestic wastes
Class V	Food wastes, garbage, construction wastes

Source: Pokhlebaeva and Nikiforova (2005).

Waste treatment

Gas industry forms some wastes, treatment and utilization of which is of special concern. Oil-contaminated waste (sludge) is formed during gas well operation, gas treatment and transportation, treatment of waste-water containing petroleum products and cleaning of tanks and other equipment. At present there is a large volume of oil sludge accumulated at gas industry's facilities, including UGS. Generally, oil waste is stored in oil sumps or burnt at gas flare devices thus resulting in considerable pollutant emission into the atmosphere. Mechanical admixtures are removed from tanks by hand and taken out to land fill for further utilization. In some cases oil containing waste is transferred to third-party organizations. Among known treatment technologies for the above wastes the following methods were found the greatest practical application:

- thermal treatment in furnaces of different types and design;
- biodestruction of oil-containing waste on the basis of special strains of bacteria;
- Chemical treatment with caustic limestone-based reagents.

At standard waste water treatment stations an oil sludge utilization unit consisting of oil waste feed system and chemical reagent are in operation. Resulting product from this unit can be used for road and foundation filling and so forth (Pokhlebaeva and Nikiforova, 2005). The other type of waste formed during UGS operation is hydrocarbons of oil separators, waste oil. The composition of these wastes allows using them in the following cases:

- as fuel for boilers, burner design of which is specially upgraded to composition of waste under utilization;
- Regeneration with return for reutilization of no less than 80% of waste oil.

Contaminated methanol and methanol water of gas separators as a type of waste are treated at regeneration units and return for reutilization thus making this process feasible both from ecological and economic points of view.

Waste waters

Waste waters formed during UGS operation are classified as domestic, surface (storm), industrial and associated (formation) water. There is a variety of methods to collect, treat, and utilize rain/waste water, brines, and other liquid wastes used in the world practice. From the concrete pads where equipment is permanently mounted, drainage water is collected to the industrial-storm water sewer or to special containers (fire ponds, concrete pits, water towers). After treatment, these waters can be supplied to the public sewer. Rainwater treatment facilities include separation systems, mechanical treatment units, and water treatment plants.

Impact on soil

In the process of UGS construction and operation chemical pollution of soil occurs due to emergency gas leaks, diffusive gas migration, formation fluid spills and discharge of fuel combustion products, leaks and spills of condensate, lubes, and/or various chemicals.

The main soil pollutants are as follows:

- liquids (oil HC, mineralized formation waters, chemical reagents and drilling muds);
- natural gas and its combustion products;
- Solids, including heavy metals.

Chemical contamination of soil may result in degradation of its physico-chemical properties, ion-exchanging properties and biological activity. Even in case of pollutants removal the sequences are not eliminated completely. Changes in soil properties caused by different types of anthropologic activity should be used as indication of soil degradation.

Table 6: Main types of UGS impacts on soil

Types of anthropologic activity	Localization of impact	Groups of soil pollutants and their composition
New well drilling and testing	Field territory, well bore zones	Drilling cuttings, mineralized formation waters (chlorides, sulfates, soda), heavy metals (Pb, Zn, Ba, Cu, Cd, Cr), combustive-lubricating materials and reagents, and natural gas and condensate blowouts
Preventive measures on wells (blowing-out, etc)	Well bore zones	Aromatic aliphatic HC, methanol, heavy metals (Pb, Zn, Ba, Cu), Formation waters, Natural gas
Well workover	- " -	- " -
Injection of production waste waters into absorption wells	- " -	Aromatic HC, wax, resin, pyrobitumen, methanol, phenol and heavy metals
Construction works; laying of flow lines, communications, etc.	Construction site zone WELL BORE ZONES	Saline soils (chlorides, sulphates) Gravel (carbonates, bicarbonate) Aromatic and aliphatic HC
Leakage from: -wellhead - poorly abandoned wells; - strata (due to excess pressure; - loss of sealing in cement stone in annular space; - lithological windows in UGS cap; -tectonic faults	Gas field area	Natural gas

Source: Vlasenko *et al.* (2008).

Table 6 gives the main types of impacts on soil resulted from UGS technological operations. The basic negative result of these impacts is soil degradation that leads to chemical contamination, desertification, swamping, etc. The intensity of anthropological activity resulted in irreversible degradation processes is different for different soils due to the difference in their buffer capacity and thus in stability to this impact. Depending on a type of degradation process (salinization, alkalinization, deflation, etc.) there appear particular combinations of unfavorable soil properties which decrease their biological efficiency. Criteria of soil pollution rate are maximum permissible concentrations (MPC) of harmful substances developed for limited range of soil pollutants. Mechanical damage of soil is related to the construction (drilling rig installation, pipeline laying, etc) and recultivation (stripping excavation, refilling of trenches, layout of sumps, etc.) work. A scale of soil cover damage, caused by mechanical impacts, depends both on a size and function of built objects and on natural environment stability in various ecosystems.

To restore soil to the condition applicable to its further usage **soil recultivation** is used. This process may follow HC pollutants removal. Soil recultivation consists of two stages: technical and biological. Technical stage includes land grading and soil surface preparation for biological stage. Biological stage includes soil conservation intended for fertile soil restoration.

To protect soil from waste water and solids impact a waste water drainage system and asphalting of sites near installations and tanks, which can be sources of pollution in case of their damage (glycol, HC condensate, methanol, brine or lubricating oil), are used.

Impact of well drilling, operation and conservation and rigging-down on the environment

Well construction, operation and abandonment are potential sources of negative impact on the environment in UGS infrastructure under operation. The above processes have an integrated effect on the environment, as they may influence on atmospheric air, soil cover, water bodies and other natural objects. UGS well products contain aggressive and toxic components which bring the threat to life and health of people. The factors which have harmful effect upon the environmental objects are as follows:

- upon the atmosphere – accidental gas release;
- upon water bodies - pressured mineralized waters and formation waters;

- Upon soil/geological environment - accidental gas release, oil products and chemical reagents spillages, drilling mud, wastes and injection of waste water into formation.

According to the requirements of national and corporate technical regulation, projects of well construction, operation, conservation or abandonment must include an action plan on monitoring environmental conditions and damaged ecosystem restoration. This plan is to be agreed with nature conservation organizations. A particular method of waste utilization in the process of well construction and operation shall be chosen based on technological, ecological and economic criteria. On selecting waste utilization method the following technologies are considered:

- treatment of waste flushing fluid (biopolymer-based flushing fluids do not contain toxic, explosive and fire-hazardous substances) from drilling cuttings and solids for providing appropriate rheological properties and reusability;
- utilization of flushing fluids by their injection into reservoir through absorption wells with preliminary destruction of biopolymer with oxidizer;
- Utilization of biopolymer-based flushing fluids with the help of special dehydration units and utilization of drilling mud.

Well conservation calls for the use of the following reagents and measures:

- non-freezable fluid (solar oil, diesel fuel, oil, 30% liquid calcium chloride, etc.) that is injected into the upper part of a well up to 30 m to prevent it from freezing;
- Kill fluid (drilling mud) with a given density. The use of fluids with increased corrosion activity, which may have a server impact on soil and fresh water during their spillage. During well abandonment environmental impact sources are transport, diesel power plants, gas-cutting machines, tanks for combustive-lubricating materials, boiler, circulating system, slurry pond, preventer sump, etc. Carbon oxide, nitric oxides, HC (methane), HC (diesel fuel and gasoline), ash (on conversion to C), benz(a)pyrene, sulfur dioxide, H_2S, cement and dust (barite) are exhausted into the atmosphere.

To prevent negative impact on the environment during well abandonment the following control is to be provided:

- gas or formation water release at wellhead of abandoned well;
- contamination of fresh water or gas ingress into fresh water;
- pulling of intermediate strings and casings under the absence of pressured mineralized waters (to exclude contamination of upper fresh waters);
- Insurance of timely and qualified recultivation work.

Measures on soil conservation during drilling waste utilization

All biopolymer-based flushing fluids both prepared and waste, as well as reaction products resulted from decomposition of biopolymer of microbe origin, shall be gathered into tanks of sufficient volume. Spillage of biopolymer-based flushing fluids and reaction products on soil is not permitted. If the latter occurs it is necessary to do as follows:

- gather a maximum possible amount of fluid and reaction products into a tank;
- Handle an area of spillage with oxidizer, e.g. lithium hydrochloride or calcium hydrochloride, and backfill the damaged area.

3. Findings and Discussion

The role of advanced technologies in improving environmental safety

Based on results of research, UGS facilities appear to make little environmental impact. It means that technologies applied in this business are sufficiently perfect. However, judging by the international cooperation experience in the field of technological and environment related aspects of UGS operation; there is room for further progress. The most important environmentally beneficial technologies currently applied by UGS companies worldwide need to be improved from the viewpoint of different technological aspects of UGS operation.

To fulfill this task a complex effort allowing not only reducing environmental pollution intensity but also improving technical and ecological characteristics of surface and underground facilities is under accomplishment.

Table 7: Trends in improving UGS facility operation for the environmental protection against hazardous pollutants

Trend	Technology
UGS management	UGS operation UGS safety position
Reduction in atmospheric emissions	Replacement of old gas turbine with relatively low efficiency with advanced high efficiency and environment-friendly units. State-of-the art methods of monitoring NO_x, CO_2, CO, SO_x, CH_4 emissions into the atmosphere from all facilities, including gas-compressor units, boilers and flares. New equipment for reducing flare gas emission New well drilling technologies: -Horizontal well drilling -Well drilling with motor-driven units
Greenhouse gas emission reduction	- reduction in UGS cushion gas; - reduction in reservoir gas losses; - injection of associated gas into formation
Methane emission (with leakage) Management	-system optimization of UGS operating practices - upgrading and revamping of CS units - Reduction in gas losses on CS units - Well resting without releasing gas into the atmosphere and with reduction of blowouts by optimizing gas withdrawal conditions and using gas wells in low-pressure networks
Introduction of now methods and Means of natural gas burning	Reduction of CH_4 emission from process equipment to eliminate leakages Reduction of purge gas emissions DEG and TEG regeneration

Source: Vniigaz (2008)

Table 8: Trends in improving UGS facility operation for the environmental protection against hazardous pollutants

Noise reduction (Development of low-noise gas-compressor units as compromise between technical capabilities and economic feasibility)	Acoustic upgrading of noise source (centrifugal blowers) Modular noise-damping means
Improvement of water utilization scheme:	- Waste disposal reduction - Methods of waste disposal measurement - Water disposal - circulating water supply
Production and consumption waste	Reduction of liquid and solid waste impact on the environment
Method and means of contaminated environment sanitation	Impact reduction technologies: Chemical, physical (radiation), electromagnetic, biological, thermal, mechanical (solid and liquid wastes)
UGS territory development	Soil recultivation Drainage system for facilities, soil compaction, asphalting and concreting of areas for processing units releasing pollutants
Operational and ecological control and monitoring	Under periodical contamination with oil products, methanol and other pollutants, under close location of agricultural land and residential areas sanitary protection zones, the size of which is defined on the basis of control and monitoring materials, may be required
Increase in labor productivity	Decrease in visual impact
Socioecological	All the technologies ensuring: Global warming prevention; Protection of the environment and personnel and population health

Source: Vniigaz (2008)

The trends in improving environment-related activity at UGS

The trends in improving UGS facility operation for the environmental protection against hazardous pollutants are as shown in Tables 7 and 8. The trends in improving environment-related activity at UGS facilities concern also the most urgent problems of reduction in purge and flare gas emissions. To solve these problems the following solutions were considered: bleeding gas flow rate control; sealing control; the use of mobile compressor units for gas utilization; hot tapping technology; and excess pressure blocking and bleeding-off with releasing of a minimum gas volume. Reduction in purge, bleeding and flare gas emissions, as well as reduction in natural gas consumption for technical needs, marketable product losses and energy saving can be accomplished at the expense of:

- GCU starting by air, electric or compressed nitrogen system;
- Natural gas utilization during blowing-out of wells or other process equipment;
- Gas-piston generating sets for flare gas utilization.

The experience in design, operation and reconstruction of UGS facilities has shown the similarity in approach to environmental protection in different countries and companies and relative comparability of positions and criteria of environmental safety estimation.

Thus cooperation, generalization and exchange of experience will allow:

- developing new technologies;
- protecting national, nation-wide and corporate interests in the field of
- environmental safety;
- enhancing the efficiency of management and quality of UGS operation monitoring;
- decreasing negative anthropological impact on the environment;
- developing and applying adequate technological and nature-conservative measures to prevent and reduce probable ecologic damage from natural anthropological impacts; and
- Stabilizing and improving gynecological situation in the vicinity of UGS.

4. Conclusion

At the end of this analytical research, the following conclusions can be drawn:

- It is possible to develop and operate underground natural gas storage in Nigeria.
- Gas emissions to the environment in the course of operating the underground gas storage are inevitable.
- It is possible to regulate the effects of the greenhouse gas emission with the modern gas handling facilities.

References

Coffin, P. and Genevieve, L. (2007), *Converting the Pecorade Oil field into an Underground Gas Storage*, Genevieve Lebas, France.

Dietert, J. and Pursell D. (2008), *Underground Natural Gas Storage*, Texas: Simmons and Company International.

Echefu, N. and Akpofure, E. (2003), 'Environmental Impact Assessment in Nigeria: Regulatory Background and Procedural Framework,' in *UNEP EIA Training Resource Manual: Case Studies from Developing Countries*.

Katz, D.L. and Tek, M.R., (1981), 'Overview on Underground Storage of Natural Gas', SPE 9390 – PA, Vol. 33, No. 6, USA.

Moroni, N., Bellarbarba, M., Belleggia, E., Illuminati, R. and LeRoy-Delage, S (2008), 'Preserving Stored Gas Reserves: Self Repairing Cement Sheath Protects Underground Gas Storage Investment', *International Petroleum Technology Conference*, 3-5 December 2008, Kuala Lumpur, Malaysia.

Pokhlebaeva, T.Yu. and Nikiforova, L.O., (2005), 'Intensification of Treatment of Waste Waters from Gas Transportation and Storage Facilities', *Gazovaya promyshlennost 11*, Russia.

Reis, J. C. (1996), *Environmental Control in Petroleum Engineering*, Houston, Texas: Gulf Professional Publishing Publication.

Shell Petroleum Development Company of Nigeria Limited (2003), *Environmental Impact Assessment (EIA) Process: Stakeholders' Guide*. Nigeria.

Shell Petroleum Development Company of Nigeria Limited (2007), *Shell Nigeria Annual Report 2006: People and the Environment*, Nigeria.

Vlasenko, N., Sergey, K., Gretta, A., Onderka, V. and Marion, P. (2008), *Environmental Safety Aspects of Underground Gas Storage*, Gazprom Vniigaz Ltd, Russia.

VNIIGAZ Ltd. (2008), 'Analytical Section by Sources and Volumes of Greenhouse Gases Emissions at Gazprom's Facilities under the Kyoto Greenhouse Gases Protocol', *Report on research effort,* Gazprom Vniigaz Ltd, Russia.

African Journal of Science, Technology,
Innovation and Development
Vol. 4, No. 2, 2012
pp. 210-213

Book Review 1

Anthony O. Agwuele*

Sanya Osha, *Postethnophilosophy*, Amsterdam Value Inquiry Book Series, Rodopi Publishers, Amsterdam, New York; 2011: 265 pages; ISBN: 978-90-420-3317-7.

African philosophy at its outset grappled with a question that is a clear and reliable indicator of its existence. That is, the question of the existence of African philosophy. This and the debate it generated, I believe, are proof of the existence of African philosophy. Every philosophical system, no matter what claims it makes for itself, must derive its authenticity from self-examination. It does not matter, ultimately, whether this meta-philosophical exercise is conclusively resolved. The question of what is African philosophy, in contrast to any other kind of philosophy, is a question which permits no simple answer. Consequently, the attempt to answer this question produced two distinct discursive formations, that of universalists and traditionalists.

Paulin J. Hountondji, an African philosopher who advocates the scientific method for African philosophy, denigrates the traditionalist approach to African philosophy as ethnophilosophy, because it follows Placide Tempels' Bantu Philosophy (1949), in which African philosophy based on African culture was paradigmatic. Undeterred, the traditionalists took

* Liberal Arts Program, Seneca College, Toronto, Ontario, Canada.
Email: tagwuele@yahoo.com

ethnophilosophy as a badge of honour and patriotism and kept it as a major current of African philosophy. The construction of an African identity became a major task.

The concept of identity is beset with conceptual difficulties. The basic difficulty is the lack of understanding of how the concept of identity and its unconscious process of becoming developed within the discourse. And without making this any clear, there emerged an articulation of identity as the knowing subject. This has, consequently, influenced ethnic, racial, social, cultural and national conceptions of identity. As a result, searching critiques and deconstructive criticisms of the essentialist approach to the concept of identity have emerged. This has in turn, prompted a two way response. One, are attempts to replace insufficient concepts of identity or the knowing subject with ample ones. Two, are efforts to offer a theory of discursive practice rather than the theory of the knowing subject. This is the approach of Foucault, because it avoids a "transcendental consciousness" (Foucault, 1970: xiv). However, what is not at issue in this debate is discarding identity or the agency of the subject.

This is what Sanya Osha, a SARChI Fellow at the Institute for Economic Research on Innovation (IERI), Tshwane University of Technology, Tshwane/Pretoria, South Africa, does in his new book *Postethnophilosophy* (2011). He attempts to dismantle the foundational hold of ethnophilosophy on African philosophical discourse. Osha feels that the focus of ethnophilosophy on the problem of identity and self-conception has stalled African philosophy. Consequently, in a bold move, the kind that gives rise to discursive rupture and instantiates paradigm shift, Osha tries to set a broad new agenda for African philosophy.

The imperative of Osha's book is in its second chapter where Osha discusses the need to resist "The Lure of Ethnophilosophy", based on Paulin Hountondji's critique of ethnophilosophy. Ethnophilosophy has acquired a reputation of a "we" versus "them" discourse which only breeds racial exclusivity and status definition. It is also seen as bringing ethnocentric baggage to bear on African philosophical discourse, through its perennial quest for African identity. On account of these problems, and the alleged western origin of ethnophilosophy, Paulin Hountondji railed relentlessly against it (ethnophilosophy). For the most part, Osha accepts Paulin Hountondji's assessment of ethnophilosophy and dismisses its two popular critics, Olabiyi Yai (1977) and Oyekan Owomoyela (1987). While the former charges that Hountondji's work has no political value, the latter contends that it undermines African tradition. Osha labels the two critiques Marxian and nativist, respectively, and discards them thus:

> To identify and appreciate the value, richness, and range of Hountondji's

> philosophical contributions in Africa we have to look beyond Marxian and nativist critiques to refocus on the historical conjuncture in which took shape in terms of cultural, political, and intellectual parameters ... (p. 46)

And with a note of finality, he dismisses the critics: "Consequently, both Yai and Owomoyela have little of enduring value to say of Hountondji's work" (p. 47). Osha goes on to offer a reading of Hountondji's "The Struggle for Meaning" (2002) as a way to account for the intellectual influences that shaped his views. Furthermore, Osha praises Hountondji for the useful discoveries he made in the evaluations of William Amo and Kwame Nkrumah. All in all, Hountondji's critique of ethnophilosophy becomes the basis for Osha to reject ethnophilosophy in order to set a new agenda for African philosophy.

Some of the topics Osha wants to be the fulcrum of African philosophy are: "decolonization", his favorite topic, others are, "globalization", "race", "culture" and "sexuality". In advancing these topics, Osha offers criticism of philosophers before him and his contemporaries too on a very high theoretical level. This results in an entirely new, highly original approach to the understanding of African philosophy.

However, the attempt to set a new agenda for African philosophy away from the problem of identity is fraught in particular ways. One, Osha's problem with the concept of identity, is not based on its essentialist nature, but on the idea that it is not a good way to think ethnophilosophically. Two, taking away the concept identity from African philosophical discourse strips it of its dominant theme. Every tradition of philosophy has a dominant theme, i.e., British philosophy (rationalism), American philosophy (pragmatism), French philosophy (existentialism), and German philosophy (idealism). The theme that has proven to be germane to African philosophy is identity. Even though it has attracted searing critiques, it is a theme without which the question of what is an African philosophy can neither be thought of nor answered. Without doubt, therefore, it remains a foundational tool of African philosophy. Like other traditions of philosophy, African philosophy can take on other themes without necessarily abandoning its dominant theme.

In the final analysis, Osha's book provides a tool to understand African philosophy. It challenges all the authoritative positions in the domains of African philosophy and offers new ones. As such it is sure to give rise to debate beyond African continent and African philosophy.

References

Foucault, M. (1970), *The order of things: an archaeology of the human sciences,* trans. A. Sheridan, New York: Vintage Books.

Hountondji, P. J. (2002), *The Struggle for Meaning: Reflections on Philosophy, Culture, and Democracy in Africa,* Athens, Ohio: Ohio University Press.

Owomoyela, O. (1987), 'Africa and the Imperative of Philosophy: A Skeptical Consideration', in *African Studies Review*, 30: 79-99.

Yai, O. B. (1977), 'Theory and Practice in African Philosophy: The poverty of speculative philosophy', in *Second Order*, 2: 3-20.

African Journal of Science, Technology, Innovation and Development
Vol. 4, No. 2, 2012
pp. 214-216

Book Review 2

Oghenerobor B. Akpor* and Maxwell K. Boakye**

Strydom, H. A. and King, N. D. (editors), ***Fuggle & Rabie's Environmental Management in South Africa*****, 2nd edition, JUTA Law, Cape Town, 2009: pages 1142, ISBN: 9780702181344.**

This book comprehensively addresses current environmental management issues in South Africa from a multidisciplinary perspective. Both legal and scientific aspects of key environmental management themes in South Africa including agriculture, air quality, biodiversity, energy, climate change, the coast, freshwater and marine resources, mining, protected areas, rivers, soil and waste management are covered by different authors, who are experts in their field. The book addresses these themes in 28 chapters.

The book, dealt with issues of environmental management from the perspective of economics, governance biodiversity and legal perspectives. The key concepts of environmental management and its contextualisation within the South African context were explored and analysed. A reflection on the challenges facing environmental management and governance were also discussed. In addition, the application of resource economics in

* Institute for Economic Research on Innovation, Tshwane University of Technology, 159 Skinner Street, Pretoria 0001, South Africa. Email: AkporBO@tut.ac.za

** Department of Environmental, Water and Earth Sciences, Tshwane University of Technology, Pretoria 0001, South Africa. Email: BoakyeM@tut.ac.za

addressing environmental problems and philosophy, coupled with the challenges of environmental governance, in South Africa against global trends and practices were covered. The book explored the concepts of biodiversity conservation and evolution from a sectoral legislation perspective. It also argued the importance of safeguarding resources and activities to integrated conservation measures, which could help in the preservation of species for the intrinsic values and use for future generations.

With respect to legal aspects of environmental management, the book dealt with aspects national, regional, and international. The sources, binding nature, limits and concept of international law were explained in terms of the municipal law analogy. Historical perspectives of environmental law at both international and regional levels were also discussed in the book. The South African National Environmental Management Act (NEMA) was discussed from a historical context (covering the pre-constitution, constitution and post-constitution eras), environmental management principles and cooperative governance contexts. The legal principles governing environmental law, requirements for the proper exercise for the general powers and functions of administrators, implementation of environmental law by individual and state, discrimination against environmental harmful goods and processes and complexities in trade and environmental debate within the framework of multilateral trade rules were also discussed.

Also discussed in the book are issues relating to soil, plants, animals, water (fresh and marine systems), minerals, air, waste management, pesticides, energy and climate change. With respect to soil in South Africa, the book discussed it as a fast deteriorating fundamental natural resource that sustains economic development and human wellbeing. The legal provisions (statues and legislation) that relates to agriculture and the future of farming in South Africa were also discussed. With the case of water, the book looked at the subject from different areas: freshwater, marine, coastal, rivers and wetland. Several aspects of water within the South Africa context that were discussed include: the South Africa National Water Act, the Integrated Coastal Management Act 24, water management/planning, water availability, water quality and ecological integrity in South Africa, the South African marine environment, including water its use, governance and knowledge base. Other issues of water that were also discussed include pollution, legislative tools and policy options in water management, current challenges and opportunities in water management and the need for the preservation of rivers and wetland. In addition, the key features of the South Africa coast, evolution of the costal management. The book proposed a legal regime for integrated coastal management in South Africa.

With respect to plants and the environment, the book focused on indigenous plants in South Africa. The driving ecological variable of the South Africa plant life, patterns of plant diversity within the Southern Africa biomes, degradation, plant resources conservation, legislation for conservation and analyses of the adequacy of the South African legislation for plant protection were covered. In the case animals and the environment, the book explored the protections and status given to the South African wild life animals under international, national and provincial laws and legislations. The book explored the effects of pollution, The Atmospheric Pollution Prevention Act 45, NEMA: Air Quality Act of 39, management of air quality, atmospheric chemistry, modes of dispersion of pollutants, significant of pollution in the South Africa context with respect to air. Several technologies for emission of air pollutants were also reviewed.

Integrated approach to waste management, current status of waste management and effects of emissions of waste in South Africa were also discussed in the book. In the area of mining, evaluation of residual biophysical aspects, economic and social impacts as well as overview of mining operation in South Africa were discussed in the book. The book also covered aspects of environmental impact assessment. The legislative framework that deals with integrated environmental management and community health, broad guidelines that distinguish human health considerations in environmental assessment and management of public health were also discussed.